外国语言文学与文化研究

Studies on Foreign Language, Literature and Culture

徐 枫 主编

云南大学出版社

序　言

在大学里，教师应该以教书为主还是以研究为主，这是一个长期以来一直有争论的问题。

我认为（而且我想大多数人也都这样认为），教师主要的职责当然应该是教书。教师就是要教好学生，把知识传授给学生，为学生释疑解惑，帮助学生掌握正确的思维方法和学习方法。确实，一个不认真教书、不好好上课的教师，绝对不是一个合格的教师。话虽这样说，但实际情况是，近年来一些大学过分强调科研，对教师的考核、评职称、评奖等，都有非常具体的科研项目、科研成果、论文数量的指标规定。这就使得许多大学老师越来越“重研轻教”，只想着多出成果、多发论文，对日常教学提不起兴趣，花在教书育人上的精力越来越少。这样的办学导向，我认为肯定是不正确的。

但是，同时我也认为，一个只会教书而不会作研究的大学教师，肯定不是一位优秀的大学教师。我们都知道，现代大学具有三大功能：人才培养、科学研究和社会服务。也就是说，大学的任务不仅仅是培养学生，同时还承担着从事科学研究和为社会提供服务的任务。现代大学除了培养人才、传播知识外，还应该深化知识、更新知识、创造知识，用自己所拥有的人才和知识为社会的发展作贡献。因此，作为一名大学教师，仅仅教好书是不够的，还必须从事科学（或学术）研究，还应该为社会提供服务。这也就是大学教师与中小学教师不一样的地方。

国外的大学教师也面临着同样的问题，除了教书，还必须作研究，必须发表成果。美国大学里就有这样的说法：“publish or perish”（发表或灭亡）。这句话说得好听一些是“（在大学里）不发表科研成果就没有立足之地”，说得不客气一点就是“写不出东西就滚蛋”。大学里各个专业的老师，除了要把本专业现有的知识全面、系统地介绍给学生，把学生带到本专业领域的最前沿地带之外，教师自己也要努力研究，探索未知，创造新知识，开拓本专业的新领域。

那么，大学里的外语教师是否也应该搞研究呢?

与其他专业的教师相比，大学外语教师确实有一些特殊性，要搞科学研究可能比其他专业的教师确实要困难一些。这种特殊性和困难性表现在这样几个方面：一是他们主要是从事语言能力（听、说、读、写）的教学，这在很大程度上是一种技能性的实践活动。也就是说，他们的任务是通过大量、反复的模仿、练习来帮助学生掌握外语这门工具，这种语言习得（language acquisition）的活动过程本身强调实践性，并没有太多的学理性和学术性。二是外国语言文学学科本身的特殊性。在我国，外国语言文学固然早已是一个自成体系且较为成熟的学科领域，但是能供发表研究成果的外国语言文学类的学术刊物却比较少，与我国庞大的外语教师队伍是不成比例的。这样，就造成了外语教师科研成果发表难、出版难的现状。三是一般而言，大学外语教师上课的任务都很重。无论是外语专业（如英语、法语、日语等）教师，还是公共外语教师，教学工作量都比较大，安排的课时都很多，大家都疲于应付教学。这样一来，他们也就很难再抽出多少时间来作研究了。

尽管有这样、那样的困难和特殊性，但却不能成为大学外语老师不搞科研的借口。事实上，国内许多著名的大学者都做过外语教师，有的甚至一辈子都是外语教师。如梁实秋、叶公超、冯至、卞之琳、朱光潜、吴宓、钱钟书、杨周翰、戴镏龄、梁宗岱、李赋宁、许国璋、王佐良、吴景荣等。他们大都学贯中西，不但培养了许多高水平的学生，而且取得了大量后人难以超越的学术成就。

今天，我们大学外语教师应该如何搞研究做学问呢？在我看来，至少可以从这样几个方面来努力：

一是在语言学和文学领域里进行研究。语言文字是一种社会现象，是人类最重要的交际工具，而文学则是语言和文字的艺术。语言文学是有生命力的，也是在不断发展变化的，只要有人类存在，就有语言文学。因此，人类对语言和文学的研究是永无止境的。对我们外语教师来说，外国语言文学的学术空间几乎是无限的。

二是对外语教学方法、教学技能的研究。外语教学是一门艺术，一名好的外语教师，从备课、讲课、作业、讨论、考试等各个教学环节中都可以发现问题，进而研究问题、解决问题，最后总结出经验和规律，甚至还可上升成为有指导意义的理论。

三是利用自己的外语工具，对其他学科领域的问题进行研究。许多外语教师往往狭隘地把自己的眼光局限在“外国语言文学”领域里。其实，外语既是一门学问，也是一种工具。我们既可以对外语本身进行研究，也可以把外语作为一种工具，来研究社会、政治、经济、文化、民族、宗教、军事、科技等问题。学外语的人有外语优势、有独特的视角，一旦选择了某一专业领域后，较容易深入进去，也较容易出成果、上水平。现在有许多学科领域的专家，原来都是学外语出身的，或者本身就是外语教师。

四是翻译。我始终认为，翻译是一门大学问。谁敢说，好的翻译不需要研究，不是创造，不是艺术呢？著名学者钱钟书先生甚至认为，翻译的难度超过了写专著、写论文。大学外语教师既可以将一些外文名著、专著译为中文在中国出版，也可以将国内的中文论著译为外文介绍到国外去。翻译领域也是可以大有作为的。

云南大学外国语学院的前身是云南大学外语系，是一个已有60多年历史的老系，有着深厚的历史积淀。最老的英语系创建于1942年，国内知名学者吴富恒、凌达扬等都曾在英语系任教。经过半个多世纪的发展，云大外语学院形成了自己的学术传统和办学特色，在省内外有良好的学术声誉，为国家培养了大批外语人才。现在，外语学院有英语系、西语系（法语、德语）、东语系（日语、阿拉伯语）、研究生公共外语教研室四个教学单位，另外还有一个美国研究室；学院有英语和法语两个硕士学位点。

学院现有一支年龄、职称和学历结构都比较合理的教师队伍。近年来，在学院的引导和鼓励下，教师既注重课堂教学，也积极从事学术研究。本论文集就是学院老师们近两年来在繁忙的教学工作之余开展研究活动所取得的一些成果。其中，既有语言文学领域的研究心得，也有跨文化交流方面的思考和探索，还有关于教学理念和方法的讨论。作者既有中年骨干教师，也有不少年轻教师。这批论文既有用中文完成的，也有用外文完成的，水平亦有高有低。但无论如何，都是老师们辛勤劳动的成果，其中都凝聚着他们的心血和汗水。经过认真的审读和加工，现结集出版。

我们之所以出版这批论文，是希望达到两个目的：一是与学术界同行交流切磋，共同提高；二是鼓励学院有更多的老师投身研究，产生更多、更好的学术成果。我相信，经过努力，云南大学外国语学院不仅在人才培养方面硕果累累，在学术研究方面也能取得骄人成绩。

肖　宪

2008年5月

目 录

序 言 …………………………………………………………………………… 肖 宪(1)

第一部分 外国文学研究

Double Focalization in "A Rose for Emily" ……………………… Wang Ling (3)
The Significance of Names in Toni Morrison's Novels ………… Wang Jinmei (17)
A Complete Rejection of Men
——An Analysis of Katherine Anne Porter's "Theft" …………… He Jingming (31)
A Black Divinity in a Moral Wasteland
——A Textual Analysis of Dilsey in William Faulkner's *The Sound and the Fury*
……………………………………………………………………… Xie Ping (38)
Lecture d'*Hamlet et Œdipe* de Jones …………………………… Xu Feng (42)
A Critical Study on Zhu Guangqian's Aesthetic View of Tragic Pleasure
……………………………………………………………………… Li Yue (59)
渴望"洁白的床"
—— 浅析《占有》中的两性和谐意识 …………………………… 邢 凌 (69)

第二部分 外语教学研究

Effective Extensive Reading: Principle and Practice ……………… Ma Ling (79)
To What Extent can We Make Best Use of Metadiscourse in Teaching
English Writing? ……………………………………………………… Li Jia (86)
A Critique of the Claim that Nothing of Any Real Substance has been
Developed in Language Teaching Since the Rise of Communicative
Language Teaching in the 1970s and 1980s ………………… Wang Wenjun (94)
谈谈朗读在大学英语教学中的作用 ………………………………… 张彩庆 (102)

提高学生法语学习兴趣的几种方式 …………………………………… 聂云梅（111）
英汉翻译量化教学法研究 ………………………………………………… 徐覃荪（116）
浅析佛教对 GMS 地区大学生学习特点的影响 ………………………… 尹可秀（125）

第三部分　外国文化及跨文化交际研究

In Socioculturally Defined Boundaries: On Joking Relationships
………………………………………………………………………… Liu Xiaohong（135）
Cultural Analysis of Chinese and American Views on Charity
………………………………………………………………………… Liu Xiaoyuan（141）
态度、知识、技能并重，培养跨文化交际能力 ………… 周 真　马 玲（153）
女歌人小野小町 ……………………………………………………… 张丽花（158）
浅议阿拉伯书法艺术 ………………………………………………… 马利章（166）
权威与可信：中、英学者学术语篇中的人际附加语 ………………… 田有飞（171）
日本战争题材电影对战争责任的概念偷换 ………………………… 赵毅达（191）

第四部分　翻译研究

现代旅游宣传对中国古典文学翻译的影响浅析
——以美秀博物馆《桃花源记》译本为例 ………………………… 董丹萍（201）
宗教词汇翻译：准确理解与灵活变通
——对 witness，sect（cult）和 ministry 译法的探讨 ………… 尹可秀（211）

第五部分　外国语言研究

法庭交叉讯问中问句与权势的关系
——对法庭交叉讯问中问句的多层次批评性分析 ………… 王晋军（223）
浅论阿拉伯语的若干特点 …………………………………………… 蔡春阳（237）
「うち」与「そと」之词义浅析 ……………………………………… 饶琼珍（244）
日本語動詞アスペクト「……ている」の意味
——中国語との対照において ………………………………… 劉 一（252）

编后记 ………………………………………………………………………（259）

第一部分　外国文学研究

Double Focalization in "A Rose for Emily"

Wang Ling

1. Introduction to Theoretical Background

"A Rose for Emily" by William Faulkner (1897 – 1962) is a short story about an eccentric spinster, Emily Grierson, set in the early twentieth century. With the great storyteller, "the telling never becomes the tale... but the design of the telling continually determines secondary fictional effects."① In the story which is "carefully calculated and complicatedly constructed"②, an unnamed narrator details the strange circumstances of Miss Emily's life, including her odd relations with her father, the man whom she loves, the atmosphere of the southern town of Jefferson, and the horrible secret that she hides. In the narration the writer successfully adopts a number of narrative strategies, such as managed and variable narrative distance, the cultivation of variant empathies, and the function of time and timing③.

According to Michael Toolan, in the process of narrating a story, with almost inevitable and copious specification of time and space, some perspective or other has to be adopted as the vantage point from which the spatiotemporally determinate events are related④. Focalization is used to refer to "this inescapable adoption of a (limit-

---

① Reed, Joseph. *Faulkner's Narrative.* New Haven and London: Yale University Press, 1974, p. 8.

② Reed, Joseph. *Faulkner's Narrative.* New Haven and London: Yale University Press, 1974, p. 19.

③ Reed, Joseph. *Faulkner's Narrative.* New Haven and London: Yale University Press, 1974, p. 19.

④ Toolan, Michael. *Narrative: A Critical Linguistic Introduction.* London: Routledge, 1988, pp. 67 – 68.

ed) perspective in narrative, a viewpoint from which events are seen, felt, understood, assessed"①.

In the following analysis, Rimmon-Kenan's theory of focalization in narrative will be constantly referred to. Rimmom-Kenan not only distinguishes between external and internal focalization, but also develops a typology of focalization which consists of perceptual, psychological and ideological facets. Focalization has the focalizer as its vehicle and the focalized as its object. The focalizer is the agent who orients the presentation through his or her perception while the focalized is what the focalizer perceives②.

2. Analysis of the Three Facets of Focalization in "A Rose for Emily"

William Faulkner himself calls "A Rose for Emily" a ghost story. "The heart of the ghost story is suspense... Revelations are controlled, and the readers' involvement and identification are managed, and they are led along by the storyteller. "③ The story in "A Rose for Emily" is told by an unspecified first-person narrator, apparently one of the residents in the town where Emily lives. However, the narrator almost always speaks using the first-person plural pronoun "we", a strategy to evoke the readers' empathy and belief in the narrator and the story.

It is questionable whether the whole text of "A Rose for Emily" is internally focalized as Rimmom-Kenan puts it④, or externally focalized, or both. The style of focalization in "A Rose for Emily" will be examined to see how it contributes to some artistic effects. Right from the very first sentence the narrator says, "Our whole town went to her funeral. "⑤ The opening statement seems to suggest that all the towns-

---

① Toolan, Michael. *Narrative: A Critical Linguistic Introduction*. London: Routledge, 1988, p. 68.

② Rimmom-Kenan, Shlomith. *Narrative Fiction: Contemporary Poetics*. London: Routledge, 1983, p. 74.

③ Reed, Joseph. *Faulkner's Narrative*. New Haven and London: Yale University Press, 1974, p. 13.

④ Rimmom-Kenan, Shlomith. *Narrative Fiction: Contemporary Poetics*. London: Routledge, 1983, p. 78.

⑤ Faulkner, William. "A Rose for Emily", in Malcolm Cowley (ed.), *The Essential Faulkner*. London: Chatto & Windus, 1967, p. 1.

people love Emily, but in actuality such is not the case at all. The writer's use of an anonymous narrator who has no active role in the story is a subtle way of showing how the townspeople truly regard Emily. The narration of the story in "A Rose for Emily" is from the perspective of the townspeople as a whole, with the narrator as one of them, thus a participant or a character in the narrated events. Therefore, it can be said that the text is internally focalized, or in Rimmom-Kenan's words, the text has internal focalization with a character-focalizer as its vehicle. Now the focalizer is different from the narrating agent, as will be seen.

The narrator of "A Rose for Emily" also keeps an eye on different subgroups of the townspeople and refers to them respectively on various occasions as follows: "the Board of Aldermen", "all the ladies", "the older people", "some of the ladies", "the newer generation". At this point, the narrator is more like an observer outside the narrated events, perceiving what is happening to Emily and how those subgroups treat Emily. Moreover, the narrator seems to have a very thorough knowledge about Emily since he can easily select the events in Emily's life, for example, the tax issue and the smell incident when she is in her seventies and early thirties respectively, and present them in the reversed chronology without confusion. All the above facts and some others indicate that "the focalization is felt to be close to the narrating agent"①, so it can also be said that the text of "A Rose for Emily" has external focalization with a narrator-focalizer as its vehicle. In the following three subsections the relevant three facets of focalization in "A Rose for Emily" will be examined one by one.

2.1 The Perceptual Facet

According to Rimmom-Kenan, the perceptual facet of focalization refers to the perception (sight, hearing, etc.) of the focalizer, and should be examined from two aspects, namely space and time. In spatial terms, the external position of the focalizer takes on a bird's eye view, whereas the internal position of the focalizer takes on

---

① Rimmom-Kenan, Shlomith. *Narrative Fiction: Contemporary Poetics*. London: Routledge, 1983, p. 74.

the view of a limited observer[1].

In "A Rose for Emily", the narrator does not have a panoramic view since he cannot see the inside of Emily's house, just as he mentions at the very beginning: "... the women most out of curiosity to see the inside of her house, which no one save an old manservant—a combined gardener and cook—had seen in at least ten years"[2]. The delayed description of the inside of Emily's house is understandable because it also helps to create suspense. The readers may be eager to know what is inside. The outside of Emily's house is an image of "decay", and with Emily's death, the inside of her house cannot be something pleasant, so an atmosphere for a ghost story is gradually constructed. When the inside is focalized, the narrator invites the readers along with him to perceive it from the perspective of the tax delegation. Such a choice of internal focalization adds credibility and objectivity to the narration since it is not the narrator's own perception.

The room above the stairs in Emily's house is the spot where the enigma in the story is to be unravelled eventually after so many suspenses and mysteries (the smell, poison, disappearance of Homer Barron, etc.), and hence the point where the ultimate climax of the story lies. Any early revelation of the room would be detrimental to the creation of the rhetorical effects. Therefore, internal focalization is chosen again to allow the readers, along with the participating characters, including the narrating agent, to experience the climax of the story. At this point, the narrator follows the focalizer, moving his viewpoint "from one detail to another, and the readers are given a task of piecing together the separate descriptions into one coherent picture"[3].

After Emily's room is forced open, "we find a tomb, a rose colour, a frozen mo-

---

① Rimmom-Kenan, Shlomith. *Narrative Fiction: Contemporary Poetics*. London: Routledge, 1983, p. 77.

② Faulkner, William. "A Rose for Emily", in Malcolm Cowley (ed.), *The Essential Faulkner*. London: Chatto & Windus, 1967, p. 433.

③ Uspensky, Boris. *A Poetics of Composition*. Berkeley: University of California Press, 1973, p. 60.

ment. "[1] In perhaps the most brilliantly economic instance of William Faulkner's exercise of stopped-action description, the objects which the readers see are frozen, each for a moment, like stills spliced into a movie. The writer makes the narrator pile horror upon horror in a tour de force of climactic revelation. The readers see "the man" himself; then he is "in the attitude of embrace"[2]; then he is in a nightshirt; then "the indentation of a head on the second pillow; finally a long strand of iron-grey hair"[3]. Internal focalization in "A Rose for Emily" not only helps to bring the story to its climax, but also demonstrates the storyteller's delicate and subtle craftsmanship.

Examined from the temporal aspect, "an external focalizer has at his disposal all the temporal dimensions (i. e. past, present and future) of the story, whereas an internal focalizer is limited to the 'present' of the characters. "[4] Suppose William Faulkner adopts the implied time of Emily's death as the opening of the story sequence in "A Rose for Emily", then the "present" of the principal character as well as that of the text, and other narrated events which happen before Emily's death, like her father's death, her love affair with Homer, her buying poison, the smell issue, the visit of the tax delegation, are all considered flashbacks; then the "past" of the protagonist, such as Emily's funeral, the forced opening of the upstairs room, the discovery of Homer's death, are all regarded as the "future" of the protagonist.

Because "A Rose for Emily" is narrated in retrospect, the text time is different from the story time, and their differences can be demonstrated by the following evidence. In Part I the narrator begins his narration with Emily's death, the description of her frame house and the street, and then flashes back to the time when she was a-

---

① Faulkner, William. "A Rose for Emily", in Malcolm Cowley (ed.), *The Essential Faulkner.* London: Chatto & Windus, 1967, p. 130.

② Faulkner, William. "A Rose for Emily", in Malcolm Cowley (ed.), *The Essential Faulkner.* London: Chatto & Windus, 1967, p. 130.

③ Reed, Joseph. *Faulkner's Narrative.* New Haven and London: Yale University Press, 1974, p. 18.

④ Uspensky, Boris. *A Poetics of Composition.* Berkeley: University of California Press, 1973, p. 67, p. 113.

live: "Alive Miss Emily had been a tradition, a duty."① The past perfect tense in the quotation shows that this part of the narrated event is a flashback. What follows is a scene of Emily's encounter with the tax delegation, which initiates another event in Emily's life with a clear time specification, which is the smell issue thirty years ago: "That was two years after her father's death and a short time after her sweetheart … had deserted her."② If the above story events can be chronologically arranged as follows: A (the smell issue)—B (Emily's encounter with the tax delegation)—C (Emily's death), then the text time is C—B—A, a complete violation of the chronology, or an chronological reversal of the events in time order. It is obvious that the narrator counts time and organizes the events from his own perspective.

The narrator can have all the temporal dimensions of the protagonist at his disposal. In Part III Emily's purchase of poison is also described with a clear reference to time: "That was over a year after they had begun to say 'Poor Emily', and while two female cousins were visiting her."③ So much evidence in the text suffices to show that the narrator is omniscient about Emily, so he is an external focalizer in terms of the temporal dimensions of the story. However, he chooses not to disclose his retrospective understanding, restricting his perceptions to those of the townspeople rather than the narrating agent, so the text has an internal focalizer as well.

In "A Rose for Emily", William Faulkner employs the element of time to enhance details of the setting and vice versa. By avoiding the chronological order of the events in Emily's life, the writer first gives the readers a finished puzzle, and then allows them to solve the puzzle piece by piece, step by step. By doing so, he enhances the plot and presents two different perspectives of time held by different characters. The first perspective is in the world of the present while the second is in the world of past tradition. The first perspective is that of Homer and the modern generation while

① Faulkner, William. "A Rose for Emily", in Malcolm Cowley (ed.), *The Essential Faulkner*. London: Chatto & Windus, 1967, p. 433.

② Faulkner, William. "A Rose for Emily", in Malcolm Cowley (ed.), *The Essential Faulkner*. London: Chatto & Windus, 1967, p. 435.

③ Faulkner, William. "A Rose for Emily", in Malcolm Cowley (ed.), *The Essential Faulkner*. London: Chatto & Windus, 1967, p. 439.

the second one is that of the Confederate soldiers and the older members of the Board of Aldermen. Emily clings to the second view.

The central theme in "A Rose for Emily" is to "let go of the past". Emily has a tendency to cling to the past and a reluctance to be independent. William Faulkner regards the past not only as a repository of the images of great human effort and integrity, but also as the source of a dynamic evil. He is aware of the pull of the romantic past and realizes that submission to the past romance is a form of death. In "A Rose for Emily", the writer contrasts the past with the present era. The past is represented by Emily, Colonel Sartoris, the old Negro servant, and the Aldermen who accept the Colonel's attitude toward Emily and rescind her taxes. The present is expressed chiefly through the words of the unnamed narrator. Homer and the new Board of Aldermen all represent the present era. Referred to as a "fallen monument" in the story, Miss Emily is a "monument" of Southern gentility, representing ideal values of the past, but she is fallen because she has shown herself susceptible to death and decay. The description of her house as "lifting its stubborn and coquettish decay above the cotton wagons and the gasoline pumps—an eyesore among eyesores"① reflects a juxtaposition of the past and the present and is an emblematic representation of Emily herself.

Emily has already completely retreated into her world of the past. When the representatives of the new, progressive Board of Aldermen wait on her concerning her delinquent taxes, Emily declares that she has no taxes in Jefferson, basing her belief on a verbal agreement made with Colonel Sartoris, who has been dead for ten years. Just as she refuses to acknowledge the death of her father, Emily now tries to deny the death of Colonel Sartoris, who has given his word, which knows no death according to the local tradition. It is the past pitted against the present—the past with its social decorum while the present with everything set down in the books.

When she is threatened with desertion and disgrace, Emily not only takes refuge in the past world but also takes Homer with her in the only possible manner—death.

---

① Faulkner, William. "A Rose for Emily", in Malcolm Cowley (ed.), *The Essential Faulkner.* London: Chatto & Windus, 1967, p. 433.

Emily's room above the stairs is that timeless "meadow" where living Emily and dead Homer remain together as though even death could not separate them. The story says that death conquers all, but what is death? Death is the past tradition, whatever is the opposite of the present.

Homer Barron, a Yankee who lives in the present, represents the Northerners' attitudes toward the Griersons and the entire South. He is ready to take his pleasure and depart, and apparently unwilling to consider the possibility of defeat. In a sense, Emily conquers time only briefly by retreating into her "rose-tinted" world of the past in which death is denied at the same time when it is shown to have existed. The story implies that such a retreat is hopeless since everyone, including Emily, is finally subject to death and the invasion of his or her own world by the clamorous and curious inhabitants in the world of the present.

2.2 The Psychological Facet

The psychological facet of focalization is related to the focalizer's mind and emotions, and determined by the cognitive and emotive orientations of the focalizer towards the focalized①. On the cognitive level, the external focalizer and the internal focalizer take on the form of possessing unrestricted and restricted knowledge respectively. When the external focalizer knows everything about the narrated world but restricts his knowledge, a rhetorical effect is achieved②.

As is shown above in the subsection concerning the time component of the perceptual facet, despite the knowledge of the external focalizer or narrator-focalizer, the narrator limits his knowledge about the focalized Emily to that of the townspeople. For instance, he knows the source of the terrible smell from Emily's house according to his retrospective understanding, but he chooses not to divulge it. Instead he follows Judge Stevens's reasoning that "it's probably just a snake or a rat that nigger of hers

---

① Rimmom-Kenan, Shlomith. *Narrative Fiction: Contemporary Poetics*. London: Routledge, 1983, p. 79.

② Rimmom-Kenan, Shlomith. *Narrative Fiction: Contemporary Poetics*. London: Routledge, 1983, p. 79.

killed in the yard"①, and withholds the truth. As a result, the smell issue narrated from the internal focalizer's perspective creates suspense, arouses the readers' curiosity and desire for the truth. Just as the first part of the story presents an unpleasant atmosphere of death, decline and decay, the terrible smell also suggests something sinister. The same is true of the poison case. The narrator definitely knows what Emily would use the poison for again from his retrospective knowledge, but he chooses to follow the townspeople's view: "... so the next day we all said, 'She will kill herself'."② The unknown reason for Emily's buying poison thus helps to build up a kind of horrible, fearful atmosphere for the ghost story.

In both the smell issue and the poison case, the narrator tells what the townspeople perceive instead of what he himself perceives, so he changes from the external focalizer to the internal one. According to Rimmom-Kenan, "the choice of an internal focalizer lends plausibility to the withholding of information and creates shocking effects when the discovery of Homer's corpse is narrated."③ Therefore, it is obvious that William Faulkner deliberately selects two different types of focalization out of rhetorical considerations. Actually he has carefully calculated what to tell, how to tell, and when to tell in narrating the story.

Regarding the emotive component of the psychological facet, the subjectivity of the internal focalizer can be observed from several perspectives. First of all in Part I, Emily's house is described from the perspective of the townspeople (including the narrator) as follows: the house is "lifting its stubborn and coquettish decay above the cotton wagons and the gasoline pumps", with its "cupolas and spires and scrolled balconies in the heavily lightsome style of the seventies"④. The description indicates

① Faulkner, William. "A Rose for Emily", in Malcolm Cowley (ed.), *The Essential Faulkner*. London: Chatto & Windus, 1967, p. 436.

② Faulkner, William. "A Rose for Emily", in Malcolm Cowley (ed.), *The Essential Faulkner*. London: Chatto & Windus, 1967, p. 440.

③ Rimmom-Kenan, Shlomith. *Narrative Fiction: Contemporary Poetics*. London: Routledge, 1983, pp. 78-79.

④ Faulkner, William. "A Rose for Emily", in Malcolm Cowley (ed.), *The Essential Faulkner*. London: Chatto & Windus, 1967, p. 433.

an obvious attitude of the focalizer (the townspeople as a whole) towards the focalized Emily, who is here portrayed as an isolated, out-dated and decadent image.

Then from the perspective of the tax delegation as a representative of the new generation, the description of the inside of Emily's house is subjective, too: "... a dim hall ... It smelled of dust and disuse … when the Negro opened the blinds of one window, they could see that the leather was cracked; and when they sat down, a faint dust rose sluggishly about their thighs, spinning with slow motes in the single sunray..."① The old, broken, dusty house is viewed as a symbol of the decline or decay of the older generation with Emily as their representative. "She looked bloated, like a body long submerged in motionless water, and of that pallid hue. Her eyes, lost in the fatty ridges of her face, looked like two pieces of coal pressed into a lump of dough as they moved from one face to another."② The unforgettable description of Emily signifies that the protagonist is separated from time, fashion and encroachment, and regarded as an isolated, lifeless still point, a walking corpse in the rushing world.

Emily's love affair with Homer also receives different responses from different subgroups of the townspeople. Firstly, it is viewed from the perspective of "the ladies": "At first we were glad that Miss Emily would have an interest, because the ladies all said, 'Of course a Grierson would not think seriously of a Northerner, a day labourer'."③ Then, it is discussed from the older people's perspective: "... older people who said that even grief could not cause a real lady to forget noblesse oblige—without calling it noblesse oblige. They just said, 'Poor Emily. Her kinsfolk should come to her'."④ Afterwards when the townspeople come to know that Homer is not a

① Faulkner, William. "A Rose for Emily", in Malcolm Cowley (ed.), *The Essential Faulkner*. London: Chatto & Windus, 1967, p. 434.

② Faulkner, William. "A Rose for Emily", in Malcolm Cowley (ed.), *The Essential Faulkner*. London: Chatto & Windus, 1967, p. 435.

③ Faulkner, William. "A Rose for Emily", in Malcolm Cowley (ed.), *The Essential Faulkner*. London: Chatto & Windus, 1967, p. 438.

④ Faulkner, William. "A Rose for Emily", in Malcolm Cowley (ed.), *The Essential Faulkner*. London: Chatto & Windus, 1967, p. 438.

marrying man, and that Emily is still with him in the glittering buggy "with her head high", it is seen from the perspective of "some of the ladies": "Then some of the ladies began to say that it was a disgrace to the town and a bad example for the young people... at last the ladies forced the Baptist minister ... to call on her. "① Based on the above emotive orientation of "the ladies", "older people", and "some of the ladies", it is evident that Emily is emotionally distanced and alienated from the townspeople. She is the attention target of the townspeople because of her "right and mighty", "real lady" aristocracy. Moreover, with the help of his string of "we*s*" in the fourth and fifth parts, the narrator gains the readers' allegiance and their empathy with the attitudes of "our town". However, when Emily's tragic fate is revealed in the end, the empathy with "our town" is instantly converted to that with Emily, the hitherto distanced individual. Therefore, the readers' conventional empathy with the first-person narrator turns out to be only a prelude to their ultimate sympathetic response to "the isolated subject"②. The cultivation of variant empathies is largely attributable to the choice of internal focalization in "A Rose for Emily".

2.3 The Ideological Facet

The ideological facet of focalization, which is often referred to as "the norms of the text", consists of "a general system of viewing the world conceptually, in accordance with the events and characters of the story which are evaluated"③. The ideology of the dominant focalizer or narrator-focalizer is the authoritative one from which other ideologies in the text are evaluated. ④

Since the story in "A Rose for Emily" is told by a first-person narrator who speaks as "we", holding a kind of collective view and gradually gaining allegiance from the readers, the readers tend to adopt as their own the narrator's view of Emily or the townspeople's collective view of Emily. Meanwhile, other views also exist because of the various subgroups among the townspeople, such as "the young", "the

---

① Faulkner, William. "A Rose for Emily", in Malcolm Cowley (ed.), *The Essential Faulkner.* London: Chatto & Windus, 1967, p. 440.

② Reed, Joseph. *Faulkner's Narrative.* New Haven and London: Yale University Press, 1974, p. 19.

③ Uspensky, Boris. *A Poetics of Composition.* Berkeley: University of California Press, 1973, p. 8.

④ Rimmom-Kenan, Shlomith. *Narrative Fiction: Contemporary Poetics.* London: Routledge, 1983, p. 8.

old", "the Board of Aldermen", "the ladies", "some of the ladies", etc. The subgroups are "definite with their characteristic opinions"① about Emily, and their views certainly influence the judgement of the readers. However, most of the subgroups' views are negative while the narrator's view seems to be more objective, comprehensive, and thus more acceptable. The negative views help to alienate Emily from the townspeople and to contrast Emily with them.

3. Conclusion

In the perceptual facet, the short story "A Rose for Emily" by William Faulkner has internal focalization, which limits the spatial perceptions to those of the participating characters, or the townspeople, in an attempt to build up horror or fear—an atmosphere for a ghost story. Though the narrator has all the temporal dimensions of the heroine at his disposal and appears to be an external focalizer, he chooses to withhold the truth by restricting his perceptions to those of the townspeople in order to create suspense and arouse curiosity in the readers. The same is truc of the cognitive component of the psychological facet. On the level of the emotive component of the psychological facet, the text is internally focalized. The relations between Emily and the townspeople are depicted, and the readers' empathy is first established with the townspeople but then converted to empathy with Emily. As a result, some unexpected effects are achieved, and Emily's tragic fate is highlighted. In terms of the ideological facet, though various ideologies are offered both explicitly and implicitly, the narrator's ideology is the dominant one.

To sum up, the style of focalization in the text of "A Rose for Emily" is no simple scheme. On the contrary, it is subtly handled by William Faulkner. The text has both internal and external focalization, and the presence of both types serves the writer's rhetorical purposes to create suspense and to arouse empathy and hence belief from the readers.

The range of narrative techniques used by William Faulkner in "A Rose for Emily" is remarkable. He would never step between the characters and the readers to

① Reed, Joseph. *Faulkner's Narrative.* New Haven and London: Yale University Press, 1974, p. 15.

explain, but let the characters explain themselves and hinder as little as possible the readers' direct experience of the work of literature. He deliberately broke up the chronology of his narrative by juxtaposing the past with the present. William Faulkner was good at presenting multiple points of view. Instead of having one person or the main character tell the story, he adopted the collective "we" that represents all the townspeople and their version of the story. The collective narrator gives the story more life because the readers are less concerned with what or who the narrator is.

The plot structure of "A Rose for Emily" is different from that of most of the stories that one reads. Most stories start from the beginning of the tale, go through a certain period of time, and normally end in a resolution. On the contrary, "A Rose for Emily" begins at the end of the story and tells the plot through various flashbacks. Instead of following the normal plot structure (the exposition, rising action, climax, falling action, and the resolution), "A Rose for Emily" includes those components throughout the tale in a precariously different order. The upsetting ending gives the story depth and air of reality while the variation of the plot structure gives it mystery. All in all, thanks to William Faulkner's ingenious techniques in writing, "A Rose for Emily" is a terrific literary work.

References:

[1] Bleikasten, Andrew. *The Most Splendid Failure.* Bloomington: Indiana University Press, 1976.

[2] Faulkner, William. *Faulkner in the University: Class Conferences at the University of Virginia* 1957 – 1958, *ed.* Frederick L. Gwynn and Joseph L. Blootner. New York: Random House, 1965.

[3] Faulkner, William. "A Rose for Emily", in Malcolm Cowley (ed.), *The Essential Faulkner.* London: Chatto & Windus, 1967.

[4] Matthews, John. *The Play of Faulkner's Language.* Cornell: Cornell University Press, 1982.

[5] Messent, Peter. *New Readings of the American Novel.* Edinburgh: Edinburgh University Press, 1998.

[6] Reed, Joseph. *Faulkner's Narrative.* New Haven and London: Yale University Press, 1974.

[7] Rimmom-Kenan, Shlomith. *Narrative Fiction: Contemporary Poetics*. London: Routledge, 1983.
[8] Toolan, Michael. *Narrative: A Critical Linguistic Introduction*. London: Routledge, 1988.
[9] Uspensky, Boris. *A Poetics of Composition*. Berkeley: University of California Press, 1973.

The Significance of Names in Toni Morrison's Novels[①]

Wang Jinmei

Typically names function as designators to distinguish one person or one thing from others. In her novels, Toni Morrison depends on the names of characters, places and titles to build their characteristics and give the reader a deeper understanding of characters, themes. This paper aims to analyze some names of characters, locations and the novels' titles, to explore the significance of naming in delineating the characters' personalities and in bringing to light the thought—provoking themes of the novels.

Naming usually plays a dynamic role in shaping identity. To name the characters, Toni Morrison takes advantage of allusions, from classical history or mythology (Valerian, Ajax, Circe), Judeo-Christian sources (Ruth, First Corinthians, Hannah, Shadrack) to African folklore. She names some characters ironically or symbolically to bring out the depth of their personalities. The ironic naming of characters can be seen in the case of the Breedlove, Peace, Wright, and Dead families.

In *The Bluest Eye*, the two words "breed" and "love" are intertwined in the name. Generally "breed" is a biological phenomenon, a physiological occurrence, while "love" is a social, religious, or spiritual phenomenon. Actually what the Breedlove family lacks is love; self-hatred marks this family:

---

① 本文受美联基金会出国进修项目、云南省教育厅青年教师科研基金项目(编号:by0182E)、云南大学人文社会科学研究项目资助。

> You looked at them and wondered why they were so ugly: you looked closely and could not find the source. Then you realized that it came from conviction, their conviction. It was as though some mysterious all-knowing master had given each one a cloak of ugliness to wear, and they had each accepted it without question. The master had said, "You are ugly people." They had looked about themselves and saw nothing to contradict the statement; saw, in fact, support for it leaning at them from every billboard, every movie, every glance. "Yes," they had said, "you are right." And they took the ugliness in their hands, threw it as a mantle over them, and went about the world with it ①.

There is no love among the family members. Pauline Breedlove is "Mrs. Breedlove" even to her husband and children, but "Polly" to the white family. Being born into this loveless family marked by self-hatred, Pecola Breedlove is humiliated by schoolmates and disdained by other black people. Even worse, she is raped by her own father. In this novel, the biological occurrence does not bring about love, but tragedy-Pecola's madness.

In *Sula*, Sula Peace, who is not as her name suggests, is rebellious and upsets the black community. When she is eleven years old, she cuts off the tip of her finger to demonstrate to a gang of threatening boys what she can do to them if she can do that to herself. She swings a child around by the wrists and half intentionally lets him slip out of her grasp into the river, where he drowns. In the shadows of her porch, she watches in an "interested" way while her mother burns to death. The adult Sula refuses the conventional roles of wife, mother, and dutiful family member. "I don't want to make somebody else. I want to make myself,"② she says when Eva asks her when she is going to get married and have children. Sula puts Eva in a nursing home, and even hurts her best friend, Nel, by casually sleeping with her husband, who then takes the opportunity to desert his wife and their three children. The betrayal of the act itself is surpassed by Sula's inability to comprehend why she might have left him alone for the sake of friendship. She retorts to Nel's accusations: "I didn't kill him, I just fucked him. If we were such good friends, how come you couldn't get

---

① Toni Morrison, *The Bluest Eye* (New York, 1970), 34.

② Toni Morrison, *Sula* (New York, 1973), 92.

over it?"[1] Sula also perceives the Bottom people as objects of contempt and actively shames them. When Sula asks Nel how she is and Nel says that she must be "all right" because she "ain't strangled nobody yet," Sula remarks that half the people in the town need to be killed while the rest are a "drawn-out disease"[2].

The name Wright suggests conformity to socially-accepted values and codes of behavior. Unlike Sula Peace, who is "a rule-breaker, a kind of law-breaker, a lawless woman", Nel Wright knows and believes in the values and the laws of the community. If we ignore the "r" instead of the "w", the name implies conformity to white norms. Helene Wright, Nel's mother, is a pillar of middle-class respectability in the Bottom community, who carries with her a deep and inherited sense of shame. The daughter of a Creole whore, Helene was raised in New Orleans "under the dolesome eyes of a multicolored Virgin Mary" by her respectable grandmother, who counseled Helene "to be constantly on guard for any sign of her mother's wild blood"[3]. In repudiating her mother's "wild blood" and becoming a proud and utterly respectable middle-class woman, Helene attempts to escape the sexual shame of black women. Bell Hooks, remarking on the humiliations endured by black women in American society, describes the still common tendency of whites to view black women as sexually loose and thus as not worthy of respect, this shaming stereotype of African-American women being historically rooted in the slavery system in which whites "justified the sexual exploitation of enslaved black women by arguing that they were the initiators of sexual relationships with men"[4]. Helene defends against her inherited shame by becoming an "impressive woman" who wins all social battles with presence and a conviction of the legitimacy of her authority. Abhorring the circumstances of her own birth to a Creole prostitute, and in order to "be as far away from the Sundown House as possible"[5], she also exchanges her name, Helene Sabat, with its exotic associations with the witch's Sabbath, for Helene Wright, with its implications of both "rightness" and "whiteness". Here the choosing of the name can also represent a re-

---

① *Sula*, 145.
② *Sula*, 96.
③ *Sula*, 17.
④ Stephen Steinberg, *The Ethnic Myth: Race, Ethnicity, and Class in America* (New York, 1981), 52.
⑤ *Sula*, 15.

jection of black race and culture.

Dead is not the true name of the Dead family in *Song of Solomon*, who are dead in the spiritual sense as well as in name. The name of Macon Dead is created by a slip of the pen. Failing to fill the information in the correct boxes, the Yankee clerk at the Freedmen's Bureau takes the place of origin as the first name, writing the condition of the father in the box for the surname. Though one point about this history of naming is that a careless drunk official has the power to change the name of a family, another more significant point is that the new name further emphasizes the death of the father. The fact that Macon, Jr, has inherited this false name highlights the way in which he is a grotesque distortion of his father. His father's real name was Jake, but his son is more like his biblical namesake, crafty and patriarchal. For Jake, property was not mere property, but the symbol of a bond between the land and the community. Macon Dead, Jr, is a grotesque fairytale character whose lust for gold has made him one of the most affluent and most hated black property owners. However, his name epitomizes how much his fixation with white-defined respectability and has cost him in personal, social and spiritual terms, even though his accumulation of wealth is part of his attempt to overcome oppression, prejudice, poverty and lack of a formal education. Guitar makes explicit the connection between the imposed name, Dead, the appropriation of white values, and a more generalized and pervasive white control: "White men want us dead or quiet—which is the same thing as dead-They want us, you know, 'universal', human, 'no race consciousness'"①. In the Deads' house, the women cower and Milkman is bored. Ruth suffers under Macon's rule, her creativity stunted, her flowers dying. The two daughters, Magdalene called Lena and First Corinthians, pine for lack of love and life, since no man in the community is good enough for Macon Dead's daughters. According to the standard black middle-class narrative, the college-educated Corinthians, who had been taught how to be "an enlightened mother and wife," should have been able "to contribute to the civilization—or in her case, the civilizing—of her community," and she should have been "a prize for a professional man of color." But despite her education and class privileges, she remains unmarried, for such men prefer wives unlike the "elegant" Corin-

① Toni Morrison, *Song of Solomon* (New York, 1977), 222.

thians, who is accustomed to black middle-class life and thus lacks the necessary "ambition", "hunger", and "hustle" such men look for in a wife①. The granddaughter of the distinguished Dr. Foster, the forty-four-year-old Corinthians ends up working as a maid for a white woman. In the genealogy of the Deads, the trauma of paternal loss reveals one father who flew away and one who died violently at the hands of whites while trying to make good in America. The two instances record different responses to life in racist America, each of which entails traumatic consequences—Solomon miraculously flies off, becoming a symbol of transcendence and escape, but bequeathing also a legacy of bereavement, loss and forgetting; Jake stands his ground but is cut down, leaving his family similarly bereft. Both modes raise the question of how black men in America survive and how they position themselves in relation to dominant social and political structures.

Milkman's nickname has ignominious origins; because his mother breastfed him for much longer than normal it was given to him by Freddie, the janitor. Indeed, his name suggests infancy and the egocentricity of the young child, from which Milkman has to develop. In the early part of the novel he tries to avoid commitment. At the age of thirty-one, Milkman is still a narcissist; his life is stagnant and his growth suspends. Once overnourished by his mother's milk, he fails to grow until the interjection of Lena's accusation that he has victimized others with his egotism. The name also serves to exacerbate the tension between Milkman and his father. Although his father Macon doesn't understand the origins of the name he recognizes that it sounds "dirty, intimate, and hot" thereby reminding him of his wife's abnormal fixation for her father and the passion which he denies in himself and in his children. His son's name compounds the shame of his own name.

Another symbolic and significant name in *Song of Solomon* is Pilate. African values and African culture, exemplified in Pilate, are privileged in the text. Pilate has all the qualities Morrison associates with an ideal African woman: She has stature, and strength. Pilate is tall, as tall as her brother Macon, with black skin and wine-colored lips; moreover, she constantly has a "chewing stick" between her lips,

---

① *Song of Solomon*, 188.

much like a West African market woman. Her father's initial selection of the name is auspicious: "He saw in them the letters a large figure that looked like a tree hanging in some princely but protective way over a row of smaller trees. "① Indeed, Pilate embodies this protective function, so that when Milkman sees her for the first time, she looks like "a tall black tree"②. Finally, Pilate's father accepts the name as a form of heroic anathema (using the name of Christ's betrayer) addressed to a God.

Thus, the contradictory aspects of Pilate's identity—protectiveness, authoritativeness, and marginality with the parodic surcharge of "pie-late"③—are enacted in her life story, and she preserves the material trace of that triple invocation in a casket made out of her mother's snuffbox containing the paper on which her father had painstakingly copied out her name. For the rest of her life, she wears the name (talisman) in her left earlobe as a constant reminder of her original dedication. In contrast to the passive Ruth Dead, Milkman's biological mother, Pilate is his spiritual mother, responsible for his very existence: When "only a miracle" could have produced a pregnancy in Ruth, Pilate had given her sister-in-law a concoction that had made her briefly both fertile and sexually irresistible to her cold husband, thus presiding over Milkman's very conception. She prevented Macon from killing the baby before it was born and aided Ruth during the delivery. As his spiritual midwife, Pilate enlarges the boundaries of Milkman's suffocating world by introducing him to the sky, "so that from then on when he looked at it, it... was intimate, familiar, like a room that he lived in, a place where he belonged. "④ Eventually Milkman discovers the true family history through this woman who, though she lives in the present, is vitally in touch with the past. When he hears the name pronounced, Macon understands it as pilot, "like a riverboat pilot"⑤. Milkman's true inheritance, black cultural identity and ancestry, is provided by his aunt, Pilate. She becomes quite literally Milkman's pilot or guiding force. She challenges his indifference and initiates him into the legacy of which black womankind are the guardians, a legacy of wisdom and beliefs. In "Root-

---

① *Song of Solomon*, 18.
② *Song of Solomon*, 38.
③ *Song of Solomon*, 286.
④ *Song of Solomon*, 207.
⑤ *Song of Solomon*, 19.

edness," Morrison states that Pilate functions as the ancestor for Milkman, and it is under her guidance that he becomes responsible and humane. Pilate's house reflects her African heritage in other ways. Her house appears to Ruth as "an inn, a safe harbor", and "true to the palm oil that flowed in her veins." Pilate offers both food and hospitality to all who enter. Even Macon, who deserted his sister, sees the house as a place of music, warmth, and caring, not realizing that he has destroyed the music in his own house. The two houses stand in stark contrast.

In *Sula*, Chicken Little is an important character. The name suggests childhood and short life. His death is the novel's central symbol of loss. One moment he is there, laughing as Sula swings him, holding him by the wrists; the next he is gone: "The water darkened and closed quickly over the place where Chicken Little sank."① Chicken Little's sky falls in, recalling the hapless chicken of the barnyard fable who thought the sky was coming down on his head when he was hit by an acorn. The text emphasizes how the women mourners relate to the event by identifying with the child as "innocent victim". They are reminded of the "oldest and most devastating pain there is: not the pain of childhood but the remembrance of it"②. The funeral foregrounds childhood as a time of vulnerabilities, pain and loss, just as, we might say, Chicken Little's death is a symbol of Sula's own childhood hurt and loss. Shortly before she and Nel go swimming, Sula overhears her mother's conversation with friends about the problems of child rearing. Hannah's comment can be interpreted as a determining factor in Sula's personality formation. The moment functions as a turning point for Sula. What Hannah says is that children are a nuisance. Her friends agree—they may love their children but they do not like them. Hearing her mother's pronouncements, Sula is stung, immersed in "dark thoughts" until Nel calls to her to go swimming. Chicken Little, then, may be seen as the childhood that slips from Sula's grasp that day. Chicken Little's death may represent the pain of losing innocence and childhood, but it also represents, the permanence of childhood captured and secured by death.

---

① *Sula*, 61.

② *Sula*, 65.

Pauline Breedlove in *The Bluest Eye* provides another example of Morrison's concern with the significance of naming. Known as "Mrs. Breedlove" even to her husband and children, she is "Polly" to the white family for whom she works, and the diminutive name is totally appropriate in this case, for Pauline has diminished herself through her obsequious dedication to whiteness. Thus nicknames are often appropriate in Morrison's novels, denoting truths about character, revealing secrets, determining how a person is viewed by a particular community. Elihue Micah Whitcomb, also in *The Bluest Eye*, is called Soaphead Church by the community, a name mysterious to him but nevertheless reflective of his perverted sexual preference for "clean" little girls: "His sexuality was anything but lewd; his patronage of little girls smacked of innocence and was associated in his mind with cleanliness. He was what one might call a very clean old man"①.

In *The Bluest Eye*, the three whores' names—China, Poland and The Maginot Line—are suggestive of their refusal to be coopted. In their occupations as whores, the women bear the same relationship to patriarchy that the occupied territories of China, Poland, and France (the Maginot Line bearing a synecdochic relationship to France) had to Japan and Nazi Germany in World War II. A significant fact about China, Poland, and France is that "these places were not annihilated and their cultural values did not crumble." Besieged though the women are, they are not merely walls to be broken or lines to be transgressed; the three whores are at war with men: "these women hated men, all men without shame, apology, or discrimination... Black men, white men, Puerto Ricans, Mexicans, Jews, Poles, whatever—all were inadequate and weak, all... were the recipients of their disinterested wrath."②

In *Tar Baby*, Jadine is hard, as her name suggests, and self-indulgent, seeking only to live in the present, disregarding her obligations to others and turning her back on her ancestral line. Her commitment to her own individual fulfillment rather than to a sense of solidarity with other black people is evident in her favoring of the interpre-

① *The Bluest Eye*, 132.

② *The Bluest Eye*, 47.

tation of the mythic horse riders on the island told her by a neighbour: That rather than a hundred ex-slaves there is only one French soldier on a horse. Her surname, Childs, indicates that Jadine is, in different ways, as immature as Son, who is accused by Jadine of thinking "like a kid" and whose name emphasizes that he has failed to wean himself away from Eloe.

The primary significance of the name Son is not to denote an individual self ("He did not always know who he was, but he always knew what he was like")①, but to place that self in a context of relationship: Son is a son of Africa and also a son of the American black male experience, the "Nigger Jims... Staggerlees and John Henrys. Anarchic, wandering, they read about their hometowns in the pages of out-of-town newspapers"②. Like Pilate and any number of Morrison's other characters, Son is dispossessed, permanently "out-of-town", his name being his only connection with community and black tradition.

Naming can also imply a form of reciprocal relationship between namer and named. To name is to have power over the individual named. Like the biblical Eve in *Sula*, Eva both gives life and takes it away. Her power is symbolic of her function as the phallic mother to destroy as well as to create life. There is no question that she loves her children; she has sacrificed even her leg to provide for them; to relieve the baby Plum's life-threatening constipation, as Eva recites ritualistically and repeatedly, she has taken a lump of lard and "shoved the last bit of food she had in the world up his ass"③. But Plum returns from war to his mother's house a drug addict, helpless as an infant again. She murders him, burns him alive in his bed, because he "wanted to crawl back in my womb". That Eva murders her son is an extension of the symbolic fact that she has already emasculated and rendered him infantile by calling him "Sweet Plum". Tar Baby, Morrison implies, might have lived more effectively if Eva had not ridiculed his white skin and infantilized him in the same stroke with whimsical naming. And the Deweys would have been at least somewhat individu-

---

① Toni Morrison, *Tar Baby* (New York, 1981), 142.

② *Tar Baby*, 143.

③ *Sula*, 29.

ated, perhaps even normal in stature, if Eva had not reduced them, truncated their potential, through her assignment of the same name for all three: "What you need to tell them apart for? They's all deweys"①. Finally, the name is not even capitalized, and "them deweys" become a "trinity with a plural name"②, indistinguishable in their appearance as in their childlike behavior.

In *Beloved*, Sethe's name is one of the few in this novel chosen by a mother, and that name is a mark of blackness and of acceptance into tribe and culture. Whether this name is derived from that of the Egyptian god, Seth, or from the biblical Seth, it represents, like most of the names that Morrison designates as chosen, a sense of heritage and a context of relational identity.

Stamp Paid, born Joshua under slavery, has chosen and devised his own symbolic name, which represents a rejection of a tradition of white naming as well as a celebration of freedom. His name is also and more specifically a symbol of freedom from debt; because he suffered under slavery and because he "handed over his wife to his master's son"③, he has paid in misery any obligation to humanity, he believes, although his continued activity as a conductor on the Underground Railroad would indicate otherwise. All African Americans are, in essence, "Stamp Paid," Morrison implies.

Nicknaming and name calling are traditions relevant to the shaping of black character, which reflect patterns of caring and incorporation into community. Pauline is pained that she does not have a nickname and blames it on the family's pity for her, for the "slight deformity" she suffers, left from a nail puncture in her foot when she was two years old. The nickname is an old and venerated tradition in the black community, and not having been given one, Pauline feels excluded. Pauline "never felt at home anywhere, or that she belonged anyplace"④. Without a nickname, Paul-

---

① *Sula*, 32.

② *Sula*, 33.

③ Toni Morrison, *Beloved* (New York, 1987), 184.

④ *The Bluest Eye*, 88.

ine feels unclaimed by her family in any special way. When the rich white family for which she works in Ohio assigns her a nickname—Polly—it serves in part to explain Pauline's attachment to them: "They gave her what she never had"① and thereby claim her attention and her loyalty more than anyone in her family has done. The white family tells anecdotes about her, of how they could "never find anybody like Polly," of how "she will not leave the kitchen until everything is in order", and of how she is ultimately the "ideal servant"②. As a counterexample of the functions nicknames serve in black communities, Pauline, as Polly, illustrates the potential identity-shaping purpose such naming provides. She desperately clings to her relationship with the Fishers, but fails to see in her daughter a similar need to be claimed in a special way.

Another meditation on the larger meaning of names and naming comes in a comic catalogue of the nicknames that constitute a distinctive feature of black culture, nicknames representative of yearnings, gestures, flaws, events, mistakes, weaknesses: Macon Dead, Sing Byrd, Crowell Byrd, Pilate, Beba, Hagar, Magdalene, First Corinthians, Milkman, Guitar, Railroad Tommy, Hospital Tommy, Empire State, Small Boy, Sweet, Circe, Moon, Nero, Humpty-Dumpty, Blue Boy, Scandinavia, Quack-Quack, Jericho, Spoonbread, Ice Man, Dough Belly, Rocky River, Gray Eye, Cock-a-Doodle-Do, Cool Breeze, Muddy Waters, Pinetop, Jelly Roll, Fats, Leadbelly, Bo Diddley, Cat-Iron, Peg-leg, Son, Shortstuff, Smoky Babe, Funny Papa, Bukka, Pink, Bull Moose, B. B. , T-Bone, Black Ace, Lemon Washboard, Gatemouth, Cleanhead, Tampa Red, Juke Boy, Shine, Staggerlee, Jim the Devil, Fuck-Up, and Dat Nigger.

Most of the other characters in *Tar Baby* have at least two names, which Morrison indicates is symbolic of their fragmentation. Lost between the white and black worlds, Jadine is Jadine to her aunt and uncle but a more exotic Jade to the white Streets who have educated her and imbued her with their questionable values. Ondine is Nanadine to Jadine, but Ondine to the Streets, just as Sydney is Sydney to the per-

---

① *The Bluest Eye*, 101.

② *The Bluest Eye*, 101.

son he calls Mr. Street, years of intimacy not being sufficient to challenge racial and class protocol.

Names are important, not only as ironic comments on the characters who bear them, but as emblems of the black community's resistance to the white culture's negation of its world. In *Song of Solomon*, geographical locations like Not Doctor Street and No Mercy Hospital (where, until Ruth Dead's son was born, black people were denied admittance) are forms of counternegation of the white world that delimits the black one. They are symbols of black resistance, poignantly commenting on the yearning for some linguistic validation of black achievement and professional cachet. This reflection also registers the subversive resources of language; this subversiveness is a well-known feature of language as spoken by the oppressed or socially marginalized. The prologue to Sula points out that the black neighborhood is called "the suburbs now, but when black people lived there it was called the Bottom"①. This linguistic shift emphasizes how language can be and has been manipulated by those in authority to maintain their advantage and protect their positions, a concern developed in all Morrison's work.

The title *Song of Solomon* suggests the biblical song of ancestral wisdom, and from the beginning the novel is presided over by the figure of Milkman's forefather. Indeed, it has the epigraph: "The fathers may soar/ And the children may know their names." Song of Solomon is framed by the African-American vernacular tradition of the flying African. The song Pilate sings to accompany Milkman's birth is a variant of this Gullah folktale of the ancestor who flew back to Africa to escape the trap of slavery, and Milkman's leap at the end of novel aligns him with Solomon.

The title of the novel *The Bluest Eye* pinpoints the focus of the novel-Pecola's tragedy resulting from her desire for blue eyes. "Blue" doesn't only mean color. It has a deep meaning, referring to white culture. The single "eye" sounding "I" rather than the plural form "eyes", suggests some kind of solitude and distance from the black tribe, black culture.

---

① *Sula*, 3.

Names are of great importance in West Africa. The power of a name is strong in much of Africa and the diaspora. As Morrison has said in an interview with Thomas Le Clair: "If you come from Africa, your name is gone. It is particularly problematic because it is not just your name but your family, your tribe. When you die, how can you connect with your ancestors if you have lost your name? That's a huge psychological scar"①. It is difficult in a discussion of Morrison's works to ignore their preoccupation with names. In her novels, names function not only as designating, but as delineating the personalities of the characters ironically or symbolically, resisting the hegemony of white society and revealing the themes of the novels.

References:

[1] Morrison, Toni. *The Bluest Eye.* New York: Washington Square Press, 1970.

[2] Morrison, Toni. *Sula.* New York: Vintage International, 1973.

[3] Morrison, Toni. *Song of Solomon.* New York: Penguin Group, 1977.

[4] Morrison, Toni. *Tar Baby.* New York: Penguin Group, 1981.

[5] Morrison, Toni. *Beloved.* New York: Knopf, 1987.

[6] Bouson, J. Brooks. *Quiet as It's Kept-Shame, Trauma, and Race in the Novels of Toni Morrison.* Albany: State University of New York Press, 2000.

[7] Furman, Jan, ed.. *Toni Morrison's Song of Solomon, A Casebook.* New York: Oxford University Press, 2003.

[8] Gates, Henry Louis ed.. *Toni Morrison: Critical Perspectives Past and Present.* New York: Amistad, 1993.

[9] Grewal, Gurleen. *Circles of Sorrow, Lines of Struggle: the Novels of Toni Morrison.* Louisiana: Louisiana State University Press, 1998.

[10] Harding, Wendy and Jacky Martin. *A World of Difference: An Inter-cultural Study of Toni Morrison's Novels.* Westport: Greenwood Press, 1994.

[11] Karenga, Maulana. *Introduction to Black Studies.* Kawaida Publications, 1984.

[12] McKay, Nellie Y.. *Critical Essays on Toni Morrison.* Boston: G. K. Hall &

① Toni Morrison, *Rootedness: The Ancestor as Foundation in Black Women Writers* (1950 - 1980) (New York, 1984), 28.

Co. ,1988.

[13] McKay, Nellie Y. ed. . *Approaches to Teaching the Novels of Toni Morrison.* New York: The Modern Language Association of America, 1997.

[14] Middleton, David L. , ed. . *Toni Morrison's Fiction: Contemporary Criticism.* New York: Garland Publishing, 1997.

[15] Morrison, Toni. *Rootedness: The Ancestor as Foundation in Black Women Writers* (1950 – 1980) . New York: Anchor Books, 1984.

[16] Peach, Linden. *Toni Morrison.* New York: St. Martin's Press, 2000.

[17] Rigney, Barbara Hill. *The Voices of Toni Morrison.* Columbus: Ohio State University Press, 1991.

[18] Steinberg, Stephen. *The Ethnic Myth: Race, Ethnicity, and Class in America.* New York: Atheneum, 1981.

A Complete Rejection of Men

——An Analysis of Katherine Anne Porter's "Theft"

He Jingming

Katherine Anne Porter was a brilliant contemporary American writer and a radical feminist. Her well-known short story "Theft" is often used to explain her views on the world and her artistic features, but as it is such a short and compact story and written in the modernist way, there are still some misinterpretations of it even in the comprehension of some minor details. Typically, we see misunderstanding of some sentences: Zu Ci-liu's explanation of the first sentence is "the heroine holds the purse when she comes in her sitting room from the bathroom"①. But if the heroine carries the purse with her all the time and from the sitting room into the bathroom and again into the sitting room, she needn't have come "out of the bathroom to get a cigarette from the package in the purse" (Para. 35). In fact we have learned that immediately after entering her own flat "she had taken the letter out of the purse before she spread the purse out to dry" (Para. 31). Thus the heroine hasn't carried it into the bathroom. Moreover, when the heroine emerges from the bathroom, one of her hands is "holding her bathrobe around her" and the other, "trailing a damp towel" (Para. 1), she has no free hand to hold the purse at the same time. Furthermore, it is not in her manner to guard the purse by carrying it all the time as "she had never locked a door in her life" (Para. 40). Last but not least, if the heroine carries the purse

① Zu Ci-liu. *Roads and Ways to Better English* (*Teacher's Book*) 4. Beijing: Higher Education Press, 1990, p. 4.

with her all the time, the whole story cannot have taken place as the janitress, who never enters the bathroom, cannot have taken it away.

If this misunderstanding will cause trouble only in our comprehension of details of the story, other misinterpretations will hinder us from the grasp of its theme. Just like Zu Ci-liu, Elizabeth Booz explains that the janitress' removal of the purse is an act of theft. Booz further explains that the heroine "belongs to the professional middle class" and the janitress "belongs to the lower class" and she "feels justified in stealing it for her niece"①. She thus concludes that the story reflects "contrast and conflict between social classes"②. Admittedly the heroine supposes the janitress has stolen the purse so she speaks to the janitress in a very sarcastic way, but the janitress also takes the heroine for a thief: She "closed the door very sharply" (Para. 34) when taking the purse away. All through the scene the janitress is in hot anger. When the heroine asks the janitress to give back her purse, the janitress' face is red with anger, saying "What do you mean, your purse?" (Para. 36) "Before God I never laid eyes on your purse, and that's the holy truth" (Para. 38). The janitress doesn't deny having taken away the purse, she only hints that the heroine is not its rightful owner. The janitress returns the purse to the heroine on hearing the latter's sarcastic remarks, "Oh, well then, keep it, keep it if you want it so much" (Para. 39). Even a shameless thief would never behave this way. A more reasonable explanation should be like this: the janitress, in a hot temper and perhaps not properly educated, cannot hope to speak to the point until at last when she tells the heroine: "It's not from me, it's from her (the janitress' niece) you're stealing it" (Para. 49). Only on hearing this does the heroine realize that she has been fooled by the man who steals the purse from the janitress's niece and presented it to her.

Booz says that story is a reflection of class struggle, and Zu Ci-liu says that it reflects the hard life of American people in the Depression. Of course their opinions are

① Booz, Elizabeth. *A Brief Introduction to Modern American Literature*. Shanghai: Shanghai Foreign Language Education Press, 1982, p. 266.

② Booz, Elizabeth. *A Brief Introduction to Modern American Literature*. Shanghai: Shanghai Foreign Language Education Press, 1982, p265.

prevailing, but the present author have a different opinion. Their views are based on misinterpretation of details and therefore are not reliable. And we will miss much fun from a hasty and careless reading of such a story. Now let us follow the heroine's train of thought as triggered by her loss of the purse, and have a close look at the men who come to her mind one after another in a way very much like a stream of consciousness.

The story is set in the depression. The heroine attended a party on the previous evening. Early in the morning she finds her purse missing. Naturally she begins to recall the immediate past to make sure when and where she loses it. The first man that comes to the heroine's mind is Camilo. Judging from the context, Camilo is an admirer of the heroine. On a raining night such as this, it is usual for a man to accompany and give help to his girl friend. This is what Camilo tries to do. "'It is written that we must be rained upon tonight,' said Camilo, 'so let it be together'" (Para. 3). Yet the heroine doesn't need his company, as his presence only gives her more trouble: She "had walked with him to the station in a pouring rain" (Para. 2), whereas without him she might have been running to the station and thus would suffer less from the rain. As she knows, "he was almost as poor as she was, and when he insisted on a taxi, she immediately refused it, saying, 'You know it simply will not do'" (Para. 2). It is to save Camilo's face that the heroine agrees to let him come with her. "If she had not feared Camilo would take it badly, for he insisted on the practice of his little ceremonies up the point he had fixed for them, she would have said to him as they left Thora's house, Do go home. I can surely reach the station by myself'" (Para. 2). Camilo's helpfulness turns out be "a set of smaller courtesies" and "the practice of his little ceremonies". He is a dandy. If most men are careless about their clothes as Eddy is, Camilo is an exception. "If he (Camilo) wore a shabby hat it would be merely shabby on him, and he would lose his spirit over it" (Para. 2). "Thinking that tomorrow morning he would gaze soberly at his spoiled hat and soggy shoes and possibly associate her with his misery" (Para. 5). In an effort to save his hat, she asks him not to accompany her up the stairs leading to the Elevated, and he "made three quick bows", "and leaped off through the rainy darkness" (Para. 5). This reveals his instinctive eagerness to protect his new hat from being further ruined by the rain. Her further observation justifies her understanding of Camilo: "As she watched, he stopped at the far corner and took off his hat and hid it under his overcoat." (Para. 5) This suggests Camilo's foolishness as well as his vanity and shallowness. On the contrary, the heroine's understanding, sympathy and consideration as well as penetrating insight are seen here.

Roger is the second man she has met the night before. He is another admirer of the heroine. Unlike Camilo, he is frank. He tells her directly that he hides his hat in his overcoat (Para. 6). He is, however, ill-behaved, conceited, stubborn and indecisive. When the taxi is running too fast, he curses the driver: "This bird is a homicidal maniac, and I could do with a cocktail myself this minute" (Para. 8). He uses swearwords to the three pedestrians who have nothing to do with him (Para. 10). He has not got enough money for a taxi fare, yet he will not sell his play below the price he sets. In an effort to get rid of his wife, Roger cannot take initiative action but has to wait for the mercy of his wife (Para. 13). And intimate as his relation with her is, his concern for the heroine is shown only in his words about the minor details of life, and when it is time to pay taxi fare, he asks the heroine to share it. Needless to say, Roger doesn't leave us a good impression.

The third man she encounters is Bill. He is also a playwright (Para. 23). He is wretched, vain, "self-pitying and tightfisted"①. He invites the heroine to his home only to let her know the reason why he cannot pay the money he owes her (Para. 23). But his flimsy excuse is soon betrayed by his own boasting of his newly-bought luxury item (Para. 25) with a sum of money much larger than what he owes the heroine. The latter now has not a single coin to jingle in her pocket, yet she doesn't tell anyone else about it. Now she cannot keep silent any longer. She asks him to pay what he owes her. As a gesture of refusal to repay the money, he even sobs while complaining and expressing his grievances (Para. 23) against his wife. Seeing no hope of getting back her money, she just leaves him without any more words with him (Para. 26).

---

① Booz, Elizabeth. *A Brief Introduction to Modern American Literature*. Shanghai: Shanghai Foreign Language Education Press, 1982, p. 265.

The three men give her nothing but verbal service. Yet they are better than those unnamed men in the story. Among them are three drunken pedestrians in shabby clothes. They are not serious about love and talk in a silly way (Para. 9). No wonder Roger calls them "pure nuts" (Para. 10). Their counterparts are two properly dressed girls. They are well behaved and very reasonable and serious about love (Para. 11).

Another nameless man is the writer of a letter to the heroine. He may want to save the love between them, but his letter is full of clichés, they sound sweet, but they don't mean anything. He puts all the blame on her for the trouble in their relationship. This justifies her decision to break with him (Para. 33).

The worst of all the men in the story is the one who gives the purse to the heroine as his present①. She must have entertained some sincere affection for him as she prizes the purse very much as a present. She is naturally very upset when she at last knows this purse belongs to the janitress' niece (Para. 48). As the purse does not belong to the man who presents it to her, his affection for her is also worthless. Thus the man has not only stolen the purse from another girl but also stolen the heroine's heart. Her only fault in it is her trust in this man, which exposes her to his traps.

By now we get the heroine's general impression of men: shabby, dirty, hypocritical, rude, conceited, wretched, vain, foolish and above all, insincere. When women are in a difficult situation, they cannot hope to get any help from men. This is a world without any protective man that women can admire or depend on. Men, despite their strong physical bodies, are nothing but "scarecrows" (Para. 9).

Women on the contrary have all the good qualities: sincerity, consideration,

---

① Zu Ci-Liu holds that the janitress has stolen the purse. But why should a thief announce her coming and close the door with a loud and sharp noise (para. 34). She has taken the purse from the heroine's room, but it is not stealing. In the consequent argument the janitress and the heroine only mean justify each's rightful possession of it and to prove the other is the thief, but as the heroine is only insinuating and the janitress is too angry to express her point well until the end of the argument, the heroine and the reader get the truth only at the end of the story.

honesty, sympathy, and penetrating insight, dignity, integrity, independence, self-respect, cleverness, graceful manners, and beauty. The heroine here well displays all these fine qualities. The very fact that she has so many admirers suggests her beauty. She is broad-minded: When Bill refuses to pay her the money of which she is in desperate need, she just "let it go" (Para. 30). She doesn't expect men's help. She is clever and knows well Camilo's mind (Para. 2). She knows how to contradict Bill when he is complaining about his difficulties. She is poor but she will not let her admirers pay a single cent for her. She is capable: She is a writer and earns her own living. She never asks for mercy from other people. She has good manners: No matter what she thinks of these men, she pays them due respect. Her confrontation with the janitress is a model of self-control. And their quarrel suggests that if there is any conflict among women, it is caused by men's evil deeds.

This artificial attribution of all bad qualities to men and all good ones to women is reinforced by Porter's deliberate use of nameless characters. The heroine is nameless not because it "helps the reader to identify himself with her" (Booz, 265), but because she represents all women in general. The same is true of the nameless men: the letter-writer, the three pedestrians and the thief of the purse, they represent the general character of men. The ones who are given names only suggest some minor differences among men.

Why should the heroine, with so low an opinion of men, still get on with some of them and show due respect? The names of these men may suggest the answer. Eddie sounds like eddy, circular movement of air or water, which may suggest the overwhelming current: Yes, most men pay little attention to clothes just as Eddy does. So women will disregard most men just as the heroine does. Camilo sounds like camellia, a decorative flower pleasing to the eye, which is one function of those few dandies. The heroine gets along with him only for this reason, as Camilo is a rare exception. Roger is a British euphemism for having sexual intercourse with someone, this name suggests another function of men: satisfying women's sexual desire. Bill means an amount expended or owed. So women have to deal with some men in economic activities, but in many cases it is the men who owe the women rather than vice versa. In short, if women still have contact with men, it is only to satisfy women's basic physical needs and there is no honorable man in women's spiritual world.

Thanks to this writer's great artistic power and subtlety, we often read her story superficially, without realizing its hidden message: the radical disgust for the men. No general statement of the author's or the heroine's opinion of men is made, but it is shown through the combination of details provided here. The third person limited point of view makes the story sound more objective and thus easier for the reader to accept. The rain definitely adds to the gloomy atmosphere. Thus her great art has masked the absurdity of the conclusion. In an age of male dominance, this story, together with many of her other short stories, is an outcry of awakened and discontented women against sex superiority.

References:

Porter, Catherine Anne. "*Theft*", *Roads and Ways to Better English* (*Student's Book*) 4, compiled. By Zu Ci-liu. Beijing: Higher Education Press, 1990. 10.

A Black Divinity in a Moral Wasteland

——A Textual Analysis of Dilsey in William Faulkner's *The Sound and the Fury*

Xie Ping

It is not until the last part of The Sound and the Fury that Faulkner allows us to adopt a view detached from the commotion of the Compson brothers' obsessive interior monologue. From such a comparatively objective point of view, our attention is directed most of the time toward Dilsey, about whom Faulkner writes nothing when he adds the "Appendix" to make things more clear. The reason, I think, is that Dilsey is almost a god-like figure on the moral wasteland of the Compsons. Although she is a Negro cook for the once aristocratic family and thus of a much humbler social stratum, her moral intergrity raises her high above their moral deterioration. She believes in God, which gives her power to survive the corruption of the Compsons. Her omniscience about the family, her tolerance of their moral degradation, and her endurance of their discrimination are just like the merits of God she believes in and we generally know so that they do not require an entry in the "Appendix" to clarify.

At the beginning of this chapter, Faulkner gives us a detailed and highly symbolic description of Dilsey that focuses on her surroundings, appearance, and facial expression. It is on the "bleak" and "chill" morning of Easter Sunday that we first see Dilsey in the house of the Compsons (165). While it is the day commemorating the resurrection of Christ, to Dilsey the light of the morning "seem[s] to disintegrate into minute and *venomous* particles, like *dust* that, when Dilsey open[s] the door of the cabin and emerge[s], *needle*[*s*] laterally into her flesh" (italics mine, 165).

The malicious light is like the foul air Dilsey breathes in the Compsons' realm. Jason (the son) regards her as "somebody in the kitchen to eat up the grub the young ones cant tote off" (116). Caroline Compson protests against setting the cradle for Quentin (the granddaughter) in Dilsey's room for fear of being "contaminated by that atmosphere" (125). Quentin (the granddaughter) "knock[s] down" Dilsey's hand and calls her "You damn nigger" right after Dilsey shields her from Jason's attack (117). Although Dilsey is the person who "raised ev'y one" of the young Compsons, her contribution is not recognized or appreciated by them (125). Instead, she is always despised and repeatedly insulted. Standing in such malicious light, Dilsey appears as a person whose "muscle and tissue [are like] courage or fortitude which the days or the years ha[ve] consumed until only the *indomitable skeleton* [is] left rising like a ruin or a landmark above the somnolent and impervious guts" (italics mine, 165). Dilsey's flesh can be consumed by the demanding Compsons, but her skeleton shows no sign of failing. Its rigidity is like Dilsey's moral integrity that protects her from the erosion of her surroundings, and makes her the "sworn enemy" of the vicious Jason (the son) and the only person he "fear[s] and respect[s]" (212). Dilsey lifts her face to the light "with an expression at once *fatalistic* and of a *child's astonished disappointment*" (italics mine, 165). Dilsey's fatalistic expression marks the difference from Jason's pessimistic obsession with his ill fate. She accepts life as it is, and her placid and honest attitude towards life constitutes a sharp contrast to the chaotic confusion characteristic of the Compsons. At this moment Dilsey is disappointed because she finds the weather is not good on this Easter Sunday when she is going to church to attend the Easter Sermon, which is almost the most important thing in her life. But in describing her disappointment as a "child's" and later her way of descending the stairs as "a small child does", Faulkner seems to imply a touch of guilelessness in Dilsey's character that makes it possible for her to adopt an indiscriminate and tolerant attitude towards the Compsons (165, 169). With her integrity and tolerance, the Dilsey we see on this Easter Sunday morning witnesses, endures, survives and contrasts with the degradation of the Compsons.

When Dilsey catches Caddy in the tree on the night Dammudy dies, she calls Caddy, "You, Satan" (29). This spontaneous response has almost the effect of prophecy. Caddy's loss of virginity is the direct cause for her brother Quentin's suicide, which in turn makes the sacrifice of Benji's pasture go in vain. Her pre-marital pregnancy costs Jason the promised job and thereby initiates his obsession with his ill fate. Her daughter Quentin also suffers from her motherless upbringing and becomes wild at an early age. Despite the misfortune Caddy has caused, Dilsey does her justice in allowing her to see her daughter secretly. She even interrogates Jason: "I like to know whut's de hurt in letting dat po chile see her own baby" (130). Like an omniscient God, Dilsey foresees evil before it takes place, endures evil when it cannot be avoided, and takes care of the sufferers as best as she can.

Not only is Dilsey like an omniscient God, she believes in the power of God that penetrates every lie and gives everyone his due. When the one-hand clock in the kitchen strikes five times, Dilsey knows and says that it is actually "[e]ight o'clock" (171). That she restores time to its order contrasts with Quentin's effort to twist and destroy time. Quentin lives in his lie of committing incest with Caddy, and therefore is afraid of facing time that cannot lie and cannot be reversed. Dilsey's matter-of-fact attitude towards time comes from her belief that what is important is the ultimate time when every soul has to face the Judgment. When Caddy tells her that the change of Benji's name will bring him good luck, she says, "Name aint going to help him. Hurt him neither" (37). She believes there is a time when her name "will be in the Book" and "they'll read it for [her]" (38). While Quentin imagines he can lie about committing incest and cheat God, Dilsey believes that nothing can escape His eyes. That's why she thinks there is no point in changing Benji's name, because God knows everything.

Dilsey is the opposite of Jason (the son) in almost every way. While Jason thinks "nothing whatever of God one way or the other", Dilsey "[sits] bolt upright" during the Easter Sermon (212, 183). She is so moved by the sermon that "[t]wo tears slid[e] down her fallen cheeks, in and out of the myriad coruscations of immolation and time" (183). Dilsey's tears are what are missing in Jason's emotional wasteland where feelings have given way to the calculating of fortune and the futile defending of family honor. Jason can feel nothing but "sort of funny" at the funeral of his father (127). His theory of "[o]nce a bitch always a bitch" betrays the cruelty and unforgivingness that contrast with Dilsey's tolerance of Caddy and care of Miss

Quentin(113). While Jason declares, "I give every man his due, regardless of religion or anything else", he is in fact the very person who thinks "what this country need is white labor"(120). Whereas Jason hides Benji from the public view to protect the family honor, Dilsey takes him to church because he is also the "Lawd's child"(117). As Jason is obsessed by the idea that he is unfairly deprived of what should have been his share of privilege, he is always oriented towards the past—towards how to take advantage of every opportunity to make compensation for his lost fortune so as to restore justice for himself. On the contrary, Dilsey is future-oriented in the sense that she believes in the Day of Judgment, which allows her to assume a calm, confident and tolerant attitude towards her daily life. Despite her inferior social status, Dilsey finally gains the upper hand over Jason, whose clawing for every bit of money that comes to hand only makes his loss more deplorable when his niece outmaneuvers him.

Dilsey's sphere in the Compsons' realm is the kitchen. She cooks food there to feed the Compsons. She reads the correct time from the broken clock there to restore the order of the chaotic world. She sees what is happening around her from the window of the kitchen and understands what that means. She looks upwards towards the realm of the Compsons "as if her eyes [can] and [do] penetrate the walls and ceilings"(168). She tells Frony, "I've seed de first en de last", and it is true that she witnesses "the rotten family in the rotting house" and endures their discrimination (185,212). But she is not a helpless victim. Instead, as she says to Jason, she "got mo heart dan dat, even if hit is black"(130). She believes in God and she is like God safeguarding the moral debris of the Compsons.

References:

Faulkner, William. *The Sound and the Fury*. Ed. David Minter. New York: W. W. Norton & Company, Inc., 1994.

Lecture d'*Hamlet et Œdipe* de Jones

Xu Feng

Hamlet, chef-d'œuvre de Shakespeare, est sans doute une des pièces les plus jouées sur les scènes de nombreux pays du mondc. Tous ceux qui ont reçu un peu d'éducation connaissent la tragédie du prince danois, malgré leurs différences de races ou de cultures. Car Shakespeare a créé un des drames les plus propres à séduire les hommes d'aujourd'hui, comme ceux de son époque. Touchés profondément, les spectateurs et les lecteurs y croient retrouver l'écho de leurs propres incertitudes, de leurs propres angoisses et de leur désespoir. *To be or not to be,* la question qu'Hamlet s'est posée avec angoisse, a obsédé, obsède et obsédera toujours des milliers et des milliers de personnes de chaque époque. Cet attrait universel s'explique peut-être par le fait que Shakespeare a dépeint, telle qu'elle est, la personnalité d'Hamlet et a reflété profondément le conflit violent en son for intérieur.

Il est vrai que les incidents de la pièce sont violents : il y a tant de morts à la fin que la scène est jonchée de cadavres. Cependant le drame le plus intense est celui qui se joue dans l'âme du héros. Toute la pièce se construit autour du conflit qu'Hamlet éprouve intérieurement entre le devoir de vengeance qu'il doit remplir et son hésitation constante apparue au cours de l'accomplissement de sa mission. C'est peut-être pour cette raison que le héros shakespearien, plus vivant que son prototype, le vrai Hamlet historique du deuxième siècle, reste immortel et continue de vivre parmi nous.

Si la critique littéraire du monde entier apprécie à l'unanimité ce chef-d'œuvre de Shakespeare et que les spectateurs et les lecteurs de tous les pays admirent merveilleusement cette pièce émouvante, les interprétations de cette œuvre, surtout celles du personnage d'Hamlet restent loin d'être unanimes. La pièce est construite sur l'hésitation qu'Hamlet éprouve à accomplir le devoir de venger son père par le meurtre de son oncle. Mais le texte ne nous livre aucune indication explicite sur les raisons ou les motifs de cette hésitation. Pourquoi le héros, qui aime apparemment tant son père qu'il le considère comme un roi excellent et tendre, comme un homme auquel il ne trouve pas de pareil, atermoie-t-il sans cesse pour remplir son devoir filial ?

Qu'est-ce qui l'empêche alors d'accomplir réellement sa tâche ? Centrées sur ces questions, de différentes hypothèses se sont proposées les une après les autres. Ce qui est tout à fait naturel d'ailleurs, car plus une œuvre est esthétiquement valable, plus elle suscite de réflexions différentes. Un chef-d'œuvre comme *Hamlet* ne manque pas bien sûr d'attirer d'innombrables interprétations de toutes sortes. Parmi toutes les interprétations d'Hamlet, celle que Jones nous a proposée à la lumière de la psychanalyse freudienne dans son livre *Hamlet et Œdipe* nous paraît d'autant plus intéressante et particulière qu'elle ouvre un nouvel horizon à la critique de l'œuvre de Shakespeare.

Publié en 1949, l'ouvrage de Jones comprend huit chapitres : I. Psychologie et esthétique ; II. Le problème d'Hamlet et les diverses explications proposées ; III. La solution psychanalytique ; IV. La tragédie et le monde psychique de la prime enfance ; V. Le thème du matricide ; VI. Hamlet et Shakespeare ; VII. La place d'Hamlet dans la mythologie ; VIII. Les transformations d'Hamlet par Shakespeare. Dans ce petit essai, nous nous limiterons à traiter l'explication que Jones a proposée de l'atermoiement d'Hamlet, essentiellement dans les deuxième, troisième et quatrième chapitres afin d'extraire quelques particularités de cette interprétation psychanalytique après la lecture d'*Hamlet et Œdipe* de Jones.

Principales hypothèses avant Freud

En analysant les hypothèses les plus intéressantes, Ernest Jones les regroupe en trois " postulats" représentatifs dans son essai *Hamlet et œdipe.*

Le premier de ces postulats, c'est ce qui Jones appelle " le point de vue subjectif ". Selon cette hypothèse, c'est le caractère même d'Hamlet qui est la cause de son hésitation. Le héros de la pièce se voit traité comme un personnage dont les facultés intellectuelles sont abusivement développées aux dépens de la volonté, de sorte qu'il est incapable de prendre des décisions et de se jeter fermement dans n'importe quelle action.

Le célèbre portrait d'Hamlet tracé par Goethe renforce sans doute cette hypothèse. Dans son *Wilhelm Meisters Lehrjahre*, il écrit ainsi : *Pour moi, il est clair que Shakespeare entendait présenter en Hamlet une âme confrontée à une grande tâche, imposée comme un devoir, et qu'il n'était pas de taille à accomplir. Voici un chêne planté dans un vase précieux, qui n'aurait dû nourrir que les fleurs les plus délicates : les racines croissent, le vase est brisé. Une nature trop pure, noble, hautement morale, mais dépourvue de cette énergie nerveuse qui fait le héros, succombe sous le poids d'un fardeau qu'elle ne peut ni supporter ni refuser.* Un prince si fin, si subtil, élevé dans le palais royal comme " *un vase précieux, qui n'aurait dû nourrir que les fleurs les plus délicates* ", ne peut pas naturellement accomplir une mission qui exige de la volonté et du courage extraordinaire.

Après avoir exposé les points de vue de cette hypothèse, Jones les résume ainsi : "*en raison du développement très poussé de ses facultés intellectuelles, Hamlet ne peut jamais se contenter d'une opinion simple et unique ; il voit toujours les divers aspects et toutes les explications possibles de chaque question. Aucune ligne de conduite ne lui semple jamais s'imposer sans équivoque, de sorte que, dans la vie pratique, son scepticisme et ses puissantes facultés réflexives paralysent son action*." ①

Selon cette interprétation, nous avons donc affaire à un type à l'intellect développé aux dépens de la volonté. La faiblesse de caractère d'Hamlet constitue l'obstacle insurmontable dans l'accomplissement de sa tâche. La tragédie d'Hamlet est en quelque sorte la tragédie de son caractère déficient. Avant la découverte psychanalytique de Freud et l'interprétation de Jones, c'est sans doute cette hypothèse. Dans une préface d'*Hamlet*, un préfacier contemporain traite aussi le héros de Shakespeare d'un homme "*pensif et subtil, chez qui l'habitation de méditer a annihilé l'énergie et le désir de l'action*" ②.

Cette hypothèse peu plausible a suscité de nombreuses objections. A peine Goethe l'avait –il avancée que Herme a réfuté cette interprétation en 1827. En fait, même dans la pièce elle-même, on peut trouver la preuve manifeste que cette hypothèse est mal fondée. Au début de la scène premier de l'acte premier, quand Hotatio, ami intime d'Hamlet, raconte le combat provoqué par Fortinabras de Norvège, il interprète l'attitude d'Hamlet avec ces paroles : "*Dans ce combat, notre vaillant Hamlet (car cette partie du monde connu l'estimait tel) tua ce Fortinbras.*"

Il faut dire que, comme ami d'Hamlet, Horatio connaît bien le prince danois. Contrairement à ce qu'on croit, à ses yeux, Hamlet n'est pas quelqu'un de caractère lâche, indécis, mais un héros vaillant. Dans le même acte, nous voyons qu'il ne manque point de courage et de décision pour affronter le fantôme en s'écriant : "*Je lui parlerai.*" Malgré la dissuasion répétée de son ami, il suit courageusement le spectre mystérieux au risque de sa vie. Dans le déroulement de la pièce, nous pouvons voir qu'il a tué successivement Polonius, Guildenstern, Rosdencrantz et enfin Claudius. Cela prouve qu'Hamlet est "*un homme capable d'action et sans prévention particulière à l'encontre du meurtre, qu'il s'agisse d'un meurtre impulsif–celui de*

① Ernest Jones *Hamlet et Œdipe* p. 30, Ed. Gallimard.
② Shakespeare Richard III, Roméo et Juliette, Hamlet p. 250, Ed. Garnier – Flammarion 1964.

Polonius –ou prémédité comme ceux de Guildenstern et Rosencrantz" ①. Quand il se décide à organiser un spectacle présenté à son oncle, quand il rompt avec Ophélie et quand il relève le défi en duel de Laërte dont l'intention de le tuer est évidente, sa résolution est vite faite et sans aucune trace d'hésitation. De plus, son mépris et son ironie mordante envers ses ennemis, même envers la jeune fille qu'il aimait, Ophélie, la condamnation violente qu'il fait à l'égard de sa mère, son absence de remords après l'assassinat de Polonius, tout cela montre aussi qu'il n'est pas de nature faible, douce ou molle.

Fondateur de la psychanalyse, Freud, qui s'intéresse surtout aux processus psychiques de l'homme, ne trouve pas naturellement cette hypothèse satisfaisante. Dans une lettre écrite le 15 octobre 1897 à son ami Wilhelm Fliess, il a indiqué la contradiction existant entre l'interprétation de Goethe et les attitudes qu'Hamlet a montrées dans la pièce. Trois ans après, dans une longue note placée en bas de page de sa *Traumdeutung*, il refuge catégoriquement l'hypothèse selon laquelle Hamlet représente un caractère maladif, irrésolu. Il y écrit : *"Mais le déroulement de la pièce nous apprend qu'Hamlet ne doit nullement nous apparaître comme une personne complètement inapte à l'action. Nous le voyons par deux fois intervenir de façon active : d'abord, dans un rapide emportement passionnel, lorsqu'il met à mort l'indiscret qui écoute derrière la tapisserie ; ensuite, de façon concertée et même astucieuse, quand, avec l'indifférence totale d'un prince de la renaissance, il livre les courtisans à la mort qu'on lui avait destinée."* Disciple de Freud, Ernest Jones n'accepte pas bien sûr l'hypothèse de Goethe.

Le deuxième postulat, dit " objectif " consiste à prouver que ce sont les difficultés de l'acte même qui constituent l'unique raison de l'hésitation d'Hamlet. Selon cette hypothèse, les difficultés de cette tâche incombée à Hamlet sont assez extraordinaires pour décourager quiconque, si résolu soit-il. Les tenants de cette hypothèse estiment qu'il ne suffit pas à Hamlet de châtier le meurtre pour réaliser la vengeance de son père. Il faut surtout dénoncer le fratricide de Claudius devant la nation. Vu la nature particulièrement odieuse du crime, cette dénonciation publique est presque inconcevable. Hamlet ne peut pas accuser son oncle sans

① *Hamlet et Œdipe* p. 31.

avancer des preuves irréfutables. En assassinant le roi pour venger son père, il risquerait de provoquer les masses de la nation contre lui et de se voir accusé d'avoir l'intention de s'emparer du trône. Il importe donc de chercher surtout un jugement par des voies plus ou moins légales au lieu de tuer tout court le fratricide. Si Hamlet tarde à réaliser la vengeance de son père, c'est parce que les conséquences et les répercussions éventuelles de cet acte le paralysent.

Cette hypothèse exagère visiblement les difficultés du devoir qui s'impose à Hamlet et ne trouve pas de justification convaincante dans la pièce. Après avoir analysé la situation intérieure et le dénouement de la pièce, ainsi que l'attitude même d'Hamlet, Jones a affirmé d'une façon convaincante dans son *Hamlet et Œdipe* *"que cette vengeance était réalisable et qu'Hamlet lui-même en avait conscience."* ① En fait, nous voyons dans la pièce qu'Hamlet jouit d'une popularité si large que Claudius n'ose même pas le punir pour le meurtre de Polonius à cause de *"la grande affection que le peuple lui (hamlet) porte"* (acte IV scène VII). Le roi sait bien que son neveu *"est adoré de la multitude en délire, qui aime, non par le jugement, mais par les yeux"* (acte IV scène III). Par contre, le roi n'est évidemment pas aimé de son peuple. La preuve en est que ce dernier est prêt à le détrôner à la suite du meurtre de Polonius. Pourtant, quand les masses suivent Laërte en créant : *"A nous de choisir ! Laërte sera roi ! Laërte sera roi !"* (acte IV scène V) elles n'ont aucune preuve à l'appui pour justifier la culpabilité de Claudius (qui n'est pas vraie d'ailleurs) dans le meurtre de Polonius. Au cas où Hamlet, héritier légitime de la couronne, affronterait le fratricide, il est inimaginable qu'il échoue là où Laërte réussit. Le fait qu'Hamlet a tué Claudius à la fin de la pièce sans que la nation soit informée des crimes de celui–ci prouve aussi que l'hypothèse de la crainte de l'émeute du peuple contre Hamlet n'a pas de fondement bien établi.

En considérant l'attitude d'Hamlet, on voit qu'il ne se conduit pas comme quelqu'un qui se trouve devant des difficultés extérieures. Dans toute la pièce, Hamlet n'a jamais évoqué le moindre obstacle matériel qui l'empêche d'accomplir

① Idem p. 39.

sa tâche. Il n'y a fait aucune allusion. En effet, la tâche que le spectre de son père lui impose est réalisable et il est de taille à l'accomplir.

Quant aux troisième postulat, il prétend que la difficulté de vengeance réside dans tel ou tel aspect de la tâche qui la rend particulièrement ardue et répugnante pour Hamlet. Tel est le cas de Mauerhorf, qui soutient que l'ordre donné par le spectre à Hamlet ne consiste pas à tuer le roi, mais à mettre fin la dépravation de sa mère sans porter atteinte à la réputation de la reine. D'après une autre interprétation du même postulat, la mission qu'Hamlet doit remplir selon la volonté du spectre est de restituer à Fortinbras les terres injustement dérobées à son père. Ces hypothèses aboutissent jusqu'à nier la valeur esthétique de l'œuvre et le talent de son auteur. Si l'on analysait la tragédie de Shakespeare selon ces points de vue, la pièce deviendrait " *inexplicable, incohérente et discordante.* " Puisqu'elle ne se déroule pas autour de ces aspects de la tâche purement fictifs. A l'intérieur de la pièce, aucune indication ne permet de justifier ces interprétations. Il suffit d'étudier consciencieusement la pièce sans préjuger pour apercevoir l'arbitraire de ces hypothèses.

Puisqu'Hamlet est capable d'agir et que les difficultés de sa mission ne sont pas objectivement insurmontables, il doit exister une raison plus profonde aux atermoiements du héros. Néanmoins, trois cents ans après la publication de la tragédie, on n'a pas encore trouvé une interprétation cohérente et satisfaisante du chef-d'œuvre de Shakespeare. Aucune interprétation ne nous livre les raisons de l'hésitation d'Hamlet. Les motifs des atermoiements du prince danois restent obscurs et énigmatiques.

Interprétation de Freud et de Jones

Au cours de son auto-analyse à la fin du siècle dernier, Freud reconnaît dans ses propres désirs d'enfant le mythe d'œdipe. Cette découverte et ses recherches sérieuses lui permettront plus tard d'établir sa théorie du complexe d'œdipe. A la même époque, il ne cesse de faire référence à Hamlet et essaie d'interpréter le chef-d'œuvre de Shakespeare avec une conception toute nouvelle. Dans une lettre adressée à son ami le 15 octobre 1897, il propose les principes d'une interprétation basée sur ses réflexions psychanalytiques:

Sans parler des intentions conscientes de Shakespeare, je suppose qu'un événement réel a poussé le poète à écrire le drame, son propre in-conscient de son héros. Comment expliquer cette phrase de l'hystérique Hamlet : 《 C'est ainsi que la conscience fait de nous tous des lâches 》? Comment comprendre son hésitation à venger son père par le meurtre de son oncle, lui qui n'a aucune scrupule à envoyer ses courtisans à la mort et qui n'hésite pas une seconde à tuer Laërte ? Tout s'éclaire mieux lorsqu'on songe au tourment que provoque en lui le vague souvenir d'avoir souhaité, par passion pour sa mère, de perpétrer envers son père le même forfait. 《 Si nous étions traités selon nos mérites, qui pourrait échapper à la fustigation ? 》 Sa conscience est son sentiment inconscient de culpabilité. Sa froideur sexuelle, au cours de son entretien avec Ophélie, sa réprobation de l'instinct qui pousse à procéder, enfin la façon dont il transfère sur la personne d'Ophélie l'acte qui vise son père, tout cela n'évoque-t-il pas des manifestations typiquement hystériques ? Ne réussit-il pas finalement, de façon aussi singulière que mes hystériques, à attirer le châtiment sur lui-même, ce qui l'entraîne à subir le même sort que son père et à être empoisonné par le même rival ? ①

Plus tard, Freud énonce publiquement ses réflexions sur Hamlet sous une forme de note dans sa *Traumdeutung* publié en 1900. Ayant montré des lacunes de l'interprétation de Goethe, il y indique entre autres : " *Qu'est-ce donc l'inhibe dans l'accomplissement de la tâche que lui a assignée le fantôme de son père. Voici la leçon qui s'impose : la cause en est la nature particulière de cette tâche. Hamlet peut tout accomplir, hormis la vengeance qui s'abattrait sur l'homme qui a écarté son père et pris la place de celui-ci auprès de sa mère ; sur l'homme qui lui montre la réalisation de ses désirs infantiles refoulés. A l'exécration qui aurait dû le pousser à la vengeance, se substituent chez lui des accusations contre soi, des scrupules de conscience : ces reproches le persuadent, littéralement, qu'il n'est*

① Sigmund Freud : *La naissance de la psychanalyse*, Paris P. U. F., 1956, p. 198.

lui-même pas meilleur que le pécheur qu'il a mission de châtier. J'ai ainsi traduit en termes conscients ce qui doit rester inconscient dans l'âme du héros ; si quelqu'un voulait qualifier Hamlet d'hystérique, j'y reconnaîtrais seulement une conséquence de mon interprétation. " La longue note de Freud constitue après le point de départ du travail d'Ernest Jones .

Ainsi, Freud établit les bases de l'interprétation psychanalytique d'*Hamlet* dont les principes essentiels sont :

1. L'inhibition du héros n'est pas la manifestation de " la faiblesse psychologique " ou de la neurasthénie. Sauf voir la vengeance de son père par le meurtre de son oncle, Hamlet ne manque point de volonté ni de courage.

2. S'il hésite à venger son père, cette hésitation est due à son sentiment inconscient de culpabilité évoqué par son oncle qui, en tuant son père et épousant sa mère, a réalisé à sa placc scs désirs infantiles refoulés.

3. A travers des attitudes d'Hamlet, se trahissant des symptômes typiques de l'hystérie, tels que la froideur sexuelle, la réprobation de l'instinct etc.

4. Il existe un lien entre la création de la tragédie et la personnalité hypothétique de Shakespeare (freud insiste en particulier sur le rapport chronologique étroit entre la mort du père de Shakespeare et la rédaction d'*Hamlet*).

Dans cette interprétation toute différente des autres hypothèses précédentes, nous pouvons voir que Freud découvre chez le héros de Shakespeare ce qu'il appelle le complexe d'Œdipe dans son interprétation des rêves. Nous savons qu'avec cette expression, Freud fait spontanément référence à un mythe au -delà de l'histoire et des variations du vécu individuel. Il affirme d'emblée l'universalité de L'œdipe. Son auto-analyse l'amène à reconnaître en lui cet ensemble organisé de désirs amoureux et hostiles qu'il éprouvait à l'égard de ses parents, c'est-à-dire l'amour pour sa mère et envers son père, une jalousie en conflit avec l'affection qu'il lui porte. Ce fameux complexe, il le découvre en lui-même, chez ses patients, dans l'âme du personnage mythique d'œdipe, et aussi chez Hamlet. C'est là, pour lui, la clef du problème d'Hamlet. En tenant cette clef, on comprendrait mieux le pouvoir d'emprise d'*Hamlet* sur les spectateurs et les lecteurs de différentes races et de différentes époques ? Car la pièce de Shakespeare, comme celle de Sophocle,

“ met en valeur une compulsion que chacun reconnaît pour avoir perçu en lui-même des traces de son existence ” (la *Révolution psychanalytique*).

Partant des bases fondées par Freud, Ernest Jones a fait une étude profonde de l'œuvre de Shakespeare. Il nous a exposé dans son détail l'interprétation psychanalytique d'Hamlet, donnant ainsi un bon exemple de l'application de la psychanalyse dans la critique littéraire.

En admettant que l'hésitation d'Hamlet résulté d'un conflit intérieur, Jones commence son analyse par indiquer que le héros lui-même est inconscient des véritables raisons de sa répulsion vis à vis de son devoir. Toute la pièce nous montre que le héros ne remet jamais en doute son devoir filial. Il se rend compte clairement de ce qu'il faut faire. Cependant, quelque chose d'obscur qu'il ne connaît pas consciemment le retient d'agir. Dans une de ses tirades, il se reproche son inaction en se demandant : “ *Et bien ! est-ce l'effet d'un oubli bestial ou d'un scrupule poltron qui me fait réfléchir trop précisément aux conséquences, réflexion qui, mise en quatre, contient un quart de sagesse et trois quarts de lâcheté ? … Je ne sais pas pourquoi j'en suis encore à me dire : ceci est à faire ; puisque j'ai motif, volonté, force et moyen de le faire.* ” (acte IV . scène IV) ce qui prouve que “ *les atermoiements d'Hamlet étaient dus à un conflit interne entre l'impulsion du devoir et une répugnance vis à vis de ce devoir* ” . ① Un des aspects obscurs de cette tâche lui inspire une répugnance invincible et, dans son for intérieur, Hamlet ne veut pas s'acquitter de la mission que le spectre de son père lui impose. Il importe donc de découvrir d'abord cet aspect inexploré qui cause sa répugnance. C'est ce que Jones fait dans son essai.

Comme Freud, Jones prend Hamlet pour un cas de psychonévrose. Selon lui , “ *Hamlet en constitue l'exemple suprême en littérature* ” . ② La psychanalyse nous apprend que les symptômes de cette affection psychique sont l'expression symbolique des conflits infantiles et qu' “ *il est impossible d'étudier utilement un*

---

① *Hamlet et Œdipe* p. 49.
② Idem p. 68.

cas de psychonévrose – qu'il s'agisse d'un être vivant ou d'un personnage fictif – sans relier les manifestations de cette affection aux pulsions qui sont intervenues pendant la prime enfance, et qui continuent d'intervenir ". [1] Il faut donc trouver les raisons de la répugnance du héros à travers ses manifestations –c'est-à-dire les attitudes manifestes d'Hamlet – dans la période de sa prime enfance.

Comme il est un aboulique spécifique, la déficience de volonté d'Hamlet est strictement localisée : elle se manifeste uniquement devant l'obligation de tuer son oncle. Dans la vie réelle, de semblables aboulies découlent généralement d'une répulsion inconsciente pour l'acte à accomplir, ou pour un élément étroitement lié à cet acte. Hamlet ne peut se résoudre à exécuter la vengeance de son père, même s'il en a le plus fort désir conscient. En lui, se dissimule une réticence profonde dont on ne peut découvrir les motifs qu'à l'aide de la psychanalyse. Dans ses activités psychothérapiques, Freud a constaté que certains ensembles de processus psychique tendaient à se dérober à la conscience et qu' " *Il s'agissait de choses que le malade voulait oublier et qu'intentionnellement il maintenait, repoussait, refoulait hors de sa pensée consciente.* " D'après Freud, il existe chez tout homme une pulsion sexuelle dès sa prime enfance. Néanmoins, cette pulsion est l'objet premier des interdits qu'impose la société, car elle s'oppose à la morale et l'éthique de la société humaine. " *Les mécanismes psychiques les plus susceptibles de refoulement sont ceux que condamnerait la société*[2]. Tout enfant est nécessairement obligé donc de refouler ses tendances psychosexuelles. Au cas du conflit psychique aigu et profond, le traumatisme d'ordre sexuel se manifeste souvent par la dépression, le doute, le désespoir et les autres expressions transférées sur des objets plus avouables. (Chez Hamlet, on peut aussi trouver de semblables symptômes.) C'est à travers ces manifestations superficielles qu'on arrive à découvrir les vraies causes enfouies.

Jones estime qu'il existe deux tendances chez Hamlet: "tendance consciente et tendance refoulée, ou inconsciente, l'impulsion de la vengeance et la tâche pieuse imposée par le père représentent chez Hamlet une tendance morale et sociale

① Idem p. 69.
② *Hamlet et Œdipe* p. 58.

qu'approuve sa conscience ; La tendance refoulée, responsable de son inhibition, prend sa source dans des pulsions cachées. " [①] Au niveau de la conscience, Hamlet accepte la vengeance, c'est le devoir filial que la morale, l'éthique et la société lui réclament. Mais à la profondeur de son inconscient se cache le souhait secret de la mort de son père. Comme tous les garçons, Hamlet éprouvait un amour pour sa mère et considérait son père comme un rival qui empêche la satisfaction immédiate et cette contrainte comme une cruauté gratuite. Blessé d'avoir à partager l'affection de sa mère, il souhaitait secrètement la mort de son père. Ces sentiments incestueux sont évidemment incompatibles avec la morale sociale et il les a refoulés et maintenus hors de sa conscience. Avec le temps, la piété filiale et l'éducation en a effacé toutes traces, mais ils restent dans la profondeur de son inconscient.

En assassinant le père d'Hamlet et en épousant la mère de celui-ci, Claudius, un proche parent de la famille, réalise le double souhait inconscient d'Hamlet lui-même : posséder la mère et tuer le père. En ce sens, Claudius représente un Hamlet inconscient. L'assassinat du père et le remariage incestueux de la mère réveillent chez Hamlet, sous forme de dépression et d'angoisse, le conflit d'enfant. D'une part, sa conscience, son devoir filial l'obligent à s'acquitter de sa mission que lui impose son père. D'autre part, son inconscient ses vagues désirs infantiles stimulés le découragent sans cesse. Inconsciemment, il se dit qu'il n'est peut-être pas meilleur que Claudius fratricide. Ses auto-reproches, sa dépression ne sont autres choses que des manifestations de son sentiment de culpabilité. " *Il est déchiré par un conflit intérieur insoluble* " [②].

Une analyse de l'attitude d'Hamlet envers sa mère permet de déceler la nature sexuelle de ce conflit. En fait, avant de savoir, grâce au spectre, la vérité de l'assassinat de son père, Hamlet souffle déjà d'une grave dépression dont la cause primordiale est évidemment le remariage de sa mère. Au début de la pièce, il s'écrie dans son premier monologue: *Quoi ! elle se pendait à lui, comme si ses désirs grandissaient en se rassasiant ··· Avant même que le sel de ses larmes*

---

① Idem p. 60.
② Idem p. 70.

menteuses eût cessé d'irriter ses yeux rouges, elle s'est mariée ! O ardeur criminelle ! courir avec une telle vivacité à des draps incestueux ! (Acte I scène II). Dans ses paroles il est facile de trouver des signes de sexualité. Le remariage de la reine provoque une répugnance et une angoisse si profondes chez Hamlet qu'il envisage le suicide. La conduite incestueuse de sa mère éveille en lui une horreur intense. Les paroles insolentes qu'il adresse à sa mère, son dégoût mélancolique à l'égard de la vie, sa dépression noire, toutes ses réactions excessives trahissent la participation de son inconscient, à savoir la présence toujours active de son univers psychique infantile.

Selon Jones, deux traits de caractères de la reine (sa sensualité marquée et la tendresse passionnée qu'elle voue à son fils) permettent de croire que "*Enfant, le héros éprouve la plus tendre affection pour sa mère ; ce sentiment comportait – comme il est de règle – des éléments érotiques déguisés, surtout pendant les toutes premières années* " ① Ce sentiment, il l'a refoulé bien sûr, mais l'attraction infantile pour la mère continue de s'exercer. Le remariage incestueux de sa mère fait émerger à la surface l'association de la mère à une interprétation sexuelle enfouie depuis l'enfance. "*Le désir agréable et diffus de la prime enfance se traduit maintenant, sous l'effet du refoulement, par un profond dégoût. L'activité inconsciente du souhait "refoulé" de remplacer son père dans l'affection de sa mère se trouve tout à coup stimulée : il voit quelqu'un usurper cette place qu'il avait brûler de ravir* " ②Le refoulement de ses désirs anciens stimulés exige une intense dépense d'énergie, de sorte qu'Hamlet sombre dans un déplorable état psychique. Sa dépression, son angoisse, son désespoir en sont des symptômes.

De plus, dans la cour que fait Hamlet à Ophélie, on peut déceler une sorte de défi vis-à-vis de sa mère. C'est là une attitude provoquée par un amour désespéré. Dans la scène de la comédie, quand la reine l'invite à s'asseoir auprès d'elle, il refuge et va s'allonger aux pieds d'Ophélie qu'il vient de répudier en répondant : "*Non, ma chère mère, voici un meilleur aimant* " (acte III . Scène II). Cette conduite étrange ne ressemble-t-elle pas aux jeux d'amour d'un amant éconduit ? Tout se passe

---

① *Hamlet et Œdipe* p. 80.
② Idem p. 81.

comme si l'inconscient Hamlet cherche à transmettre un message à sa mère : 《*Tu te donne à d'autres hommes que tu me préfères . Je vais te prouver que je peux me passer de tes faveurs et même préférer celles d'une femme que j'ai cessé d'aimer*》[1] . Tout cela trahit ses désirs infantiles refoulés et la nature sexuelle du conflit sous-jacent.

Quant à l'hostilité d'Hamlet à l'égard d'Ophélie, c'est aussi une autre expression de sa pulsion sexuelle refoulée. Voyant que sa mère, son premier objet de désir infantile, se donne à son oncle, Hamlet éprouve à la fois un dégoût et une jalousie féroce, inconscient en raison de son origine interdite. La seule forme permise de ce sentiment inconscient se traduit par d'amers reproches et un ressentiment extrême. Il ne peut supporter que la femme qu'il aimait s'éprenne d'un autre homme. Quand Ophélie s'enfuit, suivant le conseil de Polonius et de Laërte, devant la cour, qu'il lui fait, "*il voit son amour renié comme l'avait été celui de son enfance*"[2]. Une misogynie se produit et s'exacerbe en l'occurrence. Jones indique que " *Si le 《 refoulement 》sexuel est très marqué , comme c'est le cas pour Hamlet , la femme , sous tous ses aspects , ne suscite qu'animosité : ressentiment à l'égard de la 《 dame 》 chaste et pure dont on essuie les refus , répulsion envers la créature ensuelle qui inspire de coupables tentations* "[3] . Enfant, Hamlet était obligé de refouler ses pulsions sexuelles envers sa mère, maintenant, il doit étouffer le désir qui le porte vers Ophélie. Dans cette tragédie d'amour, la pauvre fille pudique fait l'objet de ses accusations injustifiées. En fait, c'est en l'avilissant qu'Hamlet exprime la déception que lui a infligée sa mère. Sa misogynie, sa froideur sexuelle sont originaires d'un refoulement excessif.

Son inconscient une fois dévoilé, la cause de l'atermoiement d'Hamlet s'éclaircit en même temps. Nous voyons que Claudius a réalisé le souhait incestueux de la prime enfance d'Hamlet. Parallèlement à sa haine envers son oncle, Hamlet éprouve une sorte de jalousie : il lui envie son succès auprès de la reine. Inconsciemment, il s'identifie à Claudius. Il se trouve alors devant ce

① Idem p .81.
② Idem p. 83.
③ Idem p. 85.

dilemme : ou bien il répond à l'appel de la vengeance de son père, mais alors il ressent plus intensément ses propres désirs inconscients ; ou bien il oublie son devoir filial, alors il doit supporter le poids écrasant de la morale et de sa conscience. Car, plus il attaque Claudius, plus il subit les remords de ses pulsions refoulées. Plus il traîne dans son action, plus il souffre des accusations de sa conscience. Tuer son oncle, c'est se tuer lui-même en quelque sorte. D'où son hésitation, d'où son atermoiement. Ce n'est pas la lâcheté physique ou morale qui le paralysent, c'est son sentiment de culpabilité qui retient son bras sans qu'il s'en rende compte consciemment.

Avec sa théorie sur l'inconscient, Freud a apporté une grande contribution à la connaissance plus complète de l'homme lui-même. Il a découvert pour toute l'humanité un univers psychique de l'homme, jusque là inexplorable et obscur. Après de sérieuses études, il a prouvé de façon scientifique l'existence de l'inconscient, cet aspect ésotérique de la psyché humaine souvent négligé. Désormais, on sait qu'en profondeur de l'âme de chacun existe quelque chose d'agissant et qui influence sournoisement notre vie psychique comme ces laves qui bouillonnent au sein de la Terre. Toute étude sur les activités psychiques de l'homme serait incomplète, si l'on ne se rendait pas compte de son existence.

Depuis le début de son élaboration de la psychanalyse, Freud s'intéresse sans cesse aux personnages fictifs de la mythologie et de la littérature. Quand il s'est mis à établir sa théorie sur le complexe d'œdipe, il a fait aussi référence à Hamlet. En essayant de résoudre le problème d'Hamlet, il a jeté les bases de la psychocritique littéraire.

Ernest Jones, qui développe très consciencieusement l'hypothèse de Freud dans son *Hamlet et œdipe,* a donné la solution d'une énigme que des siècles de commentaires n'ont pas réussi à éclaircir. En considérant Hamlet comme une " *quasi-personne avec sa conscience, son inconscient, ses pulsions, son sur-moi, bref, tout l'appareil psychique qui se constitue en chacun de nous à travers notre histoire* " ①, il analyse minutieusement les attitudes d'Hamlet comme s'il avait

① Préface de Jean Starbinsky à *Hamlet et Œdipe*.

affaire à un de ses patients psychonévroses. Dans ses travaux, il accorde une place privilégiée aux conflits psychologiques des toutes premières années de l'enfance. Pour lui, " *les tendances les plus communément refoulées découlent de pulsions innées plutôt que d'acquis ultérieurs* " ①. Tout homme est donc condamné à subir des processus d'un refoulement plus ou moins fatal. Vu la censure de la morale et de l'éthique du cycle social, les contenus du refoulement sont le plus souvent originaires de la pulsion sexuelle. " *Plus un conflit psychique se révèle* aigu et profond, plus il y a de chances pour que l'analyste décède, a l'origine, un *traumatisme d'ordre sexuel* " ② . Utile tant à la psychothérapie qu'à la critique littéraire, cette observation facilite beaucoup l'analyse de la psychologie des personnages fictifs comme un appareil radiographique qui nous aide à dévoiler ce qui se cache en nous. Quand on fait une analyse psychologique d'un personnage, il ne suffit pas de rester uniquement au niveau de sa conscience. Cela est important et indispensable bien sûr, mais on ne devrait pas négliger un autre aspect psychique caché de son personnage, si l'on voulait le comprendre d'une façon plus complète, surtout quand il s'agit de l'œuvre où les conflits psychiques des personnages paraissent aigus et complexes. Souvent, les raisons originaires de ces conflits se cachent dans la profondeur de l'inconscient. Interpréter la psychologie d'un personnage sans se rendre compte de son inconscient, c'est comme si l'on prenait la partie manifeste d'un iceberg pour son ensemble en oubliant sa partie submergée.

Ayant résolu le problème d'Hamlet, l'interprétation psychanalytique de Jones ouvre une nouvelle perspective à la critique littéraire. Ses analyses de la cause inconsciente de l'atermoiement du prince danois sont plausibles. Cependant, cela ne veut pas dire que tous les conflits psychiques découlent exclusivement du refoulement des tendances sexuelles infantiles. Bien que la psyché humaine se compose de deux aspects, conscient et inconscient, et que les activités psychiques humaines soient inévitablement marquées par la participation de ces deux aspects, d'une façon générale, c'est quand même la conscience qui joue le rôle primordial dans la plupart de cas. Ce n'est que dans la situation extrême (comme celle

① *Hamlet et Œdipe* p. 59.
② Idem p. 59.

qu'Hamlet affronte) que l'inconscient intervient intensément dans ces activités. Tous les conflits psychiques ne sont pas des conflits sexuels. Ce n'est d'ailleurs pas la conclusion de Jones. Toute exagération du rôle de l'inconscient dans l'analyse de la psychologie des personnes, vivants ou fictifs, est problématique. C'est là peut-être une remarque à laquelle on doit faire attention au cours de la pratique de la psychocritique d'une œuvre littéraire quelconque.

A Critical Study on Zhu Guangqian's Aesthetic View of Tragic Pleasure

Li Yue

Tragedy is generally regarded as the highest form of literary art and those who have excelled in it are viewed as the world's greatest literary geniuses. They were believed to be the most profound psychologists before the science of psychology had ever come into being. Theories on Tragedy mainly concern these three questions: What is tragic pleasure? Why do people take pleasure in Tragedy? And what produces tragic pleasure? In spite of the efforts made by philosophers and critics, the solution to the problem of tragic pleasure remains as remote as ever. Du Bos and Croce lean towards the pleasure of feeling. Addison illustrates tragic pleasure as a combination of the pleasure of recognition and the pleasure of relief, whereas Burke views it as a pleasure answering a sympathetic need. Most of these theories fall short of meeting the demands of modern psychology concerning the source of human emotions. None of them except Zhu Guangqian pays attention to the power of the psychology of tragedy. In *The Psychology of Tragedy*, Zhu attempts to give a critical study of various theories of Tragedy in the light of psychology, and to define the relation and difference between the tragic pleasure and pleasure of other modes, such as that evolved by the beautiful and the sublime. Zhu patterns his theory with the realization that a solution to the origin of tragic pleasure would throw light on many other psychological questions, such as how the attraction to beauty shapes an individual's sense; and how the pleasure gained from all forms of art mirrors human spiritual reality and spiritual convictions. Whoever fully explains the nature of tragic pleasure would also discover the key to the essence of the relationship between the aesthetic sense and the psyche of human being.

In *The Psychology of Tragedy*, Zhu argues that the enjoyment of Tragedy, a concrete feeling, not a mere abstract notion, essentially equates with aesthetic contemplation. In the past, some critics with little philosophical training and aesthetic taste have failed to differentiate tragedy as a form of art from the suffering experienced in real life. Tragedy represents an idealized life or a life set in an artificial frame. We should not respond to the calamities and misfortunes in tragedy in the same way as we respond to those in reality, just as we do not respond to the image of a beauty in a picture by Manet in the same way as we respond to a similar beauty in the street. And a realistic account of murder that we can find every day in newspapers never gives the same impression as Macbeth. Therefore tragic emotion distinguishes itself from such real-life responses as mourning the death of a beloved person or rejoicing over the defeat of an enemy.

By applying Bullough's theory of "Psychological Distance", Zhu assesses the main trend of European aesthetic thought from Kant to Croce, and characteristics of formalism that have inherent weaknesses. The great merit of "Psychological Distance" lies in that while it emphasizes the autonomy of aesthetic experience it does not neglect the conditions favorable to its initiation and maintenance. According to Zhu, we may describe "distance" as a metaphorical expression for the detachment of the aesthetic object from its association with everyday life. Beautiful things generally distinguish themselves by remoteness as one of their characteristics. For instance, a traveler from China who finds himself for the first time in Egypt generally has the impression that everything there has a peculiar charm of its own. Therefore, the secret of the success of art lies in a proper adjustment of distance. As Adorno indicates, "What is most desirable both in production and appreciation is the utmost decrease of distance without its disappearance."① Frye also indicates that if the imaginative powers do not prevail over emotional impulses, a contrary effect would result: without the power of poetic expression, tragedy actually intensifies sorrowful emotion instead of

① Fred Rush, *The Cambridge Companion to Critical Theory* (Cambridge University Press, 2004), 147.

converting it into something pleasurable[1]. For instance, a woman who has recently lost her child would dissolve into tears on seeing the representation of a mother with a dead child. Such a spectacle, instead of giving her pleasure, would only aggravate her grief. Zhu comes to a conclusion that the properties of realism often threaten the spirit of Tragedy. The misfortunes and calamities in tragedy can never confound themselves with those in real life, for the misfortunes and calamities in tragedy exhibit the qualities produced by temporal and spatial remoteness, such as the exceptional nature of the tragic characters, situations and actions, artistic conventions and techniques, an intense lyrical note, a supernatural atmosphere, and finally any unrealistic but suggestive staging and acting.

Zhu also examines some of the most important theories of tragic pleasure proposed by previous studies. He starts with the "Malevolence Theory", which holds that in human nature there exists something of primitive savage cruelty and something essentially egoistic and sadistic, by virtue of which man exults at the defeat of an enemy, takes delight in the infliction of pain and even extracts a satisfaction from the suffering of friends. Therefore, to rejoice at the misfortunes of our fellows demonstrates a clear sign of malignity. Taking pleasure in the representation of tragic events implies that people tend to rejoice at the misfortunes of others. Tragedy captivates us because it foregrounds our own better fortune by representing the distress and suffering of men and women who in every aspect outshine us. We would respond that, conversely, tragedy brings us into contact with nobility and grandeur and thereby awakens the noble sense in our nature and finally lights up a divine spark in our own soul.

Contrary to the malevolent view, Burke, the leading exponent of Sympathy Theory, holds that the noble spirit in man reveals itself in tragedy and man takes pleasure in the sight of suffering because he sympathizes with the sufferer. Tragic pleasure results from the pity awakened in us by others' misfortunes. In tragedy, pleasure and pain do not neutralize each other, and they often blend with each other to form a mixed feeling. The pain does not remain to the end and it turns into pleasure so as to swell the positive pleasure produced by pity, fear and the visualization of beauty.

---

① Northrop Frye, *The Educated Imagination* (Toronto, CBC Enterprises, 1985), 51 –53.

Burke seems to claim that the more tragic the situation, the greater sympathy we need, and consequently the higher pleasure we experience. But in fact, as Zhu points out, there exists a limit to the pleasurability of a tragic situation. Beyond that limit, tragic situation gives pain instead of pleasure. On a stage, such a conversion of pain into pleasure owes much to the relief of pain through actors' bodily activities. It also owes much to artistic expressions: the pain subdued and transfigured by the artists' creative imagination projects the emotions onto their artistic representations. Tragedy would not melt pain into pleasure and would turn pessimism into a heightened sense of life without an excellent artistic representation. Besides, a proper appreciation of tragedy requires a fine taste and aesthetic culture. Everyone may experience a kind of the pleasure at the sight of cock-fighting or a gladiatorial show, but few could really experience the pleasure peculiar to tragedy. The ordinary man who lacks imagination and aesthetic detachment is likely to be shocked by a catastrophe and unable to reconcile his moral sense with the unhappy event. For instance, one can recall that terrible scene in King Lear where Corn and Regan pluck out Gloucester's eyes on the stage. This horrible scene offends an ordinary man's moral sense and replaces aesthetic pleasure by disgust and indignation.

Zhu then discusses pity and fear together with the sense of sublimity. Some critics regard pity in tragedy as a kind of moral sympathy directed to some distinctly external object. Zhu refutes that and argues that by virtue of sublimity the enjoyment of tragedy equates with an aesthetic emotion, and tragic pity consequently parallels an aesthetic sympathy. In real life, the dread of pain always preoccupies man in a world full of evils and miseries. So freedom from pain becomes the greatest blessing that man can expect. The sublime element in tragedy forces its way into our imagination and emotion, expands and uplifts them to its own dimensions, enabling us to transcend our own limits, identify ourselves with it, and share its immense greatness. Therefore, while the tragic hero struggles against miseries in the hope of escaping the pain produced by sufferings and evils, spectators do not direct their pity to the tragic hero as a distinctly external object, but as with whom they sympathetically identified with the spectators themselves. In this sense, sublimity more or less likens self-pity which one sometimes feels for oneself when he has to face an irretrievable fate.

Fear, an indispensable element in the sense of the tragic, does not parallel with the fear experienced in actual life. Mere fear does not inspire us but leaves us gloomy and depressed. On the contrary, the heroic quality in tragedy inspires us by its nobility and grandeur. Mere terror thrills us with fear, whereas the heroic quality thrills us without. The tragedy must produce both terror and the heroic quality simultaneously. In tragedy, the object that moves us possesses extraordinary greatness either in extent or in power as its essential feature. And images of immeasurable magnitude thrust upon us a sense of our own feebleness and insignificance. The tragic differs from mere sadness in that it possesses an inspiring or uplifting power which the latter lacks. Zhu then defines tragic pity as a sub-species or a mode of the sublime, sharing with all of the qualities inherent in tragedy the common property of fear-inspiring but uplifting power. The sense of sublimity excites two different emotions: fear first, and then admiration. The sense of sublimity qualifies as the most important ingredient of the tragic.

Zhu believes Hegel's theory on tragedy has its weakness too. Hegel maintains rational laws can explain or justify everything in the universe. He believes that "above pity and fear, there soars a feeling of harmony"① which tragedy gives by revealing eternal justice. Though this justifies that tragic conflict arises from the collision of two equally justifiable but one-sided ethical forces and ends in the triumph of eternal justice, the weakness of this view is obvious, because Hegel seems to base his affirmation on a highly developed humanity and makes desperate efforts to show that in tragedy the hero embodies some ethical value and the catastrophe in tragedy still symbolizes a triumph of eternal justice. The hero's personality is shaped merely by external forces and it has nothing to do with his own spiritual convictions. The flaw in this hypothesis lies in that it inflates the external and ideal forces and overlooks the power of the individual's own spiritual reality and the psyche.

In *The Psychology of Tragedy*, Zhu tests the validity of the theories of hedonists, vitalists and Hegel by applying them to the problem of tragic pleasure. His solution to

① Frederick. C. Beiser, ed.. The *Cambridge Companion to Hegel* (Cambridge University Press, 2004), 97.

the problem of tragic pleasure, the adequate analysis of the relation between pain and pleasure in the terms of psychology and the definition the relation and difference between tragic pleasure and pleasure of other kinds, such as those derived from the beautiful and the sublime, contribute much to aesthetics. His interpretation of the Apollonian and Dionysian Spirits coined by Nietzsche further marks the significance of his view. Zhu attempts to define an intrinsic value of tragedy that distinguishes itself from the value of goodness and truth-values found outside of tragedy. However, deeply influenced by Nietzsche's preference for disinterestedness and aesthetic detachment, Zhu unconsciously overestimates the intellectual and rational role in aesthetic contemplation.

Some questions arise from Zhu's assertion that a great actor, while simulating the dramatic emotions in a life-like manner, should not experience them as actual emotions. Good acting and proper appreciation require both sensibility and judgment, as well as participation and detached contemplation. Can judgment and emotion coexist side by side in the aesthetic experience? Do they fuse together and will their fusion cause the spectator to weep pleasurably before the representation of a tragic event? Here, the question merits our attention: What role do aesthetic pleasure and emotional pleasure respectively play in the contemplation of tragedy? We may define aesthetic pleasure as a sort of pleasure in which people stand aloof and unmoved by the whirlpool of passions which carries away their naive and sentimental feelings. People engross themselves in a thousand intellectual considerations which would wipe away all traces of emotions. With the absence of emotional involvement, people analyze the drawing of characters, criticize the diction and versification of the lines, ask themselves whether the scenery effect matches the dramatic atmosphere, think of the different interpretations of certain passages, and wonder whether the authors mean to have a moral in the play.

However, one has to remember the fact that when the importance of the intellectual is overstressed, excessive criticism often spoils the appreciation of a good tragedy. Zhu overemphasizes the intellectual elements in an aesthetic experience without taking sufficient account of the emotional. He supposes that pleasure and pain appear independent of innate properties of tragedies that have nothing to do with our interest and attitudes. For him, emotional elements would vitiate aesthetic pleasure. This preference for the intellectual and rational elements to the emotional and sensuous may stem from Nietzsche's claim that "only as a pure intellectual phenomenon exists, the world would be eternally justified."① This implies that intellectuality has the greatest power to make life worth living. Zhu denies the existence of emotional elements in the aesthetic experience, falsely attributes aesthetic pleasure to pure intellectual responses and utterly excludes passions and sensuous particulars from aesthetic contemplation. Actually, aesthetics has much to do with the emotional and sensuous reception of an aesthetic object. If aesthetic contemplation disconnects itself utterly from man's desires and passions, how can rationality alone move actors to enthusiastically engross themselves in acting and spectators to sympathize with tragic heroes on the stage? Things become pleasant or painful only when they in some way relate to our interest and only when they call forth a definite mental attitude. According to Adorno, "Aesthetic contemplation involves our cognitive faculties in some other way and we often deploy a sentimental reaction for understanding the world."② It seems that Zhu confuses the aesthetic attitude with the critical attitude. He holds that tragic pleasure mostly results from an intellectual realization of moral significance instead of an immediate feeling. In fact, when the spectator does set himself to reflect on the moral significance of a tragedy, he has to do so cold-heartedly without experiencing the true tragic pleasure. Aesthetic value is not the equivalent of moral, practical and philosophical value. A work of art may contain part or all of these values; but these values do not constitute its unique value as art. "Artworks are things whose value appears to lie in their very nature; hence they appear intrinsically valuable, valuable in and of themselves."③

In addition to the refuting of the existence of the emotional elements in aesthetic experience, Zhu believes that what the lower sensations can sense are but nonaesthetic properties and one cannot have a real aesthetic experience in theatre unless he a-

① Bernd Magnus and Kathleen Higgins, ed.. *The Cambridge Companion to Nietzsche* (Cambridge University Press, 2004), 17.

② Fred Rush, ed., 161.

③ Rush, ed., 159.

bandons the lower senses in appreciating the beauty of a play's music, action and verse. Let us take sensation in the light of aesthetic contemplation. Sensation is a door through which we enter into the experience of beauty; and it serves as the foundation upon which all aesthetic tastes and judgment rest. "Beauty does not float free. Certain nonaesthetic properties are responsible for the aesthetic properties and without those nonaesthetic properties, the aesthetic properties would not have been instantiated."① One cannot think that beauty is bare and it is essential to aesthetic thought to realize that the aesthetic properties of a thing arise from its nonaesthetic properties. From the time of Plato, who argues for "fair sights and sounds" only, people have recognized vision and hearing as the preeminently aesthetic senses. These two senses provide the basis for all the arts. The theatre-performed play, a combination of sound and sight, deploys vision and hearing as the natural media to express its meaning. Sounds—words or tones—convey thoughts and feelings; so do visual sensations—the facial expression or gesture communicate the inner life of the speakers. The unalienableness of sight and sound results from their expressiveness and their connection with the life of feeling and thought. Thus, a tragedy performed on stage without enthusiastic action and well-constructed verse would obscure the excellence of the tragedy, and fail to inspire spectators to response aesthetically. Similarly, one who abandons the values of sensations would sink into a position of some extreme theoreticians who take universal law into account only and indulgently disregard individual enjoyment and judgment. In an aesthetic experience, sensations essentially parallel a power to free people from their concerns for the practical or the instinctive and to lift them into the higher region of sentiment. For instance, fine wines and perfumes offer tastes and odors sought and enjoyed apart from the satisfaction of hunger. In a cathedral, the odor of incense fusing with the chorale and architecture, instead of a mere odor pleasing the nostrils, may appear as an important element in religious devotion. Therefore, every kind of sensation, however low, may become aesthetically beautiful, not degrading aesthetic contemplation, but enriching and ennobling it.

Furthermore, as is generally believed, both content and form play their parts in art. The content of an artwork consists of the essential and universal interests of hu-

---

① Bernd Magnus and Kathleen Higgins, ed., 97.

manity and the spiritual forces which rule the world of man's will and action. But art cannot be based on pure abstraction but has to express itself through a certain medium, namely, form. The spiritual forces in content have to be materialized in the form of human emotions such as love, hatred, jealousy, parental tenderness, honor, duty, loyalty, patriotism and devotion to religion. The personages in tragedy incarnate these emotional forces. Each of the tragic characters identifies himself or herself with at least one of these emotions and carries it through to the end with an uncompromising self-consistency. People who attach too much attention to intellectual elements and give up emotional excitement would fail to share these emotions with the playwrights and actors. Deprived of the feeling for the values of sensation, men may appreciate artworks rationally and intelligently, but they may overlook the aesthetic value of such artworks. They may, for example, appreciate the profound or interesting ideas in poetry, but unless they can connect them with the rhythm-values of the sounds of the words, they have only an intellectual or rational, not an aesthetic experience.

Despite such limitations, Zhu comes perhaps nearer to the truth of tragic pleasure than most previous theorists. For one thing he has the advantage over most theorists on tragedy: He collects the different arguments of previous theorists and weaves them into an organic whole, and finally defines tragic pleasure with his unique formulation. As he justly remarks, though tragedy tries to solve the same ultimate problems of Good and Evil as religion and philosophy, its spirit is alien to both. Religion and philosophy reduce the sense of sublimity to a religious faith and a philosophical dogma, whereas tragic pleasure distinguishes the sense of sublimity on the strength of its aesthetic detachment. Tragic pleasure does not content itself with any result of judgment or emotional relief. It indeed stems from aesthetic contemplation which is neither logically explicable nor morally justifiable. By emphasizing the aesthetic value of tragedy, he has contributed to the theoretical development of the study on tragic pleasure. Zhu, more than any previous theorists on tragedy, makes it clear to us that the enjoyment of tragedy springs primarily from an aesthetic experience independent of any personal reference. He rightly identifies pity and the sense of sublimity with aesthetic sympathy and analyzes the notion of tragic pleasure, taking human psychology into account.

References:

[1] Fred Rush, ed.. *The Cambridge Companion to Critical Theory*. Cambridge university press, 2004.

[2] Paul Guyer, ed.. *The Cambridge Companion to Kant*. Cambridge university press, 2004.

[3] Bernd Magnus and Kathleen Higgins, ed.. *The Cambridge Companion to Nietzsche*, Cambridge university press, 2004.

[4] Frederick. C. Beiser, ed.. *The Cambridge Companion to Hegel*, Cambridge university press, 2004.

[5] Northrop Frye, *The Educated Imagination*, Toronto, CBC Enterprises, 1985.

[6] 朱光潜. 悲剧心理学——各种悲剧快感理论的批判研究 [M]. 北京：人民文学出版社，1983.

[7] 朱光潜. 西方美学史 [M]. 北京：人民文学出版社，2003.

[8] 朱光潜. 文艺心理学 [M]. 北京：生活·读书·新知三联书店，2005.

[9] 尼采. 悲剧的诞生 [M]. 周国平，译. 太原：北岳文艺出版社，2004.

渴望"洁白的床"

——浅析《占有》中的两性和谐意识

邢　凌

前　言

小说家 A. S. 拜厄特是当今英国文坛最耀眼的一颗星。她于 1936 年出生于英国约克郡的一个书香世家，成年后在剑桥和牛津接受了系统的文学训练。集学者、批判家和小说家于一身的拜厄特曾获得过多项文学大奖，并获英国女王所授英帝国二等勋位爵士头衔。

拜厄特迄今已出版了近十部长篇小说以及若干中、短篇小说集。她的代表作当属 1990 年出版的长篇小说《占有》。这部小说一经出版就在英语世界引起了轰动。英国、美国、加拿大等国的一些文学批评家纷纷撰写文章评论这部小说，并一致认为这是一部非常成功的小说。当年，这部作品获得了英国文学最高奖——布克奖。但该书至今尚未见到汉译本，实为遗憾。

一

女性主义运动经历了一个漫长的历史，从总体上讲，它可以分为两个阶段。第一个阶段，从 19 世纪到 20 世纪初，女性主义在英、法发展成了一股实质性的力量。女性争取选举权的运动是其中至关重要的内容。其中有两个重要人物：弗吉尼亚·伍尔芙（Virginia Woolf）和西蒙·德·波芙娃（Simon de Beauvoir）。在伍尔芙看来，性别、身份只不过是社会建构起来的东西，而非某种自在之物。她一直关注的就是当一个女性作家写作时所要承受的身份焦虑，这种焦虑呈现在她的许多作品中。波芙娃对“是一个女人”（being a female）和“被建构成一个女人”（being constructed as a woman）作了重要区分。这显然有来自伍尔芙的影响，而她又对其理论作了一定程度的拓展。波伏娃在她的代表作《第二性》中严厉抨击了男人在生理、心理与经济上对女人的歧视，也昭示了女性主义第二阶段的到来。同时，波芙娃也把自己的眼光投向了种族歧视这个话题。这表明女性主义者所关注的绝不仅仅是“女性”的话题，举凡有关性别、身份的问题都在她们的质疑、批判的范围之内。这个阶段的女性主义也被称做“激进女性主义”。女性主义运动从马克思主义、精神分析学说、解构主义、符号学等理论那里寻求话语资源，主要代表人物有米利特、克里丝蒂娃等。她们竭力颠覆传统的父权制社会和男性话语权威，解构“阳具中心主义”的神话。女性主义批评关注文学作品中的女性人物，常常注意勘察女性的经历和经验在男女作家那里究竟得到了怎样的表现，倡导一种以性别经验为基础的写作。激进女性主义的强调重心转向了生殖的政治，女性的“体验”、性的“差异”，并引发了西方20世纪60年代以来的性革命。

小说《占有》就是在这样的背景下展开叙述的。作者对女性主义的关注是这部小说的一个重点。

作为一名女权主义者，拜厄特自然会受到前面提到的女性主义思想的影响，强调女性应有的独立性，而不是作为男性的“他者”而存在。正如有人所说的：“拜厄特对女权主义和争取妇女自由特别感兴趣……认为女人们要将性和日常生活分隔开来，要区别情人和朋友。……她还认为一个人想要与另一个人的精神和肉体融为一体的想法是荒谬的。”① 这一点在小说中也有体现。比如书中有一个重要符号，神话长诗《梅卢西娜》（这是拜厄特借拉摩特之手歌颂女性生命和力量的创作）描述了半人半蛇的女神梅卢西娜。她极具权威性，能知世事始末；她在水边以蛇身出现，象征着一个雌雄同体的完整形象，一个能为自己创造生命意义而无需外界帮助的形象。

然而，作为受过高等教育的新一代女作者，拜厄特在《占有》中没有过多地表达女性主义的不满，也没有停留在单纯地批判男性中心主义，或重建女性的话语模式之上，而是对女权主义作了较为深入的反思，对实现两性和谐及平等交流进行了更多的思考，从而传达出诸多不同于上述引文的信息。这也是本文所要分析的重点。

---

① 蒋显文：《占有》前言，外语教学与研究出版社2000年版，第vi页。

二

书中的女主人公之一莫德博士（Dr. Maud Bailey）年轻貌美，她的工作是从女权主义的视角去专门研究一位19世纪的女诗人拉摩特（Christabel LaMotte）。莫德独立、冷漠而常带傲慢。虽然已是研究拉摩特的专家，可是在充满嫉妒的学术同仁之间，她的成功却很容易被刻意看成是凭借姿色所得，甚至她本人也会被戏称为“洋娃娃”。在20世纪中后期“性解放”的大背景下，莫德实践着性和感情应当分离的观念。她既和另一位女权主义学者有同性恋的互慰行为，又有异性性伴侣，但是在这一副标准的后现代女权主义者的做派之下，莫德内心深处却隐藏着空虚和不安，还有连她自己也难以言明的渴望，正如她那总是严密包裹在头巾之下的美丽金发。

这种空虚、不安和隐隐的渴望是透过一个在书中反复出现的意象即“白色的床”（a white bed）逐渐向读者传达出来的。在一次学术交流会上，莫德结识了一位年轻的男性学者弗格斯（Fergus）并和他有了一段交往。这种缺乏真爱而仅仅基于生理需求的性伙伴关系，加剧并凸显了她内心深处的空虚和不安，也令她对欲望本身产生了厌倦（“... desire lies on the other side of repugnance”①），甚至在和弗格斯结束这样的关系之后，只要见到、听到或联想到他，仍会使她脑海中浮现出一幅尴尬的画面：“一张宽大、凌乱、带有污迹的床，床单被蹂躏得遍布折皱，像被鞭子抽打过的鸡蛋白（a huge, unmade, stained and rumpled bed, its sheets pulled into standing peaks here and there, like the surface of whipped egg - white）”②，“……像肮脏的雪”（“... like dirty snow”③）。类似的对被污染了的“白色的床”这一意象的描写在书中多次出现，强烈暗示着空虚的性在莫德内心深处留下了鬼魅般挥之不去的阴影，让她对这种放纵的生活方式产生了潜意识里的厌恶。

书中的男主人公罗兰特（Roland）也是一位年轻学者，他专门研究与拉摩特同时代的一位重要诗人伦道夫·亨利·阿舍（Randolph Henry Ash）。罗兰特文弱而腼腆、清贫而执著，他和同居女友瓦尔之间问题重重。除了共同负担生活费用和性，他们之间便没有什么共同语言，也根本不存在爱情（“He took

① ［英］A. S. 拜厄特：《占有》，外语教学与研究出版社2000年版，第63页。
② ［英］A. S. 拜厄特：《占有》，外语教学与研究出版社2000年版，第63页。
③ ［英］A. S. 拜厄特：《占有》，外语教学与研究出版社2000年版，第155页。

hold of her. It was will and calculation, not desire"①)。罗兰特有时会幻想独自睡在洁白的床上，摆脱了这样死气沉沉让他产生窒息感、不洁感的生活（"If there had been more than one bed in the flat he could have used his natural defence, which was self-enfolded inattention. He woke now most mornings stiff with keeping himself to the edge of the mattress"②)、("—because—I have this vision of the white bed"③)。

一次偶然的机会，罗兰特发现了阿舍曾经给拉摩特写过的两封激情洋溢的信稿。出于学术敏感和好奇，他决心弄清楚阿舍和拉摩特之间究竟发生过什么，于是找到了莫德，希望得到她的帮助来查寻两位诗人之间的秘密。起初，莫德对罗兰特的态度谈不上友好。这主要是由于她对诗人阿舍存在偏见，称他写过"nasty anti-feminist poem"④。这种对阿舍的敌意似乎也殃及了罗兰特。而罗兰特心中对女权主义的那一套也不以为然，但他却只能隐而不发。尽管如此，莫德还是对罗兰特的发现颇有兴趣，同意和他一起调查。她先让罗兰特阅读了保存在她的研究中心的拉摩特当年志同道合的好友布兰奇·格洛弗小姐（Blanche Glover）的日记，又和他一起到拉摩特当年居住的塔楼里，在她房中的木偶席子底下的一个洞里找到了拉摩特保存下来的她和阿舍当年的信件，从而揭开了阿舍和拉摩特之间一段鲜为人知的罗曼史。

伦道夫·亨利·阿舍是19世纪英国维多利亚时代一个杰出的诗人，他不信仰宗教，热爱科学，想探索生命的起源⑤。阿舍和妻子艾伦（Ellen）婚后40多年过着平静、和睦的生活。可是这表面波澜不惊堪称模范的婚姻生活并不完美，甚至还隐含着深深的遗憾。由于对阿舍的宗教态度不甚满意以及父亲的不赞同，艾伦没有在风华正茂的年龄与阿舍结合。当她的两个妹妹都走在她前面幸福地结了婚时，艾伦感觉自己境况窘迫，遂与阿舍结婚。那时，阿舍已苦苦等待了16年，时年34岁，艾伦36岁。激情不再的年龄加之宗教、时代等因素使艾伦对性心生恐惧和排斥（"She had never spoken of it to anyone, not even to Randolph... precisely not to Randolph... An attempt. A hand not pushed away, the locked gateway, the panic, the wimpering flight. Not once, but over and o-

① ［英］A. S. 拜厄特：《占有》，外语教学与研究出版社2000年版，第140页。

② ［英］A. S. 拜厄特：《占有》，外语教学与研究出版社2000年版，第238页。

③ ［英］A. S. 拜厄特：《占有》，外语教学与研究出版社2000年版，第294页。

④ ［英］A. S. 拜厄特：《占有》，外语教学与研究出版社2000年版，第48页。

⑤ 该角色的这些特征和英国历史上的真实诗人罗伯特·勃朗宁带有明显相似性。此外，拜厄特在书中假借阿舍之手创作的大幅诗作也极具勃朗宁风格。

ver and over. When did he began to know that however gentle he was, however patient, it was no good, it would never be any good? ... The eagerness, the terrible love, with which she had made it up to him, his abstinence, making him a thousand small comforts, cakes and tidbits. She became his slave"①)。对于阿舍经常兴致勃勃地念诵诗文给她听的做法，艾伦在日记里记下了自己的真实感受："I can never say enough in praise of Randolph's unvarying goodness and forbearance with my feebleness and inadequacies."② 由此可见，阿舍和艾伦缺少爱人间正常的性的亲密和谐，而柏拉图式的情感交流也未能有效地消弭这种不和谐。当艾伦回首往事之时，她感叹道："二十四岁的妙龄女子实不该等到芳华已尽的三十六岁再嫁人（A young girl of twenty-four should not be made to wait for marriage until she is thirty-six and her flowering is over）。"③

在遇到拉摩特之前，阿舍在这没有多少实质内容的、伪善的婚姻中已经度过了 11 年。他们是在和一个评论家朋友共进晚餐时相识的。拉摩特的诗人名气不如阿舍，她的主要作品是神话长诗《梅卢西娜》。拉摩特原本和好友布兰奇·格洛弗有着共同的理想和抱负，无心世俗婚恋。与阿舍相识之后，两人都被对方的精神气质和见识所吸引。后来阿舍主动写信给拉摩特，他们通过书信谈论诗歌、人生、信仰等话题。飞鸿频频，点燃了两位诗人的灵魂。阿舍最终启迪并打开了拉摩特的心扉，他们共同找到了有生命的爱情。他们先是在公园约会，进而发展到去约克郡旅游，在那里度过了他们的"蜜月"。

然而，拉摩特知道，在她那个时代，虽然宗教信仰在一点点地丧失，人们的观念仍很陈旧，社会对他们仍有着极大的压力，因此他们的爱情不会有什么结果。于是，她和阿舍约定分手后他们的爱情也就此止步，永不再回头。后来，拉摩特发现自己怀孕了，为了躲避英国社会的压力，她只身到了法国布列塔尼的亲戚家，悄悄生下了一个女孩。他把孩子送回英国交由姐姐索菲娅抚养，成了索菲娅的女儿。此后 30 多年，拉摩特一直居住在姐姐家里，每天眼见自己的孩子，却不能相认。她独自一人默默忍受着这样的痛苦，自始至终保持着对阿舍的一腔深情。而阿舍也没有一天不在渴望知道她和孩子的消息，并为此饱受煎熬。由于艾伦从中作梗，阿舍临终时也没能收到拉摩特写来的告白之信。

① ［英］A. S. 拜厄特：《占有》，外语教学与研究出版社 2000 年版，第 498 ~ 499 页。
② ［英］A. S. 拜厄特：《占有》，外语教学与研究出版社 2000 年版，第 128 页。
③ ［英］A. S. 拜厄特：《占有》，外语教学与研究出版社 2000 年版，第 499 页。

阿舍和拉摩特的故事主要是以书信体和日记体的形式出现在书中的，作者拜厄特假借两位诗人之手创作了许多诗歌和神化故事穿插其中，使他们之间的爱情呈现出扑朔迷离的浪漫色彩。

三

罗兰特和莫德是秘密展开他们的调查的。罗兰特隐瞒了敏感的女友瓦尔，莫德也竭力回避其他学术同仁的怀疑与试探。当调查一点点接近历史的真相时，罗兰特和莫德似乎也正一步步远离现实生活——他们原本就渴望逃避的生活。

经过一起细细温读拉摩特和阿舍的信稿和诗篇，莫德和罗兰特这两位年轻的学者渐渐加深了了解，他们的心灵慢慢贴近，并由衷地生出爱意。两位昔日诗人之间纯真的情怀和深沉的灵魂交流深深打动了他们，他们意识到自己身处的是一个情感匮乏的时代。这种领悟正是他们超越自身和时代的开始。在结伴重游当年拉摩特和阿舍相依相伴的秘密旅程时，罗兰特和莫德同行分宿，感受着客栈里洁白的床带给他们的轻松—— 一种摆脱了欲望纠缠的轻松，并且终于把这种感觉讲了出来：

"Sometimes I feel," said Roland carefully, "that the best state is to be without desire. When I really look at myself—... At my life, at the way it is—what I really want is to—to have nothing. An empty clean bed. I have this image of a clean empty bed in a clean empty room, where nothing is asked or to be asked. Some of that is to do with—my personal circumstances. But some of it's general, I think."

"I know what you mean. No, that's a feeble thing to say. It's a much more powerful coincidence than that. That's what I think about, when I'm alone. How good it would be to have nothing. How good it would be to desire nothing. And the same image. An empty bed in an empty room. White."

"White." ①

情感的贴近使他们的调查之旅带上了一层蜜月色彩，对“洁白的床”的同样渴望却使得他们一直保持着自然的距离，谁都没有跨越雷池一步。这种对

① ［英］A. S. 拜厄特：《占有》，外语教学与研究出版社 2000 年版，第 290 页。

欲望的理性把握升华了感情，并最终引领他们实现了精神与肉体的和谐统一。

小说中多次暗示了两对主人公的同一性。如，写罗兰特和莫德“步伐一致”，写阿舍和拉摩特“步履和谐”；罗兰特把莫德看成“受折磨的豌豆公主”，阿舍则觉得拉摩特睡的褥子“隔开了公主和豌豆”；就连名字，“Maud”和“LaMotte”，“Roland”和“Randolph”，也带有明显的相似性。作者拜厄特在小说第十五章描写主人公的约克郡之旅时，没有点明人物是现实中的莫德和罗兰特，还是昔日诗人阿舍和拉摩特，而是采用了“他们”、“他”、“她”、“这个男人”、“这个女人”这样的模糊人称，造成一种时空交错的感觉。这些似乎都暗示了两对主人公本来就是一对，作者着力想表现的并不是某对男女，而是一种人类历史上动态发展的两性之间的和谐问题。对历史的追问使莫德和罗兰特从阿舍和拉摩特身上获得了理解、尊重和爱等现实无法给予他们的情感力量。对“洁白的床 ”的渴望帮他们完成了精神洗礼，实现了欲望的纯洁化。同时，莫德和罗兰特的结合削减了拉摩特和阿舍之间的悲剧色彩。

作品的戛然而止为我们留下了许多要思索的东西，两性之间的隔膜永远存在，但那张“洁白的床”的梦想确实是这个世界上的男人们和女人们所渴望要实现的目标。当然，这张所谓的“洁白的床”既不是禁欲主义式的“洁白”，更不能被放纵主义的肉欲所玷污，它表征的只是男性、女性和谐相处、平等交流的梦想。当这种男性与女性、灵与肉的和谐到来之际，就消解了任何性别中心主义所设立出来的藩篱。

参考文献：

[1][英]A. S. 拜厄特．占有[M]．北京:外语教学与研究出版社,2000.
[2]王佐良,等．英国19世纪文学史[M]．北京:外语教学与研究出版社,2006.
[3]王佐良,等．英国20世纪文学史[M]．北京:外语教学与研究出版社,2006.
[4]李银河．女性主义[M]．济南:山东人民出版社,2005.
[5]塞尔登．文学批评理论——从柏拉图到现在[M]．北京:北京大学出版社,2003.

第二部分　外语教学研究

Effective Extensive Reading: Principle and Practice

Ma Ling

1. Introduction

In the EFL setting, students do not have many opportunities to use English outside of class. Their experience is mostly means to be confined to the classroom where limited time and resources are available. Reading is the primary means to extend their exposure to the target language. Reading skill has been most emphasized in traditional FL teaching, and is still the mainstay of EFL instruction in present day China. To be specific, English instruction at the university level in China is usually the "intensive reading procedure", which implies close study of short passages, including syntactic, semantic, and lexical analyses and translation into the L1 to arrive at meaning. This, as Alderson and Urquhart (1984) have argued, is not a reading but a language lesson: In other words, when reading, we engage in activities such as recalling word meanings, inferring, drawing conclusions, and so on, but these are all aspects of the act of comprehending. Freeman (1999) suggests that reading is an active, fluent process, which involves the reader and the reading materials in building meaning.

In recent years researchers and teachers involved in foreign language instruction have become increasingly aware of the importance of extensive reading. It is believed that successful readers have a positive attitude towards reading: read more, and become better readers. As better readers, they have a larger vocabulary, are familiar with the syntactical structures found in books, and have a broader knowledge base.

Good readers get better by reading more. This goal can be achieved in extensive reading as well. Studies have shown that extensive reading is the key to achieving higher reading proficiency (Krashen, 1993, Green & Oxford, 1995, Susser & Robb 1989). Hayashi (1999) argues that extensive reading provides learners with rich background knowledge, vocabulary growth, and higher motivation for more reading. Even though extensive reading can offer many advantages for language learners, how to manage the learning process and the product to make extensive learning effective has become a challenge for both learners and teachers. Moreover, most teachers would probably agree that, generally speaking, EFL students do little reading in English that goes beyond required textbooks.

2. Definition and Description of Extensive Reading

Bamford and Day define extensive reading as "an approach to language teaching in which learners read a lot of easy materials in the new language" (2004). They choose their own reading materials and read it independently of the teacher. They read for general, overall meaning, and they read for information and enjoyment. They are encouraged to stop reading if material is not interesting or if it is too difficult. These authorities further indicate that as students "become better and more confident readers, they write better. Their listening and speaking abilities improve, and their vocabularies get richer" (p. 1). This, in turn, positively affects their level of motivation and attitudes towards their language studies.

Bamford and Day (2004) suggest ten principles as a theoretical framework for the implementation of extensive reading in the language classroom. In brief, teachers provide a variety of reading materials on a wide range of topics; learners choose what they want to read and read as much as possible; the reading is rapid; the purpose of reading is related to pleasure, information and general understanding; reading is individual, silent and for its own reward; teachers orient and guide the students and serve as role models in reading. This paper concentrates on four of these points, which may offer some solution for EFL reading teachers at University level.

2.1 The Reading Material is Easy

It would be hard for foreign language learners to succeed reading extensively if they had to struggle with difficult materials, which were beyond their competence in the foreign language. The appropriate material contains no more than one or two unknown vocabulary items per page for beginners and no more than four or five for intermediate learners. Hu and Nation (2000) suggest that learners must know at least 98% of the words in a fiction text for unassisted understanding.

2.2　Learners Choose What They Want to Read

Learners selecting reading materials on their own play a role different from that of traditional classroom, where the teacher dominantly chooses one. Learners may be motivated by reading what they choose, and enjoy the reading. I usually ask my students (non-English major graduates) to choose their own extensive reading materials in their relevant subjects. As a result, they are more actively engaged in reading, benefiting not only from the linguistic knowledge, but also information on the subject matter. Further, this method encourages students to become independent learners.

In contrast, suppose the reading is an assignment. Most of us do not take pleasure in assignments. However, pleasure, like quantity, is relative. The procedure assumes that students will enjoy reading books that they have chosen on topics of interest to them more than they will enjoy assigned readings from a reader.

2.3　Reading Speed is Usually Faster Rather than Slower

If learners read materials that they can easily understand, it stimulates fluent reading. For many EFL learners, a habit of reading word by word for illusion of understanding better. Nuttall notes that "speed, enjoyment and comprehension are closely linked with one another" (1996:128). She describes "The vicious circle of the weak reader: Reads slowly; Doesn't enjoy reading; Doesn't read much; Doesn't understand; Reads slowly..." and so on. Extensive reading can help readers "enter instead the cycle of growth... The virtuous circle of the good reader: Reads faster; Reads more; Understands better; Enjoys reading; Reads faster..." (1996:127).

Mikulecky (1990) suggests that L2 readers are trapped in a feeling of security, in that they believe reading every word leads to better understanding of the text's meaning. Unfortunately, such slow reading may discourage learners. It is clear that methods that help students learn to read faster and with better comprehension may encourage them to read more and more fully utilize opportunities for growth in the L2 through reading.

2.4 Teachers Orient and Guide Their Students

Extensive reading is very different from the usual classroom practice. In the intensive reading class, for example, teachers need to explain to students linguistic points, vocabulary, and background knowledge, and follow with comprehension questions. Intensive reading often refers to the careful reading (or translation) of shorter, more difficult foreign language texts with the goal of complete and detailed understanding. Intensive reading is also associated with the teaching of reading in terms of its component skills. Texts are studied intensively in order to introduce and practice reading skills such as distinguishing the main idea of a text from the detail, finding pronoun referents, or guessing the meaning of unknown words (Wurr, 2003). However, when exposed to simple and fun materials, learners may not achieve as greatly as expected. So according to Day (2004), students need careful introduction to extensive reading. Teachers can explain that reading extensively leads not only to gains in reading proficiency but also to overall gains in language learning. Teachers can reassure students that a general, less than 100%, understanding of what they read is appropriate for most reading purposes. The teacher will keep track of what and how much students read and their reactions to what was read.

3. Practice

The teacher may conduct the class guided by the principles discussed above. The teacher's role in the extensive reading procedure is to encourage and help the students with their reading, by oral reading reports, written reading reports, and writing summaries.

3.1 Oral or Written Reports / Summaries

Oral or written reports / summaries give students an opportunity to demonstrate that they are, in fact, doing their reading. They also allow the teacher to determine if students understand their books at an acceptable level. If not, the teacher's task is to direct them to more appropriate books. The students' main task is reading, but writing summaries is valuable not only to provide a means for teachers to check comprehension, but because the writing of summaries demonstrates that comprehension is an element of the lesson rather than a precondition, and is determined by the techniques of this procedure (Susser & Robb, 1989). I have employed writing summary practice in my reading class, and find it effective in helping students with both their writing skill and reading ability.

Effective reading will lead to the shaping of the reader's thoughts, which naturally leads many learners to respond in writing with varying degrees of fluency. Elementary level students can be asked simply to write short phrases expressing what they most enjoyed about a book they read, or to record questions they wish to ask the teacher or other students in class. With intermediate students, book reports may be used, with sections for questions, new vocabulary, and for recording the main characters and events. At this level, summary writing is also a valuable practice because it allows learners to assert full control, of both the main factual or fictional content of a book and the grammar and vocabulary used to express it. Advanced students can be asked to write compositions, which, by definition, are linguistically more demanding written responses to the reading material.

3.2 Avoid the Use of Tests

One of the main purposes of extensive reading is to motivate EFL students to read by pleasure. Tests or marks will increase pressure on students. The use of tests runs contrary to the objective of creating stress-free conditions for pleasure reading because it invokes images of rote learning, vocabulary lists, memorization and homework. Extensive reading done outside of class should be under the learner's control.

3.3 Discourage the Over-Use of Dictionaries

While dictionaries certainly have a place in the teaching of reading, they are probably most useful in intensive reading lessons, where detailed study of the lexical content of texts is appropriate. If learners turn to the dictionary every time they come across an unfamiliar word, they will focus only on the language itself, and not on the message conveyed. This habit will result in slow, inefficient reading and destroy the pleasure that reading novels and other literature is intended to provide.

4. Conclusion

In order for extensive reading to do its work—build vocabulary knowledge, develop positive attitudes toward reading, and strengthen reading fluency—the reading material must be well within the students' linguistic ability. Students may choose to read for different purposes. At the same time, extensive reading is not necessarily the entire answer to the teaching of reading. Some students will need special help with certain reading sub-skills; others will need extra encouragement to read, and assistance in choosing enjoyable books at a suitable linguistic level. Most likely, skills/strategies training is also necessary. If used appropriately, extensive reading not only helps students learn to read in the second language, but also leads them to enjoy reading. In addition, extensive reading provides a means of developing autonomy in learning. As a result, students can benefit by making reading a part of their foreign language study.

References:

[1] Aebersold, J. A. & Urquhart, A. H.. Postscript on Hosenfeld. In J. C. Alderson & A. H.. Urquhart (ed.). *Reading in a Foreign Language.* New York: Longman, 1984.

[2] Day, R. & Bamford, J.. *Extensive Reading in a Second Language.* New York: Cambridge University Press, 1998.

[3] Day, R. & Bamford, J.. *Extensive Reading Activities for Teaching Language.* Cambridge: Cambridge University Press, 2004.

[4] Freeman, D.. Exploring Second Language Reading. Newbury House: Heinle & Heinle. Hayashi, K.. *Reading Strategies and Extensive Reading in EFL Classes.* RELC Journal, 1999, 30 (2): 114 – 132.

[5] Hu, M. & Nation, P.. Unknown Vocabulary Density and Reading Comprehension. *Reading in a Foreign Language*, 2000, 13(1): 403 – 430.

[6] Krashen, S.. *The Power of Reading: Insights from the Research.* Englewood, CO: Libraries Unlimited, 1993.

[7] Mikulecky, B. S.. A Short Course in Teaching Reading Skills. Reading, MA: Addison – Wesley. Nuttall, C.. *Teaching Reading Skills in a Foreign Language.*

Oxford: Heinemann, 1990, 1996.

[8] Susser, B. & Robb, T. N.. Extensive Homework. *The Language Teacher*, 1989, 13(8): 7-9. Wurr, A.. *Transfer Effects of Repeated EFL Reading on Reading New Passages*. Journal of College Reading and Learning, 2003, 33(2): 157-f169.

To What Extent can We Make Best Use of Metadiscourse in Teaching English Writing?①

Li Jia

1. Introduction

Studies on how to improve L2 learners' writing are quite productive, and among those theories, the significance of the functions of metadiscourse in oral and written English have been carried out by a great number of scholars (Xu, 2005:54 – 61)②. It seems that metadiscourse is of great use in facilitating students' writing. The author, however, would like to challenge the applicability of metadiscourse in classroom instruction. In other words, the author will examine the applicability of metadiscourse in a teaching and learning context. To answer this question, the author believes that it is necessary to first analyze the exact use of metadiscourse devices in an English textbook. As it is known to all, the textbook is normally considered an important learning resource in a Chinese speaking environment in which students and teachers have to reply on the textbook in classroom to interact with each other. In this sense it is assumed to be helpful to reveal the patterns of various metadiscourse elements emerged in the textbook. As a teacher, however, he or she has to select what to teach in class concerned with certain teaching objectives and students' learning needs. Hence the author will examine whether it is appropriate to teach students all of those metadiscourse devices in the textbook in comparison with the teaching objectives of

---

① 本文是云南大学教学改革研究项目 Jxyj 2006 – 19 的系列成果之一。

② Xu Haimin 2001. Meta-discourse: A Cross-cultural Perspective. Nanjing: Southeast University Press.

syllabus in Test for English Major-4 (TEM-4) for writing section. By so doing, the author will offer her different understandings of metadiscourse theory in facilitating students' English writing, and in the meanwhile she will provide some related suggestions on how to make best use of metadiscourse theory in teaching English writing.

2. Metadiscourse

2.1 Definition of Metadiscourse

As it is well known, any integrated discourse is composed of two parts: primary discourse and metadiscourse. Metadiscourse has been given various terms before such as "signaling devices", "signposts", "gambits", "meta-talk", "modalities of texts" (Xu:2005:54-61)[①]. The definition of metadiscourse has also experienced different interpretations. Vande Kopple claims that metadiscourse is discourse about discourse or communication about communication (1985:83)[②]. Williams takes it to be "writing about writing, whatever does not refer to the subject matter being addressed" (1981:111, quoted in Xu, 2005:54-61).

2.2 Function of Metadiscourse

Based on the above definitions, metadiscourse elements can be considered to be non-propositional since they can be omitted from the text without changing its actual meaning. According to Vande Kopple (1985), metadiscourse can help readers better understand the propositional content of a text as well as the writer's attitudes. In other words, metadiscourse can facilitate readers with text comprehension, enabling readers to interact with writers' intention.

3. Theoretical Classification of Metadiscourse and Pattern of Metadiscourse Devices Used in a Textbook

Based on numerous theoretical and experimental studies, Xu Haiming has classified types of metadiscourse and offered relevant examples of each type. What followed is the exact use of metadiscourse devices in seven texts derived from "New Compre-

---

① Xu Haimin 2001. Meta-discourse: A Cross-cultural Perspective. Nanjing: Southeast University Press.

② Vande Kopple, W. J. 1985. Some Explanatory Discourse on Meta-discourse. College Composition and Communication, 36: 81-93.

hensive English" Book IV which has been used as textbooks of English majors in many Chinese universities (Li, 1999)①. According to the syllabus, students are required to pass TEM-4 after they have finished learning this textbook, and due to the fact that there are only two writing styles required in TEM-4—exposition and argumentation (Syllabus, 2004)②, the author has collected seven expositions and argumentations in total from the textbook. The author will then employ Xu's theory and analyze the patterns of metadiscourse devices in Book IV as it follows.

The pattern of metadiscourse devices in the textbook

Textual metadiscourse	Textual connectives	times	examples
	Transitive connectives	96	However; but; whereas; yet; while...
	Logical connectives	20	Since; Because of that; So; Thus; Therefore; For...
	Sequencers	19	First…the second…the third; Also; Then; And...
	Topicalizers	6	Well; Of course; Regard; Now
	Addictive connectives	4	Moreover; Also; Then
	Contrastive connectives	3	By contrast; In contrast
	Code glosses	times	examples
	Explanatory words and phrases	9	An illustration may make this point clear...; Say; Take ... for example; For example; Such as;... which means...;... example of... is...
	Rhetorical devices	8	... like shooting sitting bird...; music like the theatre...; ... as if we don't know... as if we don't know...; It's like resuming...

① Li Guanyi 1999. A New English Course. Shanghai: Shanghai Foreign Language Education Press.

② Syllabus for TEM-4 2004. Shanghai: Shanghai Foreign Language Education Press.

<table>
<tr><td rowspan="12">Inter-personal Meta-discourse</td><td>Commentaries</td><td>times</td><td>examples</td></tr>
<tr><td>Real/rhetorical/tag questions</td><td>23</td><td>Is it false respect to...? Why is marking up a book...? Why is writing necessary? What do we listen for? ...</td></tr>
<tr><td>Validity markers</td><td>times</td><td>examples</td></tr>
<tr><td>Modal verbs</td><td>22</td><td>may; can; might; will; should; will...</td></tr>
<tr><td>Emphatics</td><td>13</td><td>Of course; Surely; Certainly; Small wonder...; no doubt; indeed; do...</td></tr>
<tr><td>Hedges</td><td>6</td><td>You are likely to...; probably; it was possible...</td></tr>
<tr><td>Attitudinal markers</td><td>times</td><td>examples</td></tr>
<tr><td>Indicating author's attitude towards the proposition made</td><td>11</td><td>I contend...; I'm arguing...; It is the height of naivety to...; Such an attitude is ridiculous...; It would be equally ridiculous to...; It is insufficient to...; I estimate...</td></tr>
<tr><td>Attributors</td><td>times</td><td>examples</td></tr>
<tr><td>Marking the source of information</td><td>1</td><td>According to...</td></tr>
<tr><td>Illocutionary markers</td><td>times</td><td>examples</td></tr>
<tr><td>Indicating an illocutionary speech act or author's intention</td><td>2</td><td>I want to persuade...</td></tr>
</table>

4. Requirements of Writing in TEM-4

According to the syllabus (2004)[①], students majoring in English in their second-year undergraduate program are supposed to be able to write a composition (either an exposition or an argumentation) with about 200 words within 30 minutes. Any

① Syllabus for TEM-4 2004. Shanghai: Shanghai Foreign Language Education Press.

qualified composition based on the requirements should reach certain standards in three main levels-*content*, *organization and grammar*. As for content, students should offer their idea or opinion towards a topic, and related reasons with supporting details are also provided. Concerning organization, three main parts (introduction, body and conclusion) are to be written, and the argument must be clear and logical. In other words, the way of arguing has to be logically coherent. As far as grammar is considered, it is composed of two parts—words and sentence structures in which words should be used appropriately and effectively and sentence structures should be various and based on grammar rules.

5. Suggestions on the Application of Metadiscourse in Teaching Writing

We have analyzed the exact expressions of metadiscourse devices in the textbook based on Xu's metadiscoursive theories; we have also revealed the requirement of writing TEM-4 according to the latest syllabus. In the combination of these two previous analyses, the author would like to show her own understanding of how to use metadiscoursive theories into English writing teaching and learning as followed.

5.1 Textual Connectives

From the pattern of metadiscourse devices shown above, a variety of connective words have been used in the textbook, and among those connectives, transitional words are most frequently used, with 96 times in the seven texts. Other connectives, such as logical connectives, sequencers, topcalizers, addictive connectives and contrastive connectives are also found with 20, 19, 6, 4 and 3 times respectively. The employment of these connectives can undoubtedly make one's writing coherent and cohesive. For example, "in contrast" can reveal something different from what has been discussed above; "consequently" may show what kind of results one wants to show based one certain reason. In a word, using these textual connectives, one's argument may be expressed clearly and effectively, which is also one of the essential requirements in TEM-4 (Syllabus, 2004). But if we carefully reexamine the pattern, we may find that there is no summative connective at all in the seven texts, which means the words such as "in conclusion", "in summary" or "in short" have not been used, and without these summative words, one can not reach another requirement of TEM-4—*organization*. In fact, Chinese students do not seem to remember to use those words to summarize their argument unless they have been trained with this aspect of learning (Li, 2007)①. Therefore, it is necessary for English teachers to remind students of using summative connectives in writing TEM-4 so that their writings might reach the requirement of TEM-4.

5.2 Code Glosses

It is obvious that using explanatory words or phrases can make one's idea or one's expression clearer or better understood by readers. In the textbook, 9 expressions have been found in this part, such as "an illustration may make this point clear"; "for example"... Students can benefit from using these expressions in their writing since the expressions can make their argument more convincing and more logical as required in TEM-4. As for the rhetorical devices including similes, allusions, metaphors etc., 8 different sentences are also used which will definitely make one's writing more interesting to read and easier to understand especially in writing expository and argumentative compositions. Thus, the author believes that code glosses should be encouraged to practice in teaching writing.

5.3 Interpersonal Metadiscourse

In this part, Real/rhetorical/tag questions (23 times) in commentaries and modal verbs (22 times) in validity markers have been used most frequently. Using real/rhetorical/tag questions, readers will find it easier and more interesting to follow what a writer is going to discuss; using modal verbs, one's writing will not appear too subjective and one's argument will be more convincing. Therefore, teachers should lay much emphasis on teaching those two aspects. The other devices in this part are also useful in expressing one's idea by using illocutionary markers; or in indicating writer's attitude by using attitudinal markers; in marking the source of information by using attributors and so on.

---

① Li Jia 2007. An Investigation of Conjunctive Devices in Chinese Students' English Writing from a Perspective of Metacognition. Paper presented in Nanchang in the 10th National Functional Linguistics Conference.

5.4 Content and Grammar

As it has been stated above, there are three main aspects in writing a TEM-4 composition. One aspect (organization) has been discussed in relation with the pattern of metadiscourse, but two other aspects, content and grammar do not seem to be related with metadiscourse theory. In fact, as Xu (2005)① has stated, metadiscourse does not involve propositional content, it is "discourse about discourse" and using it can facilitate one's understanding of a text, but without it, the original content will not be changed. Therefore, this theory can not be of any help either in producing one's viewpoint with related reasons and supporting details or in using appropriate words and a variety of sentence structures to express one's thought. To put it another way, English teachers have to consider these two aspects of learning which obviously can not be acquired from learning metadiscourse theory, but are essential as required in the syllabus(2004).

6. Conclusion

In summary, this paper has focused on the discussion of the possibility of using metadiscourse theory in teaching writing. The related definitions and functions of the theory have been stated, the specific examples from selected texts have been listed based on a framework of the metadiscourse theory and the requirements of writing a TEM-4 composition have been discussed in the hope that the combination of considering these three parts will be able to reveal how the theory of metadiscourse can be better applied in teaching writing. The author then has analyzed in detail the applicability of the theory by taking into consideration the requirements of TEM-4 and exact pattern of metadiscourse in the textbook and related suggestions on how to better teach English writing have also been pointed out. It is true that metadiscourse can be of great help in improving students' coherence awareness, but the theory is not perfect in the way that it does not teach how to reason and how to choose certain words and expression to express one's idea, and other useful connective devices. For example referencing or collocation is not included in the categorization of metadiscourse, but these devices can undoubtedly achieve the effectiveness of cohesion and coherence

① Xu Haimin 2001. Meta-discourse: A Cross-cultural Perspective. Nanjing: Southeast University Press.

(Halliday, 2001)①.

① Halliday, M. A. K. and Hasa, Ruqaiya. 2001 Cohesion in English. Beijing: Foreign Language Teaching and Research Press.

A Critique of the Claim that Nothing of Any Real Substance has been Developed in Language Teaching Since the Rise of Communicative Language Teaching in the 1970s and 1980s

Wang Wenjun

Introduction

Language teachers always try to explore the most effective teaching approaches to meet the needs of learners. Since the 1970s and 1980s, Communicative Language Teaching (CLT) has gained great popularity. Influenced by its dominance, some people are inclined to draw a conclusion that nothing of any real substance has been developed in language teaching since the rise of CLT. A critical analysis on this comment is based on two major aspects: the claim emphasizes the significance of CLT, but has ignored the nature and characteristics of language teaching; it has drawn an over-simple and vague conclusion of the development of language teaching, and has neglected the learner, teacher, and settings, all of which have played important roles in language teaching. Clearly the development of language teaching has not ceased, for there have been both new and modified approaches and a great trend towards a more realistic eclecticism.

Section 1

The quoted claim denies the objective and inevitable developments of other teaching methods. It is an arbitrary conclusion, which ignores the law of language teaching development, absolutely separates the internal connections in CLT and highlights CLT at the expense of and in the place of other existing teaching methods.

The development of language teaching approaches is dynamic and ever-changing. According to Brown (1994:51), from the methodological age to the functional age, language teaching has experienced "changing winds and shifting sands" and it is still developing towards a various and versatile perspective. The earliest and one of the most widely used methods is the Grammar Translation Method (GTM), which stemmed from the teaching practice of Latin and Greek in the nineteenth century. At the beginning of the twentieth century, another new method-the Direct Method-broke away entirely from the GTM and became widely known and practiced at the turn of the century. With the outbreak of WWII, the military's need for oral proficiency in foreign languages led to the development of the Audio-lingual Method. After the 1960s, with the development of cognitive linguistics, the Cognitive Approach came into being. Since the early 1970s, the communicative approach has been influential and has opened up a broader perspective on language. Since the last quarter of the century, there have been more and more language teaching approaches, methods and ideas springing up, for example, "Total Physical Response", "The Silent Way", "Community Language Learning", "The Natural Approach", and "Suggestopedia". The above sketch of the development of language teaching, especially of second and foreign languages, has demonstrated that applied linguists and language teachers in different periods have consistently been seeking and designing better approaches. CLT is one of these approaches. Its emergence does not mean the existing or other new methods or approaches completely lose their popularity and stop developing. The rise of CLT shows its dominance against a certain historical background, but does not mean that the eternal demise or the impossibility of developing other teaching methods or approaches.

The nature of CLT is that it is essentially a mixture of existing varied language teaching methods that aim to improve language competence. Johnson (2002:162) points out "language teachers rarely come across pure, uncontaminated examples of any method". Littlewood (1981:xii) emphasizes that "if developments since the 1970s have any special claim to the label 'communicative', it is because the implications of this goal have been explored more thoroughly and explicitly than before". Brown (2001:15) claims that "the term CLT is a byword for language teachers. Indeed, the single greatest challenge in the profession is moving significantly beyond the teaching of rules, patterns, definition, and other knowledge about language to the point that we are teaching our students to communicate genuinely, spontaneously and meaningfully". The basic idea of language teaching is that communicative ability is the goal. CLT is not an absolutely new substance rising in the 1970s and 1980s. Superficially; it may seem an illusion that little of any real substance has been developed in language teaching since the rise of CLT. In fact, different existing teaching methods and approaches have been experiencing developments of a communicative trend and have not been overwhelmed by CLT itself.

From the characteristics of CLT, it is understood as an approach, not a method. It has combined the structural and functional views of language. It has absorbed the advantages and strengths of traditional methods to develop communicative competence. Thus the potential, internal and interactive developments of traditional teaching methods cannot be ignored. First, CLT focuses on communicative competence, but also recognizes the importance of linguistic structures and does not discard the development of grammatical competence in communication. Generally, the stereotypical view of grammatical study would probably "lead to an illusion that learning grammar is often associated with the dry memorization of rules and the equally dry prospect of applying these rules in the fill in-the-blank, pattern practice, substitution, transformation and translation exercise" (Comeau, in Rivers, 2000:57). As a matter of fact, through CLT training grammatical rules can be practiced in communicational interactive activities. This activity makes learners consider language in terms of its structures (namely, grammar and vocabulary) while they are performing the communicative function. Widdowson (1998:98) argues that "a communicative approach, properly conceived, does not involve the rejection of grammar. On the contrary, it involves recognition of its central mediating role in the use and learning of language". Vocabulary and grammar are essential to make a sentence or utterance sensible and understandable in most real-life situations. Instead of memorizing abstract rules, students can master grammar via interesting and informative activities. Learners can practice dialogues and apply the underlying grammatical rules in them. CLT itself does not deny the importance of grammar as one of the basic language items. Instead, it ensures that students become familiar with these structures through innovative training techniques. Moreover, CLT shares the focus of the Direct Method and Audio-lingual approach in its goals of oral and aural/oral efficiency. The basic premise of the Direct Method is that "second language learning should be like first language learning-lots of oral interaction, spontaneous use of the language, no translation between first and second language, and little or no analysis of grammatical rules" (Brown, 1994: 55). In addition, the Audio-lingual method is intended to develop the aural/oral skills by much use of tapes, language labs and visual aids. Thus, there are at least three goals of the above two traditional methods echoing the requirements of CLT: massive oral interactions; spontaneous use of language; mimicry of real life-situational communication to realize the language function and convey information.

From the development, nature and characteristics of CLT, it is clear that CLT does not contradict other teaching methods. The title comment has neglected that all the teaching methods and approaches have contributed much to the more scientific and reasonable development of language teaching and gained vigor and new blood from academic research and the teaching practices of linguistics and language teachers. So they serve the communicative purposes of language learning.

Section 2

The quoted comment makes a simple and indistinct generalization on language teaching. The popularity of a certain teaching method or approach is influenced by three factors: learner, teacher, and setting. Methodological issues are quite diverse and complex. There is no consensus of opinion as to what is the best way to teach language. Nunan (2001) claims that the development of language education reflects different needs of different learner groups, which is in harmony with the interpretative view of knowledge being fashioned within humanistic psychology and experiential learning.

The research on learners has been of great significance in language teaching. The finding is that age level and proficiency level influence the language teaching methodology. Teachers use different methods depending on how old or advanced learners are. Diversity of age level is an impetus for diversified and multilateral development in language teaching. Teachers decide to adopt different methods according to the mature features of the cognitive abilities of different age groups. For children, the Direct Method is likely to be the most productive. Brown (1994:101) argues that "since children (up to the age of about eleven) are still at an intellectual stage of what Piaget called 'concrete operation', they have inevitable limitations with respect to learning. Rules, explanations, and other even slightly abstract talk about language must be approached with extreme caution". The "directness" requires reduced distraction from the first language, and combines second or foreign language teaching with concrete objects, pictures and activities in learning. Since children are focused on the functional purposes of language, they have little appreciation of the notion of "correctness". Adults, on the other hand, have superior cognitive abilities. "The influence of cognitive linguistics may prove valuable, because it lends theoretical support to a number of accepted teaching approaches in the fields of both vocabulary and grammar" (Unger & Schmid, 2001:267). As for students in-between (approximately from ages 11 to 18), they are at an age of transition, confusion, and self-consciousness. Language teaching for them requires more consideration in both functional and structural development (Swain, quoted by Nunan, 2001).

The proficiency level is an active factor in the development of language teaching. In the process of language teaching practice development, special attention has been focused on the proficiency levels of language learners, since it is an important factor in language learning efficiency. The proficiency level is always defined according to three bands: beginning, intermediate and advanced. The proficiency level descriptor can guide language teachers in determining their students' levels and adapting different methods and approaches accordingly. For beginning-level students, the language instruction is the most challenging, since students at this level have little or no prior knowledge of the target language. The teacher needs to become a central determiner and the teaching methods can take the form of repetition of limited words, phrases, and sentences. Intermediate-level students have progressed from the novice stage and have an ability to sustain basic communicative tasks. Teachers are no longer the only initiator of language. Students should be encouraged to put forward questions arising from their language learning process. For advanced learners, teaching techniques can be aimed to develop the full range of sociolinguistic and pragmatic competencies. In short, the age level and proficiency level are important variables in the continuous development of language teaching. The research and attention given to these variables are also significant improvements, which the rise of CLT cannot overshadow.

From the point of view of the teacher, the language teaching profession is high demanding "not merely in the mastery of rules of practice but in an exploration of the knowledge, beliefs, attitudes, and thinking that inform such practice" (Littlewood, 2000: vi). Teachers play many roles in the course of teaching as controller, director, manager, facilitator and resource. Teacher training and training education are progressing along with language teaching development. For as long as people have been learning and teaching language, there has been a continual debate about how to describe the process and how best to achieve it. Freeman (in Carter & Nunan, 2001) points out that since the 1980s, teacher education has been an important focus, which has gained enough attention during the process of language teaching development. Around the world in the 1970s and 1980s, there was greater realization of the critical importance of teacher and administrator preparation and training, though there are still examples of innovation being introduced without adequate teacher development, as in Saudi Arabia and China. CLT is influential, but it requires language teachers to have a good command of the target language and effective techniques to improve students' communicative competence. Regional and individual inequalities amongst language teachers have resulted in a variety of language teaching methods and approaches. In a broad sense, teachers' engagement in planning and carrying out their work has a direct impact on the popularity of a certain approach or set of teaching methods.

Language teaching and learning settings are another focus of continuous and substantial development. Cultures, political situations and social pressures need to be taken into consideration in adopting teaching approaches. English teaching in non-English-speaking countries is the most prevalent case. Both the traditional and newer teaching methods and approaches are being used internationally because of the diversity and complexity of language teaching development. The English teaching and learning situation in China can be a good example to demonstrate this point. The Grammar Translation Method is the major method in most teaching practice (Zuo, 2001). The "blackboard and chalk" has limited teaching to the teacher's total level of grammar and vocabulary. Even though more and more teachers are eager to master communicative language teaching, the scant availability of teaching practice, teaching facilities and teaching aids has restricted the adoptions of updated teaching approaches. Even though CLT is generally popular, the title comment obviously ignores the fact that other teaching methods and approaches are still active and progressing in different language teaching situations.

Conclusion

During the decades from the 1970s and 1980s to the twenty-first century, although no new teaching approach as influential as CLT has come into being and been globally accepted, improvement of language teaching has not come to an end. With the wide spread of second and foreign language learning, more and more applied linguists have realized that there is no absolutely bad or good method or approach on the international scene. Following the debates and compromises among the structural and functional views, research into language teaching theories and practice has diversified to include learner-centered, task-based, content-based, interactive, and other specific approaches. Nunan(1991:96) encapsulates by saying that "It has been realized that there never was and probably never will be a method for all, and the focus in recent years has been on the development of classroom tasks and activities which are consonant with what we know about second language acquisition". In the light of the current literature on language teaching and learning, significant and new theories and new ideas have developed.

I have tried to show that since the rise of Communicative Language Teaching in the 1970s and 1980s, many traditional and new theories, ideas, concerns, methods and approaches have been developed in the practice of language teaching, not just communicative language teaching. Controversies that arise in the language teaching profession are useful and insightful. Language teachers may sometimes be "confused and be buddled by a plethora of conflicting assertions and recommendation" (Rivers, 1997: 43), but they need new ideas and proposals to refresh their minds and form a reasonable view towards the developments of CLT. We must make the most of their knowledge and techniques, sifting, sorting and selecting according to the needs of learners in different particular situations.

Reference:

[1] Brown, D.. *Principles of Language Learning and Teaching.* Beijing: Foreign Language Teaching and Research Press, 2001.

[2] Brown, D.. *Teaching by Principles: An Interactive Approach to Language Pedagogy.* London: Prentice Hall Regents, 1994.

[3] Carter, R. & Nunan, D. (ed.). *Teaching English to Speakers of Other Languages.* Cambridge: CUP, 2001.

[4] Johnson, K.. *An Introduction to Foreign Language Learning and Teaching.* Beijing: Foreign Language Teaching and Research Press, 2002.

[5] Littlewood, W.. *Communicative Language Teaching.* Cambridge: CUP, 1981.

[6] Littlewood, W.. *Foreign and Second Language Learning: Language-acquisition research and its implications for the classroom.* Beijing: Foreign Language Teaching and Research Press, 2000.

[7] Nunan, D.. *Language Teaching Methodology: A textbook for teachers.* London: Prentice Hall, 1991.

[8] Nunan, D.. *Second Language Teaching and Learning.* Beijing: Foreign Language Teaching and Research Press & Heinle & Heinle/Thomson, 2001.

[9] Rivers, M.. *Interactive Language Teaching.* Cambridge: CUP, 1997.

[10] Ungerer, F. & Schmid, J.. *An Introduction to Cognitive Linguistics.* Beijing: Foreign Language Teaching and Research Press, 2001.

[11] Widdowson, G.. *Aspects of Language Teaching.* Oxford: OUP, 1990.

[12] Zuo, H.. *The Perspectives of Foreign Language Education.* Shanghai: East China Normal University Press, 2001.

谈谈朗读在大学英语教学中的作用

张彩庆

一、朗　读

朗读（reading aloud）作为一种普通和传统的语言学习方法，其有效性是无可置疑的。该方法一直以来都在被从事语言教学的教师和学习者所运用。可以说，几乎人人都有在小学阶段学习汉语时大声读书的经历。但是，在英语教学中，朗读的作用实际上并没有受到足够的重视，大学阶段尤其如此。本着这一认识，笔者认为有必要重提朗读在大学英语教学中的重要性。

朗读，顾名思义，指的就是大声地、清楚地把文章念出来，使视觉、听觉、各发声器官的感受性得到充分的整合刺激，以达到强化记忆、加深理解、增强语感的目的。中国谚语“三天不练口生”和英语习语“Practice makes perfect”点明了朗读的重要性。朗读时，口、鼻、喉、舌、腭、唇、齿等各发声器官能体验词句的轻重、强弱、爆破、浊化、连贯、停顿、节奏快慢，甚至是语气、口吻和情感。正确的发音必须以大脑和各发声器官之间能快速、准确地传递刺激反映信号，并在生理机能上形成良好的配合为前提，所以在这个意义上说，语言的学习，有一半是体力劳动。在语言学习中，“动脑不动口”是不可能真正把一门语言学好的。毕竟，以为自己开口就能读好是一回事，而实际上真正读好又是另一回事。虽然，朗读所涉及的通常是非动态的语境，而且文字材料中的交际情景真实性（authenticity）与实际的口语交际相比，有着较大的差距。但是，在能准确、流利、自然地说出单词，以恰当的句子表达思想、进行交际之前，必须先有大量的、相对而言较机械的朗读练习为基础。只有当对词、词组、常用句型达到一定的熟练程度，实现对所读材料的内化时，才谈得上发音准确、用词恰当，做到流利、自如地口头表达，实现有效的沟通。

从输入与输出理论来看，朗读作为一种强化的信息输入方式，为语感的培养提供了物质基础。Krashen 认为，二语习得必须通过理解大量反复出现的输入语，即可理解性输入（comprehensible input）才能完成；习得者在接触大量易懂的实际语言时，借助交际情景和上下文理解输入语，自然地掌握其中的句子结构，最终实现运用外语进行交际的目的。也就是说，话语能力（即有意义的自然输出）是在习得者通过理解性输入达到一定语言能力时自然产生的。朗读能提高所输入信息的可理解性，为提高话语能力潜移默化地打下基础。Bialystok（1978：69－83）的输入与输出理论集中体现在显性语言知识和隐性语言知识上。前者存在于学习者的意识层中，经过熟练掌握后的显性语言知识可以内化为隐性语言知识，隐性语言知识（或语感）水平越高，熟练运用目标语的程度就越高①。

从交际效果的角度也能说明朗读训练在英语学习上的重要性。在交际中，良好的“第一印象”是成功交际的一大步。“第一印象”包括仪表印象和声音印象。它往往是在头几秒钟形成的。实践证明，在很多交际场合中，如果说话者吐字不清、词不达意、语调不自然、说话不连贯，则会让听话者产生不耐烦甚至反感的情绪。在实际的交谈中，这种不良情绪会同时被说话者意识到，而反过来影响说话者继续交谈的信心。撇开音质、音色这些非可控因素不谈，朗读能有效地改善一个人的发音习惯，增强话语能力，使练习过程中获得的有益成分很好地迁移到具体的、生动的语境中去。

因此，毋庸赘言，朗读显然是使人“能说会道”的必要准备。可以不夸张地说：“在英语学习中，朗读不过关，口语能力无从谈起。”遗憾的是，笔者在教学中发现非英语专业的大学生朗读水平普遍较差。很多学生对于一些基本词汇的发音拿不准，对于句子中哪些词该轻读、哪些词该重读不能很好通过控制气流的强弱表现出来，甚至有些学生不会根据意群停顿……出现的问题不一而足。而且，更严重的是，这些学生在认识上存在不小偏差。他们认为朗读是小学生的事、朗读不重要、没有必要朗读，等等，因而在实践中很少有朗读的习惯。这样的认识和现状对于培养大学生的综合英语应用能力，尤其是口语能力是极为不利的。是什么原因造成朗读被普遍忽视呢？本文将从中国英语教学的几个侧面来分析该现象产生的原因。

---

① 张殿玉：《着眼大学英语课程培养目标，力求听说并举》，载《外语界》2005 年第 3 期，第 21 页。

二、中国英语教学现状

(一) 社会环境因素

从社会大环境来看，由于中国世界地位的上升，对外交往的频繁和英语在世界经济、文化领域的强势作用和我国教育政策的导向，英语教学在国内可谓方兴未艾，正值前所未有的高潮。但其中有两个最大的现实：一是英语教学始终是外语教学；二是英语教学“热”。

英语作为外语这一现实决定了目标语学习环境的缺乏，使学习者很少有机会接触课外、书本外的真实的、有任务指向性的交际语境。一般说来，学习的目标定位应该是“学以致用”。而对大多数学习者来说，英语似乎让人有一种“学了无用武之地”的尴尬。所以，除了应付各种过级、晋职、应聘这些“暂时一用”的考试之外，几乎没有什么真正的内在学习动机，形成了一种“考一次，学一次；学一次，考一次；考了完事”的低效、重复学习，学习者学习时缺乏自主性。再说中国英语教学的“热”现象。全国上下，从学前班到博士生都在学英语，数以亿计。开办各种考试培训班、辅导班、提高班蔚然成风。其实，这“热”严格说来，更多的是考试英语热和出国英语热，是一种“教育泡沫”，而绝非来自于学习者非功利的内在热情。

作为全国英语教学的重要组成部分，大学英语教学不可避免地受到了这一大气候的影响。具体表现为：（1）学习者观念不正确、自主性差。很多大学生没有意识到“学习外语成功与否很大程度上依靠学习者在课堂外寻找机会练习外语”①；没有意识到在大学阶段增强自主学习能力和调整学习策略的必要性，而过分地依赖教师。(2) 英语学习目标低。很多大学生没有从“全人教育”的高度理解英语学习与大学教育的关系，而简单地以为大学英语课只不过是中学英语课的延续，是为了过级考试，不需要达到通达（proficiency）的水平。所以在学习材料的使用上通常表现为教材、教辅、题集等为考试服务的材料，大大限制了学生接触语言（linguistic exposure）的机会而使其无法形成对英语的兴趣。“求其上，得其中；求其中，得其下”表明了目标与实际成效之间的差距。目标定位低，学生没有充分发挥他们的学习潜力。（3）困惑心理。因为学习观念和目标设定存在问题，很多学生主要是由于主观上不够努

① Lee Icy. Supporting Greater Autonomy in Language Learning [J]. ELT Journal, 1998, (4): 282-290.

力才学不好英语。而在归因的时候，却往往认为是老师教得不好、英语太难学等。这样的学生会由于英语水平出于“胶着”（stalemate）状态或是“每况愈下”而产生困惑，最终产生畏惧心理甚至完全失去对英语的信心。

朗读更多地属于自主学习的范畴，需要学生有很强的自主学习意识进行目标设定、自我监控、自我评估等能力。上述所分析的大学生学习英语的社会大环境及学生的各主观因素在一定程度上决定了他们对朗读练习的忽视。毕竟，朗读是一种勤奋学习的习惯。当然，造成忽视的还有以下原因。

（二）应试教育的“反拨”作用

测试制度中固有的“反拨”效应使学校在教学中只重视考试内容而忽视不进行检测的内容。由于长期以来，我国的教育始终以考试为教学指挥棒，尤其是初中阶段、高中阶段的教学面临的中考、高考压力过大。结合现实来看，由于每次的考试都不直接考到朗读，中学生便误以为朗读不重要，便轻易地放弃了；中学的英语教师（尤其是基层的）负荷很重，面对超级大班的常规教学，根本就抽不出时间来抓考试范围之外的内容，于是在初二至高三的教学中忽视了朗读的教学。所以，学生到了高中毕业时，朗读能力却远远达不到大纲要求。而当学生到了大学阶段，朗读及与朗读有紧密联系的口语也长期没有列入考试范围，朗读训练再一次被忽视了。因此，学生到大学毕业或到研究生阶段仍然过不了朗读关也就成了情理之中的事。

（三）各阶段的英语教育没有形成一条龙体系

“目前高校外语教学在一定程度上存在费时低效现象，其中主要原因之一在于大、中、小学外语教学在衔接方面存在一定的欠缺，不同阶段英语教学在教材和教学法等方面缺乏科学统筹。”① 笔者认为，这种衔接上的欠缺还表现为各阶段英语教学没有把对学生英语能力的培养看做前后相继的过程，而有过度的“各司其职”之嫌。从中学课程标准来看，朗读技能的训练属于中学阶段的内容。但是由于考试“反拨”作用的存在，该技能训练并没有得到实际的落实。而当学生进入大学阶段，很多大学英语教师在教学中想当然地认为朗读训练属于中学英语教师的事而不把朗读训练纳入教学环节。这样一来，朗读在很多学生的英语学习实践中便成了无人重视的“死角”和“盲点”。

---

① 戴炜栋：《构建中国特色的英语教学一条龙体系》，载《外语教学与研究》2001 年第 5 期，第 322 ~ 327 页。

（四）教师期望值低

我国的英语教学走的是专业培养和非专业培养两条路线。英语专业的学生无论从课程设置、班级规模，还是从课时量上来看，基本上达到了最优化。学生从语音，外台、外刊选读、选听，词汇，阅读，写作，翻译等方面得到了综合、全面学习的机会。事实上，绝大多数在高校从事英语教学的教师都有“科班出身”的专业学习背景。大学英语教师对非英语专业学生的英语学习语言环境、培养目标与专业学生相比有着极大的反差这一点无疑是有清楚的意识的。很多教师会自然地认为：“很多英语专业的学生在有那么好的学习条件的情况下，尚且学不好英语，更何况是非英语专业的学生呢。”这种思想在一定程度上使教学者不自觉地降低了对非专业学生的期望和对学习质量的把关意识，加剧了学生的消极心理，从而使学生忽视或干脆放弃了连教师都不重视的朗读。

（五）大学生的认知规律和年龄意识

从认知水平的发展来看，大学生已经进入了理性认知能力超过感性认知能力的阶段。很多大学生由此错误地认为英语学习同其他非语言学习课程一样，也可以更多地依靠理性思维和理解能力实现“内化”。殊不知，外语学习很多时候依赖一个人为的语言环境。这要求学习者主动地营造语言学习的氛围。而这其中，以反复的练习、体验形式出现的感性学习方式是营造这一氛围必不可少的基础。毕竟，语言学习是有其特殊性的。另外，从对学生的口头访谈发现，有些学生认为朗读是小学生的学习方法；自己年龄太大不适合朗读；朗读显得幼稚，等等。而实际上，朗读练习这一语言学习方法的有效性和必要性并不以学习者的年龄因素为转移。

以上分析表明：无论是从大的社会环境来看，还是从教学中考试制度的副作用及大学校园中英语教师和学习者的观念来看，朗读环节的确被普遍忽视。笔者认为朗读练习看似无足轻重，但它却能给学习者在综合英语能力上，尤其是在口头表达能力上带来大的突破。有鉴于此，笔者将结合我国的英语教育政策和自主学习理念谈谈加强朗读训练的策略。

三、加强朗读训练的策略

（一）充分发挥大纲的导向作用

随着我国总体英语教学水平的提高和学习者需求的变化，我国的《大学英语教学大纲》作了相应的调整。如1999年版的《大学英语教学大纲》明确规定，大学英语教学的目的是“培养学生具有较强的阅读能力和一定的听、说、读、写、译的能力，使他们能用英语交流信息”。而2004年由教育部正式颁发的新制定的《大学英语课程教学要求（试行）》则明确指出：“大学英语的教学目标是培养学生的英语综合应用能力，特别是听说能力，使他们在今后工作和社会交往中能用英语有效地进行口头和书面的信息交流，同时增强其自主学习能力，提高综合文化素养，以适应我国社会发展和国际交流的需要。”新大纲着重强调了听说能力的培养和增强学生自主学习能力两点内容。由于朗读与口头表达能力有着直接的联系，因此大学英语教师更应该在大纲的导向作用下，强调朗读的重要性，使提高听说能力落到实处。

（二）因势利导，充分利用考试制度的积极作用

中国学生学习中存在的应试心理可谓根深蒂固，在短期内很难有根本的转变。因此，可以因势利导地发挥考试“反拨”作用中的正效应。加大口语考试的覆盖面和效度，其中适当地增加对朗读能力的测试，让已经习惯于以考试促学习的大学生在朗读和口语能力上投入更多的时间和精力，以此达到增强朗读水平，最终提高听说能力的目标。当然，这与从根本上转变学习者的动机，使其有终身学习的自主学习观念相比，至多也只是一个退而求其次的选择。因此，要从根本上解决问题，还得从转变学习观念上入手。这对教师而言，提出了新的要求。

（三）逐步增强学生英语学习的自主性

教师应切实帮助学生建立自主学习的信心和能力。教师应该意识到大部分中国学生由于一直以来形成的对教师的依赖心理，不可能在短时间内做到真正的自主学习。“在实践中，自主学习的开展似乎出现了盲目的趋势，有些高校忽视学生薄弱的自主学习能力，依仗有限的多媒体教室，在没有自主学习管理规范的情况下，急功近利，大力减少教师的面授课时，导致教学资源浪费，教学效果低下。有的教师把自主学习等同于自学，忽视了教师的作用，导致学生放任自流，学习兴趣低下。有的教师教学流于形式，一味要求学生设计自主学习方式，在课堂上一味迎合学生的意愿而忽视语言知识的学习。”① 由此可见，虽然目前“自主学习”这一理念被提得越来越多，但它显然与我国的“尊师重教”的学习传统有着较大的矛盾。在这种情况下，或者说是在以教师的“教”为主向以学生的“自主学习”为主过渡的过程中，教师的作用暂时不能削弱，相反应该加强。教师的作用表现在如下几个方面：

1. 应用引导性原则，树立正确的语言学习观

教师应发挥积极的引导作用，让学生认识和体会到语言是音、形、义的统一体。其中，“音”作为语言的第一层物质外壳，在交际中往往最快、最直接地为交际对象感受到。因此，语言中“音”的因素能微妙地影响实际的交际效果。而且，由于“音”与说话者的发音器官以及听话者的听觉系统之间存在着感性联系，这决定了语言学习必须是一种“体验”。而朗读作为一种有效的体验方式，具有不可替代性，必须是学习者亲自“动口”。因此，在一定意义上可以说，语言学习比起其他学科来，更多的是靠“学”而不是靠“教”，或者说，成功的语言学习对学习者的自主性有着极高的要求。所以，大学英语教师首要的任务是培养学生“自主学习”的语言学习观，其次才是教师在“教”中起到抛砖引玉的作用。而笔者认为，要让学生获得自主学习的意识，必须以学生有兴趣为前提，变“怕学”为“乐学”。

2. 应用示范性原则

如上文所言，自主学习不是放任自流。准确的理解应该是：在教师的引导下，逐渐使学生形成对学习的兴趣并最终获得自主学习的意识和能力。英语学习在我国作为外语学习的本质决定了学生由于真实语境的缺失而无法自发形成对英语的兴趣。这要求英语教师在学生“入门”（有自主学习意识、能力；能不依靠教师独立学习）前培养学生的学习兴趣。笔者认为，教师应充分应用语言中的声音元素，以语言的听觉效果和美感来打动学生。这要求教师自身要有很高的朗读水平，能胜任示范者的角色，能以适当的语音、语调、口吻对相应的材料进行朗读，甚至在朗读文学作品时融入角色心理成分，充分表达出文字所包含的意义和情感，让学生直观地体验到声音与意义间存在的微妙联系。如，经典听力教材 *Step by Step* 中的例子“London Bridge is falling down”就很有代表性。朗读者通过不同的语调、语气、语速、音高表达了惊诧、喜悦、沮

---

① 陈冬纯：《论自主学习在我国大学英语教学中的定位》，载《外语界》2006 年第 3 期，第 32 ~35 页。

丧等不同的意义和感受。这样的例子在教师的实际教学中应是多多益善的。

3. 增强课堂教学的多维动态性

有了教师的示范作用，学生便有了模仿的参照对象。毕竟，与缺乏生气的磁带、碟片相比，教师才是最好的活例子。教师在示范时，表情、体态随之变化，能给学生最多的感性体验，从而能最大限度地激发学生的模仿欲望。虽然，一方面，朗读属于自主学习范畴，但这并不意味着教师不需要监督。考虑到大学英语教学班级规模通常较大、人数较多，教师可以定期地对各学习小组通过小组竞赛、互评等集体学习的方式（group learning）进行监督，提高学生的参与能力，形成学习兴趣，使课堂更具互动性和评估功能。这不但对朗读水平本身的提高大有裨益，而且对帮助学生形成学习英语所需的参与意识和外向型性格的塑造也具有重要意义。

四、结束语

虽然，我国的大学英语教学已取得了较大的提高，但论及学生实际的语言能力，情况却不容乐观，原因是“聋哑病”普遍存在。这与我国的英语教学的高投入是极不相称的。因为实际上过半的学生虽然通过从初中阶段算起到大学毕业的整整十年的学习，竟然还无法开口说英语。这不得不令人反思。当然，达到提高听说能力这一目的的方法不一而足，但“舍近求远”地放弃朗读这一最基本的、易于实践的手段不用而求其他，不能不说是一种遗憾。尽管，朗读教学并不具有语言教学分支这样的地位，但鉴于朗读的有效性被普遍忽视的这一实际，大学英语教师应提高对朗读的“问题意识”，共同重视朗读，以朗读为突破口，为学生消除“聋哑病”，切实提高听说能力打牢第一步的基础。

参考文献：

[1]张殿玉．着眼大学英语课程培养目标，力求听说并举[J]．外语界，2005，(3)：21.

[2]Lee Icy. Supporting Greater Autonomy in Language Learning [J]. *ELT Journal*, 1998(4)：282 - 290.

[3]戴炜栋．构建中国特色的英语教学一条龙体系[J]．外语教学与研究，2001，(5)：322 - 327.

[4]《大学英语教学大纲》修订工作组. 大学英语教学大纲[Z]. 北京:高等教育出版社; 上海:上海外语教育出版社,1999.

[5]教育部高等教育司. 大学英语课程教学要求(试行)[Z]. 上海:上海外语教育出版社,2004.

[6]陈冬纯. 论自主学习在我国大学英语教学中的定位[J]. 外语界,2006(3):32-35.

提高学生法语学习兴趣的几种方式

聂云梅

语言学习是一种比较抽象且相对乏味的过程。英国语言教学法专家亚历山大（L. G. Alexander）曾经说过："语言教学上有两个最基本的问题，首先是教什么，其次是如何教。""教什么"就是教学大纲、教学原则；"如何教"就是教学法，即教学方法。为了使学生真正有效地掌握繁复的法语知识，我们必须探索和寻求适合我国法语课堂教学的行之有效的教学方法和教学模式。其实，语言是一种极其复杂的现象，由此决定了教学过程的多元性。有效的外语教学应该吸收一切教学法中有价值的东西，考虑多方面的因素。本文作者根据自身多年的教学经验，并结合我国现行普遍的外语授课环境、硬件设施和传统教学方法，简单介绍几种提高学生法语学习兴趣的方式。

一、充分利用课前5分钟的陈述

（1）目的：锻炼学生的口头表达能力，并强调两个人之间的合作。

（2）形式：每一堂课老师留出5分钟的时间给学生；学生以两个人为一组，以自由形式用法语表达。范围可以是一首法语诗歌朗诵，一篇故事或者一首法语歌曲表演，一段对话。5分钟之后，教师就学生在法语表达之中提及的生词和主题进行讲解，并对学生的准备进行必要的点评。这种不命题的作业让学生有很大的发挥余地，有的学生可能会两个人商量着自己写一段对话，然后把它表演出来；还有的学生会到图书馆或者网络上寻找一些资料，然后通过查字典或请教老师，弄清文章的大意后，再在课堂上把它陈述出来。而在这短短的5分钟之内，教师可以看出学生在口语表达中存在的问题或取得的进步，学生也通过这样的方式展示了自己并通过教师的点评吸取经验和教训。笔者在教学中一直坚持这种方式，收效良好。

二、定期的歌曲、影片和图片欣赏

（1）目的：利用法文歌曲、影视和图片对学生进行听力和表达能力的训练。

（2）形式一：选择一首适当的法语歌曲，首先就这首歌曲的题目来进行练习。比如，笔者曾经就 *Deux pieds* 这首歌进行过实践，效果良好。在听这首歌曲之前，教师会问学生是否知道法文里有这样的表达："Je n'ai que deux pieds."学生说不知道，但是从字面的意思翻译来看，他们都知道这句话的意思是："我只有两只脚。"这时候教师再进一步问："请你们想一想，什么情况下，我们会对对话者说出这样的话呢?"学生进行思索后，会有不同的答案。这时，教师提示："当对方要求我们做太多的事情的时候，超出了我们自身的承受能力，这个时候可以对对方说'Je n'ai que deux pieds'。"于是，学生恍然大悟。接下来可以要求学生以两个人为一组，做一段对话，用上"Je n'ai que deux pieds"的表达。这是听歌曲之前的活动。在听歌过程中，第一遍完了之后，可以问问学生，这首歌里讲述了几个场景、这首歌的主角是一个什么性格的人等。在学生逐渐进入状态的情况下，不妨反复听法文歌曲，并请学生写下所听到的歌词（当然，学生不可能听出所有的歌词），然后再根据所记下的单词发挥自己的联想，想象整首歌曲所讲述的故事，用法文讲给大家听。最后，由老师公布正确的歌词，看看谁的听力好、想象力丰富。

（3）形式二：应用法语影视片段进行法语课堂教学的教学设计，必须符合创造性的、有意义的语言操练活动这个基本原则，使教学活动从传统的以"教"为中心的模式转为以"学"为中心的模式。这种教学模式是以交际培养为纲，以语言实践为主线，全面、和谐地培养学生综合的外语素质。在影视片段的选择上要注意几点：①片段不要过长，以 2～3 分钟为宜；②画面易理解；③对白要清楚，有可听度；④交际场景不要太复杂；⑤人物的面部表情、肢体语言要与对白一致。目的是为学生提供可操作的足够的语言实践材料。在课堂教学前，教师必须认真准备好教案，设计的教学活动必须能够激发学生积极参与活动的内在动力，使学生在参与活动中感到富有趣味性、实用性和挑战性。而只有当语言成为传递学习者感兴趣或相关信息的中介时，才会刺激学习者的内在学习动力。课堂步骤可以以如下方式操作：①整体理解：第一遍看某个影视片段时去掉声音，让学生们回答问题。比如："这个片段发生在哪里?""影片中有几个人物?”“这些人物之间的关系是什么?”第二遍看这个片段还是没有声音，让学生们观察人物的表情和举止，重点观察主要人物的面部表情和肢体语言。然后，老师发给学生每人一张表格，表格内容要包含填写不同人物的眼神、动作、面部表情等部分。最后，教师把参考答案抄写在黑板上，便于学生对比自己所写的东西，并进行修正。②细节理解和有选择地理解：第三遍看配有声音的片段，检查学生们的假设是否正确，重点看、听片段里的人物是怎样表达自己的。第四遍还是看配有声音的片段，让学生们一句句地听并重复人物的语言，从而在语言里可以分析人物的性格特征，并且还可以把语法现象也延伸到语言里来，看看人物使用了什么样的语式和时态。这样的学习方式是能极大地促进学生学习法语的兴趣的，因为有了声音和图像，学生的记忆就会加强。

(4) 形式三：利用图片来传授知识是最简单可行的方式。图片可以是明信片，也可以是名画欣赏或者电影宣传海报，甚至是小广告，都可以在课堂上运用。教师可以复印图片，把图片发到每一位学生手中，然后组织学生利用图片上的内容来编写对话或短文。笔者曾经把凡·高的一幅油画发给学生们——画面是一把椅子，椅子上有一个烟斗。然后，让学生们两个人为一组来写一段对话或者短文。其中，有两个学生就有丰富的想象力，对话在椅子和烟斗之间进行：椅子问烟斗：“主人哪里去了?”烟斗说：“主人永远地离开我们了。”椅子问：“为什么?”烟斗说：“主人因为大量地吸烟，患肺癌去世了。”对话简短精练，发人深省。还有的学生则通过描写一个人物最喜欢的两样东西——椅子和烟斗来揭示人物的性格。之后，教师可以就画面的背景知识、画家的经历向学生进行介绍。这也是扩展知识面的一种方式，同时也在某种程度上培养了学生的审美情趣。

三、教学中适当地加入游戏

游戏训练法的优点就在于，把相对枯燥、抽象的练习变得生动、具体；变书本上的练习集、练习题库为实际操作训练；弥补由于缺少行之有效的语言环境而形成“哑巴法语”的教学弊端；更有针对性地把书后练习变成一种喜闻乐见的娱乐形式使学寓于乐中、乐寓于学中。游戏的形式多种多样，笔者介绍几个法国学生常用的游戏。

(1) 形式一：造句接力游戏。目的是配合语法项目“关于假设句‘si’和与之相关的条件式现在时”的练习。由第一个同学做出一个假设句。如，“si

je gagnais un million euros, j'achèterais une villa à Nice"（如果我挣了一百万欧元，我将在尼斯买栋别墅）。第二个同学根据前一位同学做的假设句的结果再进行假设。如，"si j'avais un villa à Nice, je pourrais assister au Festival de Cannes"（如果我在尼斯有栋别墅，我可以参加戛纳电影节）。第三个同学根据第二个同学的假设的结论再进行假设。如，"si j'assistais au Festival de Cannes, je..."（如果我能够参加戛纳电影节，我就……）。这样，学生就可以在不断的假设中锻炼自己的想象力和正确的时态及动词变位能力。

（2）形式二：案件询问调查游戏。目的是通过练习，使学生掌握复合过去时和未完成过去时两种时态间的区别和联系。假设昨天在某地发生了一起银行抢劫案，班级所有的同学均有作案嫌疑，但每个人在案发当时都是和班级里的另一位同学在一起。请同学自行组成两人小组，共同商议案发时两人在做什么以便脱离嫌疑。准备好后，由其他组的同学扮演警察的角色分别询问两人，看两人的口供是否完全吻合。在整个调查中，无论盘问者还是被盘问者均要注意选用正确的过去时态，以便进一步区分复合过去时和未完成过去时。

（3）形式三：脑筋急转弯游戏。目的是练习学生在短促时间内的应变能力。法语和中文一样有很多的文字游戏，不妨拿出来经常练练学生的反应能力。比如有一个很简单的脑筋急转弯：老师说："我说一个单词，你们重复三遍，之后迅速地回答我一个问题。"于是，学生会集中注意力地听这个单词。教师说："blanc（白色的）。"学生听完之后迅速地重复三遍。之后，教师突然提问："Qu'est - ce qu'elle boit? la vache（奶牛喝什么）?"有的学生由于受刚才单词的干扰，不假思索地回答："du lait（牛奶）。"当然，也有学生回答正确："de l'eau（水）。"脑筋急转弯虽然看起来很简单，但是对于把法语作为外语来学习的中国学生来说，如果没有一定的基础，还是很难听懂教师的提问的。所以，这样的训练也可以提高学生的听力、理解以及运用能力。

在交际法语的课堂上，教学的最终目标是让学生在不需预先练习的情况下能产出性地和接收性地使用语言。课堂上每位同学都积极参与。由于以上的几种方式直观、生动，再加上老师尽可能地为学生创造条件（如，作为游戏的组织者），极大地调动了同学们的积极性，增强了他们的信心。在这样的课堂上看不出明显的强势和弱势，看到的只是同学们参与课堂教学的欲望。学生成了课堂的中心，法语教学变成了活动教学，整个教学过程也就成了交际活动的过程。学生通过经历这些课堂交际活动，提高了他们学习法语的兴趣和用法语进行交际的自信心及积极性。可以说，应用歌曲影视欣赏、学生的自我陈述、穿插游戏等方式进行外语教学，是交际教学方法在法语课堂教学上较好的尝试。这样的教学模式使课堂教学过程中实现了师生间的多向互动。当然，要使课堂教学搞得生动，这对教师本身也是一种挑战。无疑，和传统的教学法相比它对教师提出了更高的要求。在这种教学中，教师不仅应是知识的“呈现者”、对话的“提问者”、学习的“指导者”、学业的“评价者”和纪律的“维持者”，更重要的应是课堂教学过程中呈现各种信息的“重组者”，以及整个教学过程的“策划者”。要扮演好这些角色，这就要求教师不仅要有较全面的法语知识，而且还要不断地学习一些社会语言学、心理语言学、教育心理学等方面的知识，不断地扩大自身的知识面，培养自身的语言技巧和课堂组织技巧。只有这样，才能不辱外语教师的使命。

参考文献：

[1] 邵永真，应惠兰，等．深入探讨教学原则，促进大学英语教学改革[J]．外语界，1998（1）.

[2] Né M. F Du document authentique vidéo au document pédagogique lisible pour des apprenants Alliance française de Paris.

[3] NATHAALIE BLANC，L'image eomme support de médiation le français dans 1e monde N 330. NOV. DEC. 2003.

[4] 邵瑞珍．教育心理学［M］．修订本．上海：上海教育出版社，2002.

英汉翻译量化教学法研究

徐覃荪

一

翻译教学的内容主要由两个部分组成：宏观认识和微观运用。前者的目的是构建理论体系和确立翻译标准，后者的重点则是传授具体的翻译方法和技巧。从理论上讲，若能将二者有机地结合起来，实现教学目的就不是一件难事。但实际情况怎样呢？笔者根据自己多年的教学见闻，发现了以下一些比较突出的现象。

（一）现象之一：宏观与微观的失衡

宏观与微观的失衡主要反映在理论与实践的差距上。不少学生都能熟记学过的理论概念，考试时也能正确回答有关理论问题，但在处理具体的语言材料时，往往不能正确运用理论与技巧来指导翻译实践，译文不是显得僵化呆板就是不够严密。且看下例：

例 1：Wind is when air moves.
译文 1：当空气流动时就形成了风。
译文 2：风就是空气运动的结果。

两句译文都出自学生之手[①]。当要求学生对以上译文作出评价时，学生一

① 本文例句均取材于 2000 年云南大学外国语学院翻译教学。该年度英语系三年级有两个班，共 60 人。翻译课是合班讲授。

致认为，两句译文都是正确的，也无优劣之分，唯一的差别在于译文1采用的是直译理论，译文2遵从的是意译原则。应当说，学生的判断基本上是正确的，其理由似乎也很充分。但这是否说明学生已掌握并能正确地运用翻译理论了呢？要想得到这一答案，有必要先对照一下原文与译文的内容与形式。

不难看出，原文是对“风”一词下定义。若只是为了传达原文的大概意思，两句译文似乎都可以接受。但若以形式与内容相统一的标准加以衡量，则会发现两句译文都存在一定的问题：译文1是在描述过程，不是下定义；译文2中的“结果”一词也似是而非，不够严密，因为风的形成和空气的流动应是同步的。换句话说，学生虽然在理论上建立了直译与意译的概念，但却不能恰当地使用这些概念去指导实践，从而导致了理论与实践的脱节现象，且这种现象具有相当程度的普遍性①。

（二）现象之二：标准的困惑

翻译实践中，学生对翻译标准或多或少地都有一些困惑感，在同一原文材料出现两种或多种意思正确的译文时，这种困惑感就更加突出。试看下例：

例2：The 1967 UN document calls for the settlement of the Middle East conflict on the basis of Israeli withdrawal from the occupied territories and Arab acknowledgement of Israeli's right to exist.

译文1：1967年联合国文件要求在以色列撤出所占领土及阿拉伯承认以色列的生存权的基础上来解决中东冲突。

译文2：为结束中东冲突，联合国1967年下达文件，要求以色列撤出所占领土，同时要求阿拉伯承认以色列的生存权。

客观地说，以上两句译文的意思都是正确的，其表达形式虽有一些不同，却也能为大多数人所接受。若以忠实和通顺的标准加以衡量，可能很难判断译文质量的好坏，因为两句译文都能再现原文的意思，不但做到了忠实，而且译文的文理也是清晰的，符合通顺的要求。唯一的差别似乎只是句式长短的不同，但句式的长短属文体研究范畴，至今尚未纳入翻译标准。这是否意味着只要意思正确、文字通顺，就不必再计较译文的差异或优劣了呢？如果学生没有

① 60个学生中，除2名学生没有发表意见外，其余58人均认为两句译文没有优劣之分，只是风格不同而已。

这种要求，老师当然可以回避这一问题。遗憾的是，每当发现自己的译文有别于他人的时候，学生都会请老师当裁判，希望老师能对译文作出一个比较客观的评判。同样遗憾的是，学生并不能每次都得到满意的答案，因为忠实与通顺这把尺子也有自身的局限，它只能测出歪曲与不畅，而不能衡量译文的全貌。对于意思正确且文字顺畅的译文，这把尺子显然就不能发挥应有的作用了。

既然忠实与通顺不能鉴别一切，若一定要评判译文的差异或优劣，例如批改作业或试卷，有时就只能借助经验和语感，但经验和语感不仅存在个体差异，甚至还有主观之嫌。正因如此，在得不到令人信服的答案时，学生难免会对翻译标准感到困惑。

（三）现象之三：结构的桎梏

学生习作的另一突出现象是欧化句式。其主要特征是句子冗长、修饰语重叠、语序不当。究其原因，或受制于原文结构，或图省事、快捷。

若是为了介绍英语的句法特征，译文选用欧化句式倒也无妨，但前提是要自始至终地贯彻这一准则。若太随意，对能够把握的句子结构就采用汉化的句式，而对难以驾驭的原文结构则套用欧式句型，既破坏了原文的风格，也给读者带来费解的麻烦，那么这种做法就不可取了。遗憾的是，无论翻译作品还是学生的习作中，欧化现象都是十分突出的。例如：

例3："It's difficult to lead a competitive, individual life—as we're raised in American society—without devaluating others to some extent", says Staub.

译文1："过一种既有竞争又有个性的生活是困难的——因为我们生长在美国社会里——不在任何程度上损害他人的利益"，斯道博说。

译文2："过一种既有竞争又有个性而同时又不会在任何程度上损害他人利益的生活是困难的，因为我们生长在美国社会里"，斯道博说。

译文1是比较典型的欧化句式，其成因主要是不能摆脱原文结构的束缚，但也不排除为了赶时间而敷衍了事的可能。无论原因如何，欧化的译文总是晦涩难懂的。相形之下，译文2的欧化程度要轻一些，因为去掉破折号后，插入状语的位置也必须改变，从而使破折号前后的意思得以连贯。尽管如此，由于句式太长，译文2仍有欧化之嫌。与译文3相比，其差别就显而易见了。

译文3：斯道博说："生长在美国社会里的人，要想适应竞争、保持独立，又毫不损害他人的利益，这的确难以做到。”

这里顺便提一下，虽然国内译学界早已注意到了译文的欧化现象，但褒贬不一的争论至今仍在继续。可是，自 Chinglish 一词出现后，国人则无不处处小心，生怕犯了中国式英语的大忌。这不禁令人生疑：既然我们不能容忍中国式英语，难道就可以对译文的欧化现象置之不理？

二

针对上述现象，笔者在教学中创立了一种量化方法，经过近十年的实践证明，这种方法不仅切实可行，而且有利于克服译文僵化及欧化的现象，对消除翻译标准的困惑也不无裨益。现将这种量化教学法介绍给同仁，供教学参考，同时也希望能得到批评指正。

所谓“量化教学法”，是指在忠实和通顺的前提下，对译文的句子长度实行字数控制，并以字数的多少作为衡量译文质量的一个标准。这种要求的理由是：在确保忠实和通顺的前提下，译文质量的好坏在很大程度上取决于译文的语言效率。能用一个字就表达清楚的概念，如果用了两个或三个字，前者的语言效率肯定高于后者。高效的语言无疑是优秀的语言，而优秀的语言自然也是优秀译文必备的一个条件。

需要说明的是，由于汉语句子的概念不完全等同于英语，如英语句子一般以句号为单位，而汉语句子有时则可以以逗号或其他标点符号为单位。因此，译文句子长度的概念也有广义和狭义之分。广义的句子长度是指两个句号间的中文字数；狭义的句子长度则指每两个标点符号间的中文字数。就局部而言，教学中主要使用的是狭义概念，但在整体意义上，两个概念却是相辅相成的，因为段落或文章是由若干广义句子构成的，一旦狭义句子的字数受到限制，广义句子的字数也必然受到影响，这种影响最终会辐射到整个段落或全篇文章。

具体到教学工作中，可根据不同体裁提出不同的字数要求。例如，翻译法律条文及合同、章程时，译文句子的字数要求可适当放宽些，但狭义句长不宜超过 25 字；翻译科技文章时，狭义句长不宜超过 20 字；而翻译文学作品或其他材料时，狭义句长最好不超过 15 字。之所以提出这样的要求，完全是出于对读者负责的目的，因为狭义句长一旦超过 25 个汉字，译文读起来就很吃力，有时甚至晦涩难懂，有违简明、晓畅的准则。如：

例 4：Unpublished works of nationals of each Contracting State shall enjoy in each other Contracting State the same protection as that other State accords to unpublished works of its own nationals, as well as the Protection specially granted by this Convention①.

译文 1：任何成员国国民未出版的作品，在其他各成员国中均享有后者给予其国民之未出版的作品同等的保护，并享有本公约所专门授予的保护。

原文出自 1971 年 7 月于巴黎修订的《世界版权公约》。由于法律英语行文非常严密，句式难免偏长。但这决不意味着译成短句就不忠实于原文，或短句不如长句严密。译文 1 看似严密，但其中第二个狭义句子竟长达 30 个汉字，且不论译文是否佶屈聱牙，至少读起来非常吃力，有违晓畅的原则。若以 25 字的量化要求控制狭义句长，则可能得到下面的译文：

译文 2：任何成员国国民未发表的作品，除受本公约的特别保护外，还应受其他成员国给予本国国民未发表作品的同等保护。

不难看出，相对译文 1 而言，译文 2 不仅更符合汉语的文理，且行文更流畅，更容易理解。这主要归功于较短的句式，因为译文 2 中最长的狭义句子并未超过 25 个汉字。

即或是同一材料，也可根据教学目的逐步减少狭义句长的字数。例如，可先从 20 个汉字的句长要求开始，逐渐减少为 18 个、16 个、15 个，甚至 10 个或更少。随着字数的减少，翻译难度也越来越大，但译文质量则会越来越好。例如翻译下面这句话时，先由学生独立完成，然后汇总各自的译文进行讨论与修订，最后的定稿是译文 1。

例 5：If one realizes that our time on this earth is but a tiny fraction of that within the cosmos, then life calculated in years may not be as important as we think.

译文 1：如果一个人意识到我们生活在地球上的时间不过是宇宙之中的一瞬间，那么，以年数的多少来衡量生命也许就不像我们想象的那么重要了。(58 字)

---

① 庄绎传：《英汉翻译教程》，外语教学与研究出版社 1999 年版，第 309 ~ 311 页。

记得学生送交译文时，脸上都绽放出一种自豪的光彩。公正地说，译文1虽不一定就是上乘之作，但若以忠实和通顺的标准加以衡量，该译文则无懈可击。在肯定了学生的译文后，笔者对他们提出了量化要求，要他们分组重译这句话，第一组将狭义句长控制在20个汉字以内，第二组控制在15个汉字以内，第三组则不许超过10个汉字。数分钟后，学生送交了以下三种译文：

译文2：如果一个人意识到，我们在地球上的一生不过是宇宙之中的一瞬间，那么，以年数来衡量人生也许就不似想象那么重要了。(20字)

译文3：如果一个人意识到，人生一世不过是宇宙中的一瞬间，那么，以年数来衡量生命，其意义也许就不似想象那么重要了。(15字)

译文4：宇宙无穷而人生有限，一旦认识到这一点，再以年数来计算生命，其意义也就不大了。(10字)

对比以上四句译文可以发现，随着狭义句长字数的减少，译文似乎已从最初的“形似”过渡到了“神似”。这不能不说是一种质的飞跃。

三

作为一种教学手段，量化教学法的优点在于：(1) 可避免僵化翻译模式；(2) 能促进翻译技巧的掌握；(3) 有利于鉴别译文质量的好坏。

僵化翻译模式在译文中的具体表现是句子过长、意思晦涩。其成因可能与两个因素有关：一是机械地理解直译与意译的标准，二是受制于原文的句式结构。坚持直译准则的翻译，大多注重形式的对等，以为原文长译文就不能短，否则就不忠实于原文，于是就出现了例2中译文1的翻译形式。当然，即便主张意译，如果不能摆脱原文结构的桎梏，类似的结果也是难以避免的，因为意译只是相对直译而言的，其概念或标准也不够清晰。所谓“见仁见智”，实则无章可循，没有具体的标准，译文有时难免僵化。

既然直译和意译均不能有效地消除僵化的译文，那么量化教学法是否就能弥补这种不足呢？让我们再回顾一下例2：

例2：The 1967 UN document calls for the settlement of the Middle East conflict on the basis of Israeli withdrawal from the occupied territories and Arab acknowledgement of Israeli's right to exist.

译文1：1967年联合国文件要求在以色列撤出所占领土及阿拉伯承认以色列的生存权的基础上来解决中东冲突。

姑且不论以上译文采用的是直译或意译方法，仅就译文本身而言，恐怕不读上两遍则不能得其意。当按照16个字的句长量化标准翻译时，学生的译文则变为：

译文2：为结束中东冲突，联合国1967年下达文件，要求以色列撤出所占领土，同时要求阿拉伯承认以色列的生存权。

对比以上两句译文，不难发现，虽然译文的意思都是正确的，但客观地说，译文2比译文1更清晰、更具可读性，因此也更符合忠实与通顺的要求。

从形式上看，译文1之所以显得僵化，与其说是刻意模仿原文结构的结果，不如说是不能有意识地摆脱原文结构的束缚。因为，在没有量化要求的时候，碰到结构复杂的原文，为了省去拆分和重组句子的麻烦，一般都会避难就易，而最简单的做法就是照结构翻译。这种翻译模式一经形成，久而久之，拆分和重组句子的能力必然下降，僵化的译文也就在所难免。

相形之下，译文2则显得比较灵活，完全摆脱了原文结构的桎梏，因为要满足16个字的量化要求，就不得不拆分长句，而原句一经拆分，其结构自然改变，译文也因此而摆脱了原文结构的束缚，从而避免了欧化现象。此外，拆分后的句子需要重组。在此过程中，考虑到句子各部分之间的衔接及逻辑关系，学生会潜意识地运用其他翻译技巧，如译文2中的逆序法和增词法等。这是其他教学法难以收到的效果，因为在介绍翻译技巧时，一般教材并不指出该在何时或何处运用何种技巧，而量化教学法则能迫使学生运用各种技巧，使之由潜意识的状态演变到自觉的模式。

量化教学法的另一优点是有利于鉴别译文质量的好坏。长期以来，每当谈到翻译标准时，似乎总离不开"信、达、雅"或"忠实与通顺"。作为指导性的准则，这类标准虽然无可厚非，但实际运用时却有一定困难。最典型的问题是，译文均已达到忠实与通顺的要求，但译文之间却又存在差异，有时甚至是明显的差异，倘若将它们一视同仁，恐怕会有失公允。前面已经说过，在这种情况下，既有的标准已不能发挥应有的作用，而严复先生的"雅"字又颇有争议。与此同时，学生还要求老师对他们的译文进行公正的评价。倘若评价不当，或不能使学生信服，其结果只会挫伤学生学习的积极性，甚至造成师生间的误解。

使用量化标准，则可有效解决这一难题。如果同意高效的语言是优秀的语言，而优秀的语言又是优秀的译文必备的条件之一，那么，在满足忠实和通顺的前提下，评价译文好坏的标准当然是译文的效率。而限制译文句子长度的目的就是为了提高语言效率。换句话说，有了量化标准，老师的评价会更具说服力，学生也会对自己的译文作出比较合理的判断。让我们再回顾一下例1：

例1：Wind is when air moves.
译文1：当空气流动时就形成了风。(11字)
译文2：风就是空气运动的结果。(10字)

当要求狭义句长不超过8个字、6个字、5个字、4个字和3个字时，学生提供了如下译文：

译文3：空气流动产生了风。(8字)
译文4：空气动而生风。(6字)
译文5：气动而风生。(5字)
译文6：气动生风。(4字)
译文7：气生风。(3字)
译文8：风者，气动也。(5字)

讨论中，学生改变了最初的观点，他们一致同意，除译文7以外，译文3至译文8都强于译文1和译文2。理由是译文3至译文8不仅忠实、通顺，而且语言效率高于译文1和译文2。而其中首推的是译文8，因为它最符合原文的意思（下定义）。译文7虽然最简练，但可能会产生歧义，故不可取。能达成这样的共识实属不易，而译文8的出现更是难能可贵。虽然当今并不提倡“言必先秦”，但追求语言效率在任何时代都是不为过的。

四

作为一种教学改革的尝试，量化教学法的确能收到一定的效果：它有利于避免僵化的翻译模式，能促进翻译技巧的掌握，还能提供一种比较客观的依据鉴别译文的质量。但在使用这种教学手段时，务必注意以下事项：（1）量化教学法只是对传统教学法的一种补充，旨在树立精益求精的翻译态度，而不是仅仅满足忠实和通顺的基本要求；（2）每提出具体的量化指标之前，既要考虑文字的难易程度，也要考虑学生的语言水平，要求过高容易产生畏难的情绪，要求过低则达不到预期的效果；（3）遵循循序渐进的教学原则，只有从简到难，才能奠定扎实的文字功底。

尽管量化教学法有其独特的效果，但在实施过程中肯定会遇到新的挑战。因为，一旦确定了量化指标，不仅学生需要斟词酌句，教师也需要投入更多的备课时间，这自然会增加教学的工作量。但从另一方面讲，不在炼词、炼句上下工夫，又怎么能译出好的文字呢？此外，由于理论界和外语教学界尚未提出过量化概念，其理论肯定还有待进一步完善。

参考文献：

[1] Baker, Mona. *In Other Words: A Coursebook on Translation* [M]. Foreign Language Teaching And Research Press, 2000.

[2] Bassnett-McGuire, S.. *Translation Studies* [M]. London and New York: Methuen, 1980.

[3] Duff. A.. *Translation* [M]. Oxford: Oxford University Press, 1990.

[4] 陈廷佑．英文汉译技巧[M]．北京:外语教学与研究出版社,1980.

[5] 李四清．英汉翻译教程[M]．北京:东方出版社,2000.

[6] 刘宓庆．文体与翻译[M]．北京:中国对外翻译出版公司,1986.

[7] 张培基,等．英汉翻译教程[M]．上海:上海外语教育出版社,1980.

[8] 庄绎传．英汉翻译教程[M]．北京:外语教学与研究出版社,1999.

浅析佛教对 GMS 地区大学生学习特点的影响

尹可秀

一、引　言

GMS（大湄公河次区域）地区包括柬埔寨、中国（云南和广西）、老挝、缅甸、泰国和越南。近年来，随着中国国际地位的提升及教育和经济实力的增强，云南与五国的交流更加密切。这集中体现为泰、缅等国持续升温的“中国文化热”、云南各高校对五国汉语教学的不断支援，以及这些国家到云南的留学生人数急剧增加。由于地域上相互毗邻，文化和经济上保持联系，因此 GMS 地区拥有诸多共性。佛教的影响正是其中之一。佛教在云南拥有众多信徒，也是越南的主要宗教，还是柬埔寨、老挝、泰国的国教；在缅甸、柬埔寨、老挝、泰国，佛教徒占全国人口的比例均高达 80% 以上。佛教必然对这些国家和云南边境的文化产生重要影响。大学是文化传承和发展的重要机构。在这些地区，佛教对大学生是否有影响？这些影响具体表现在哪些方面？对这些国家的来华留学生应当采取什么样的教学和管理方法以适应教学客体的特点和需求？本文将逐一探究这些问题。

二、佛教影响下的 GMS 地区大学生的学习特点

本次研究和观察的对象主要包括泰国皇太后大学、清迈大学、柬埔寨金边王家大学、缅甸仰光大学的学生以及泰国、柬埔寨、越南、老挝到云南大学进行汉语学习的留学生。采取的研究方式主要为实际观察、访问教师和学生以及问卷调查。研究于 2004 年 11 月开始，至 2007 年 6 月结束。调查发现，由于

家境差异较大，GMS 地区的大学生在学习动力、努力程度方面呈现出较大差异。在体现出尊重师长、学习目的明确、勤奋刻苦、重视实践的良好特点时，他们的时间观念、学习方式、课外活动安排等方面也具有一些中国主流教育观念所认为的“消极特点”。事实上，这些消极特点不一定是个人意愿和努力程度的体现，它们与这些学生成长的佛教环境具有较为紧密的联系。

（一）时间观念较为淡薄

学生时间观念淡薄主要表现为上课迟到。许多在 GMS 国家以及在云南进行对外汉语教学的中国教师发现，学生上课迟到是难以纠正的一个问题。无论教师对这个问题如何重视，批评时如何严厉，学生总是要比上课时间晚几分钟甚至一二十分钟才到教室。此外，迟到的并非只有差生，还包括了许多学习成绩和课堂表现中等甚至中等偏上的学生。这一现象在广西也得到了反映：“越南留学生迟到现象非常严重。”[①] 同样，学生经常迟到的现象在 GMS 国家也较为普遍。笔者 2004 年至 2005 年在泰国北部高校观察发现，即使是一些受欢迎的核心课程，例如英语系的翻译课和写作课，全班依然有近 1/3 的学生迟到。值得注意的是，与中国教师相比，其本国教师对此的态度比较“宽容”。

当迟到成为普遍现象时，不能简单地用学习态度来进行责备或解释。在一定程度上，这种现象与佛教的时间观是有联系的。陈洁认为，与基督教相比，佛教否定时间的价值。佛教徒对时间的态度是冷漠的，甚至是有敌意的。佛教徒们把时间想象为环形，只有跳出环形无穷无尽的轮回循环，才能超然于环外。时间只是让人在其中受生、老、病、死之苦的“场所”，它本身没有价值。时间的交替变化无关紧要，悟道的人永远都活在“好的”心中，好的心看世界，任何时候都是“好时节”[②]。在佛教环境下成长的大学生，未必能够清晰地意识到这一深层次的佛教时间观，但是他们的行为却是这种观念的反映。佛教徒追求的是个人的完善，而个人的完善一方面要超越时间，达到“无”的境界，另一方面要获得自我的认可和满意。成绩和表现中等的大学生普遍性地迟到，说明他们一方面不重视时间，不认为迟到是严重的事；另一方面，他们更认可“比较努力”的学习表现，并且这种自我认可比较牢固。因此，迟到就成为一种经常性的现象，被视为小问题，无需下决心改正。

---

① 杨宁坤：《浅析来华越南留学生思想特点》，载《比较教育研究》2004 年第 6 期。

② 陈洁：《佛教时间观试析——兼与基督教比较》，载中国论文下载中心，2006 年。

（二）接受式学习占主导地位

学习方式一般可分为接受式学习和发现式学习两种。前者的特点是被动、重复训练、问题意识不强，后者的特点则是主动性高、具有探索精神、问题意识强。接受调查的云南对外汉语教师中，一半以上认为 GMS 地区的留学生依然以接受式为主，基本提不出或不提比较难的问题，很少与教师就某个问题进行深入讨论；即使提出问题，在教师解答之后也不会继续追问。与日、韩等其他国家的留学生相比，GMS 地区留学生的这一整体特征更为明显。日、韩的学生更容易提出需要教师课后认真思考才能解答的学术问题，并且他们一般不满足于只听取教师对这些问题的解释，而喜欢拿自己的观点和依据来反驳教师的解释。这与有的学者观察到的越南留学生情况相似：越南留学生在学习上体现出被动性、依赖性、大众性①。

同样，接受访问的泰国北部、缅甸、柬埔寨高校教师也反映，学生比较喜欢通过记忆就可以达到要求的教学内容。在问及“如果每节课（40 分钟）留 10 分钟来自主学习，你们喜欢由老师提出问题，然后大家一起思考和回答，还是自己提出问题来思考和回答”时，绝大部分学生选择由教师提问，理由大多是“我们不知道提什么问题”、“老师提的问题比我们自己提的有思考价值”、“我们提的问题很简单”等。可见，来华的 GMS 留学生和其国内的学生都在不同程度上呈现出偏爱接受式学习的特点。

要分析接受式学习占主导地位的原因，首先要承认，有相当多的 GMS 学生（无论其国内或是留学）具有刻苦、认真的优点。在强调发现式学习的当代教育环境中，不能简单地把他们不习惯发现式学习归咎于缺少思考、主动性差。事实上，GMS 国家大多比较认可中国的教育体制和教学模式，而中国学生也具有亚裔学生依赖教师和书本的学习特点②。既然如此，为什么与同为亚洲学生的中国和日韩学生相比，GMS 学生被教师评价为在知识上更“顺从”、更“不愿意提问题”呢？除去传统教育方式的影响以及学习动力、学习风气、个人努力程度等因素，佛教氛围浓郁的成长环境有可能是原因之一。佛教徒在人际交往中反对冲突，追求融洽（harmony principle）。“融洽”原则可能来源于“善行修来世”这一教义。传统上，人们对僧侣、教师、长辈极为敬重。在学生看来，向老师提一些“挑战性”的问题是不敬的，讨论的氛围（无论是

① 施翠芳：《对 139 名越南留学生的学习方式研究》，载《大理学院学报》2003 年第 6 期。

② 郁小萍：《中国学生留英学习体验调查》，载《现代外语》2001 年第 3 期。

师生之间还是学生之间）如果较为激烈，容易被视为冲突或不愉快、不和谐，违背了避免冲突的日常行为规则。在中国儒家文化和佛教的双重影响下，GMS国家的学生较少质疑、当面争论，因而表现出了接受式为主导的学习特点。

（三）课外活动安排较多

GMS 国家的高校大多早上 8：30 开始上课，中午 12 点到 1 点午餐，主要课程于下午 3：30 以前结束，因此学生自主学习和课外活动的时间比较充裕。学生参加课外活动的积极性很高，艺术团、戏剧社、跆拳道协会等大学社团一过晚上 7：30 就热闹非凡，学校组织的各种活动也有大量学生参加。尽管云南高校的作息时间与这些国家不同，课余时间较少，但是这几乎没有影响留学生们对课外活动的热情。在云南大学留学生院，班级或学院组织各种晚会、活动时，最积极的就是 GMS 地区的学生。有一个值得注意的现象，无论是在这些国家执教还是在云南执教的对外汉语教师均反映过，学生可以为了参加课外活动而严重影响正常学习，并且似乎他们认为这是可以理解的。例如前面提到的迟到现象，经常有学生很自然地跟老师说："我迟到是因为昨晚参加某项活动，睡晚了，所以今天起不来。"当下一次再有活动时，同样会有学生因为同样的理由而迟到。

学生从课外活动中得到了快乐，教师也较为重视学生获得快乐。2005 年 9 月，在泰国清莱举办的 GMS 地区英语教学会议上，来自老挝、缅甸的学者一再强调追求"快乐的学习"。Vongvipanond 认为，这种对快乐的追求（fun principle）有可能是佛教信奉宿命论的体现①。佛教宿命论认为，人不能改变自己的命运，个人奋斗和努力并不决定命运，要改善对人生的满意程度，应当顺从自然，修养佛性，在生活中发现美和乐趣，不主张以牺牲快乐为代价而对人生进行规划。这或许可以从一个方面解释社会节奏较慢的原因。在此文化环境或背景下，学生不愿意为了学习而牺牲课外活动似乎就不难理解了。

三、针对学习特点，采用相应的教学和管理方法

在佛教文化底蕴深厚的地区，大学教育必然要考虑宗教文化对教学客体的影响，教学管理必然要适应教学客体的特点和需求。根据学生表现出来的时间

---

① Vongvipanond, Peansiri. *Linguistic Perspective of Thai Culture*. New Orleans: Social Science Workshop of the University of New Orleans, 1994.

观念、学习方式和课外活动安排方面的特点，对来华的GMS留学生应当采用相应的教学和管理方法。这具体包括：

（一）强调时间纪律

针对时间观念淡薄的特点，一方面要对学生进行正确评价，不能仅凭迟到等现象就产生负面印象，否定其学习态度和努力程度；另一方面也要强调纪律的严肃性和重要性，促使学生用学校纪律来约束自己，共同创造守时的良好学习环境。时间观念，尤其是迟到现象，在留学生来华的初期需要着重强调和纠正，这一过程需要花费较长的时间。

（二）采用发现式学习的过程中要注意循序渐进

针对习惯于接受式学习的特点，要注意循序渐进地介绍和采用发现式学习方式。在教学的初始阶段，接受式学习具有基础扎实的优点，随着教学内容增多、程度加深，可逐步引入发现式学习，主要培养学生思考、探索和发现问题。在此过程中可以对学生说明，提问以及讨论是很好的学习方法，与老师进行学术争论绝对不是不尊重老师的行为。只要加以充分鼓励，辅之以必要的硬性要求，应当可以逐步建立起发现式占主导地位的自主学习习惯。

（三）充分利用课外活动，同时加以恰当引导

学生课外活动安排较多，有可能是佛教文化影响的表现，也有可能是其他原因，如贪玩、对学习重视不够、自律性差、不懂得安排学习与生活等。在留学生教学和管理中，一方面要尊重他们的生活习惯，充分利用课外活动来增进教师、管理人员和学生之间的感情；另一方面要加以引导，让课外活动真正有益于学生的身心健康以及提高学生的知识水平。广西民族学院在这一方面的做法值得借鉴。他们认为，湄公河流域国家的学生有较强的民族意识，因此当一国留学生达到一定的数量时，通过一定的程序产生出具有较高群众威望和热衷于为同学服务的学生作为留学生学生会干部，帮助校方对学生进行管理。让学生干部在校方的指导下，参与课外活动的组织、学习生活纪律的监督，参与对违纪学生的教育管理以及与学生家长的沟通①。除此之外，还要关心学生的课外活动是否有价值，是否有益于个人发展。但是，必须强调课外活动不能影响

---

① 雷伟中：《湄公河流域来华留学生的文化特征及其管理》，载《广西民族学院学报》2005年第2期。

正常教学。例如，不允许由于参加课外活动而不按时到课、不完成学习要求等。

四、结 语

Gudykunst 提出，在跨文化交际中，存在主体文化和客体文化。要减少两类文化的差异带来的误解，使交流获得成功，必须消除主体或客体文化中心主义①。尽管云南与柬埔寨、老挝、缅甸、泰国和越南毗邻，保持着文化和经济联系，拥有诸多共性，但是受中国主流文化的影响，云南高校的情况具有自己的特点。若不考虑这些国家的学生的特点，尤其是不考虑来华留学生的学习特点，就有可能产生一些误解，导致教学效果不佳，管理难以进行。受经济条件、传统文化、家庭教育以及宗教（如基督教、伊斯兰教）等因素的影响，这些留学生具有许多学习特点，并且呈现出较大的个体差异。本文从佛教文化的影响入手，总结了 GMS 留学生的一些学习特点，并相应地分析了原因。希望这些粗浅的总结和分析能够加深对 GMS 地区文化特点和教育情况的了解，促进大学之间的国际交流与合作，并且能够进一步为 GMS 地区留学生教育提供借鉴。由于研究对象有限，文中观点难免挂一漏万，恳请读者批评指正。

参考文献：

[1]陈洁．佛教时间观试析——兼与基督教比较[Z]．中国论文下载中心,2006.

[2]雷伟中．湄公河流域来华留学生的文化特征及其管理[J]．广西民族学院学报,2005(2).

[3]施翠芳．对 139 名越南留学生的学习方式研究及其管理[J]．大理学院学报,2003(6).

[4]杨宁坤．浅析来华越南留学生思想特点及其管理[J]．比较教育研究,2004(6).

[5]郁小萍．中国学生留英学习体验调查[J]．现代外语,2001(3).

[6]Gudykunst, W. & Young Yun Kim. *Communicating with Strangers: an Approach to Intercultural Communication.* New York: Random House, 1984.

① Gudykunst, W. & Young Yun Kim. *Communicating with Strangers: an Approach to Intercultural Communication.* New York: Random House, 1984.

[7] Vongvipanond, Peansiri. *Linguistic Perspective of Thai Culture.* New Orleans: Social Science Workshop of the University of New Orleans, 1994.

第三部分　外国文化及跨文化交际研究

In Socioculturally Defined Boundaries: On Joking Relationships

Liu Xiaohong

In discussing the social significance of joking relationships Keith H. Basso alludes to a Western Apache analogy which likens the development of solidarity in interpersonal relationships to the process by which "deerhides" are softened into pieces of fine "buckskin" (Basso, 1979). A. R. Radcliffe-Brown defines a joking relationship as "a relation between two persons in which one is by custom permitted and in some instances required to tease or make fun of the other, who in turn is required to take no offence" (Brown, 1965). Research by some other scholars also shows the structural functional importance of joking relationships. Brett O'Bannon views the "joking relationship" as a powerful cultural institution that binds families, clans or even whole ethnic groups into ties of imagined kinship (O'Bannon, 2005). Highlighting the social and political function of joking relationships Lamin Sabally said they are "treasured national pride" and a cherished national symbol that concretize the very social fabric of our societies (Sabally, 2008). In the same structure functionalist perspective, this paper emphasizes how joking relationships as a dynamic social process tell much about the cultures and societies in which they exist. It argues that what is intended in joking relationships can only be best achieved within socioculturally defined boundaries. To go beyond is dangerous and even disastrous.

A joking relationship is defined and permitted by custom. In some societies it is one of permitted disrespect. What makes a joking act possible and successful for its intended result is a joking frame the joker successfully creates and then persuades the "butt", in Basso's word, to play along. Brown's research shows that in many societies it is regarded as preferable that a man should marry the daughter of his mother's brother. This custom, known as cross-cousin marriage, is accompanied by a joking relationship between the man and the children of his mother's brother, who are thus the man's potential in-laws and wives. It is a custom in that society that when these cross-cousins meet they must try to embarrass each other. They "joke" with one another, making the most vulgar allegations with no one taking any offence. Cross-cousins who do not joke this way are considered boorish, as not playing the social game. When two people from West Africa's Ndiaye and Diop families meet, they are also required to "dis" each other. They insult each other's family heritage and eating habits: "The important thing is that they are not only required to engage in these insulting exchanges, but they are equally obligated not take offense" (O'Bannon, 2005). Including elements of obscenity though, this kind of joking is only verbal and the joking relationship underlying the joking act is symmetrical as each of the cross-cousins teases or makes fun of the other. By the "wedding-night play" custom in China, friends of the newlyweds draw all their wits to tease and make fun of the newlyweds, who, made to do what would otherwise be unacceptably embarrassing and even humiliating, can take no offence at all. Here the joking relationship is totally asymmetrical. The newlyweds, however, go right into the joking frame and play along. If they don't, or they their friends don't joke this way, the marriage may be seen as ominous.

People don't joke with each other when their relation is "stiff" as "deerhides". They joke to soften "deerhides" into pieces of fine "buckskin". Le Ly Hayslip, the well-known Vietnamese American woman writer joked with her audience as she started her speech in the lecture hall at Whitman College: "I'm 38, not young enough but still available (recorded by the author of this paper)." The audience laughed loud, feeling perhaps a satisfying sense of identification with someone who otherwise would have never been so close and real to them. Joking is thus a means of working on softening relationships and consequently a means of establishing solidarity and shortening social distance between people. More significantly, people joke to fulfill their social roles defined by society. When the cross-cousins crack vulgar jokes, they are playing the social games set forth by the cross-cousin marriage system. The friends of the newly weds make fun of the newly weds to make them less shy on their wedding night. When two old Chinese friends meet and joke over their creeping old age with one saying: "Oh, you are still alive? I thought you had been disposed" and the other one laughing back: "Oh, you know, I've been waiting for you" (recorded by the author of this paper), the joke functions to chase away the joker's inner fear of death by projecting it into the butt. When a grandchild and his grandfather joke about wishing to marry each other's wife (recorded by Radcliff-Brown), the jokes convey special meanings for both the grandchild who, in joking, pretends that he wishes to marry his grandfather's wife, and the grandfather who then pretends that the wife of his grandchild is, or might be, his wife. For the grandfather, this kind of joke must give him an irresistible pleasure of being rejuvenated while, for the grandchild, it works to satisfy his wish to grow up and enter into the world of full maturity.

Joking relationships tell much of the cultures and societies they exist in. Radcliffe-Brown proposed structural functional approach to social analysis of some strange customs whereby certain individuals (often in-laws) are expected to engage in formalized banter. He proposed that one could only understand such strange customs by studying the specific joking relationship in the context of the total pattering of social relations in the society (Brown, 1940). Cultural differences between societies create varieties in social relations and social life in general. In China where there is extreme respcct between a man and his parents-in-law, a man standing in a joking relationship with the friends of his wife is rarely in a joking terms with his parents-in-law. A man and his wife reciprocally call each other's parents "Dad and Mom" the day they become married by law. Embodying total and unconditioned respect, this address form assigns a sense of filial duty and obedience to the man and his wife who use it rather than a joke relationship which can put the couple and their parents-in law on an equal basis. The man is not even on a joking relationship with his older sisters-in-laws since he is required by custom to call them "sisters" instead of addressing them by name: there is studied respect between him and his older sisters-law in using this address form. In Australia the complete avoidance of any social contact between a man and his mother-in-law (recorded by Radcliffe-Brown) makes a joking relationship of any kind absolutely out of place even though his mother-in-law is "the greatest friends he has since she has provided him with a wife" (Brown, 1965). In the U.S, however, it is common for a man and his father-in-law who call each other by name to joke like friends. Their joking relationship embodies a sense of intimacy and equality distinctively American. Some Americans, even as kids, call their parents by their first name and they say "I love you" to their parents almost as a ritual, either as a way of ending a phone conversation or departing, which would be a thing extremely difficult and even embarrassing for Chinese children to do. The way the little boy in the American movie "Sleepless in Seattle" brings up the topic of sex in his conversation with his father and asks questions about it may seem blasphemous in Chinese culture. Parent-children relationship in China is becoming "softer" but not to the extend that they can joke like friends as some Americans do. While the intimate close relationship between Chinese parents and children is reinforced more by filial obligations and parental love and care, the solidarity between American parents and children becomes strengthened by their joking relationships. When an American girl tells her mom about her new boyfriend who is tall, gentle and handsome, instead of asking more about him to show how she cares about her daughter as a Chinese mom would probably do, the mother can joke about it: "How could you hide him from me when I'm still attractive (recorded by the author of this paper)?" The joking relationship between father and son depicted in the American movie "Indiana Jones and the Last Crusade" can be very foreign to Chinese society.

Joking, as Keith H. Basso puts it, "is a form of play" (Basso, 1979) and jokes, not meant to be serious, therefore, should be taken playfully. Funny and humorous, jokes serve to entertain and delight. Chinese cross talk shows feature on the joking relationship between the two actors at each other's expense to make them funny and entertaining. Disneyland and Universal Studios Hollywood thrive on the joking relationships their performing and entertaining personnel can instantly strike up with their visitors through live shows, guided tours and thrilling rides. The change of a cultural environment in which the jokes exist may change the playful limits of jokes and consequently their entertaining nature. The reproduction of Disneyland in and around the world, perhaps, is a good example. While Disneyland in US is a fantastic wonderland its replica in Japan is much less entertaining. What is entertaining in one culture can even be humiliating in another. The following episode is very typical of a joking relationship between the performing actors and the audience at Universal Studios Hollywood (recorded by the author of this paper). Its existence may be unimaginable elsewhere.

> "You guys have had fun?" the live show actor asked the audience, who responded: "Yeah!" "Go home!" the actor shouted. In a stunned moment, he went on: "After this wonderful live show. Uh... uh... uh... " The audience cheered, totally rejoiced in the overwhelming Hollywood atmosphere. "Anyone wants to offer a camera?" the actor shouted, inviting the butt to play along in the joking frame he created. A little girl ran to him and handed him her camera. "Ah, a cheap camera for cheap pictures!" the actor put the camera in between his legs and then shot a picture at this ass: "It sure will be a great picture!" Gleaming at the girl from his mask, he lowered his voice and said, "Be sure to have it printed!" Laughing, he handed the camera back to the little girl. The crowd became exuberated...

Taken seriously or literally this kind of jokes will cease being jokes. Instead of being funny, they may become dangerous as the Apaches claim them to be. For however amusing jokes may be, they are always amusing at someone's expense. Unless jokers are careful to keep their slurs and criticism within playful limits, their actions may be interpreted as veiled expressions of genuine hostility. Jokes badly played can easily tear down an established joking relationship. In extreme cases, they can even result in violence and death. Years ago it was reported that in one village in rural China a bride jumped into a river and drowned herself upon hearing her wedding night bridal room conversation aired over the village. What had happened was that on their wedding night after the "wedding-night play" their friends hid a microphone in their bridal room, recorded the whole conversation and played it loud for all the villagers to hear and make fun of.

Within culturally defined boundaries joking relationships have the potentials of resolving conflicts and creating peace. In demonstrating how fictive relationships can bring an end to quite serious conflicts O'Bannon documented on his presentation at an international conference on jokes and policy in Africa an instance in which a rebel group in southern Senegal actually released a carload of hostages because the driver successfully pleaded for their lives in the name of the Serer-Diola joking relationship (O'Bannon). To form and maintain balanced and dignified joking relationships in a dynamic social process is to enhance social stability and progress.

References:

[1] Basso, Keith H.: *Portraits of the white men by the Western Apache Linguistic Play and Cultural Symbols among the Western Apache.* Cambridge: Cambridge University Press, 1979.

[2] Brown, A. R. Radcliff. *Structure and Function in Primitive Society.* New York: Free Press, 1965.

[3] O'Bannon, Brett. "Joking Relationship Can End Serious Conflicts" Paper presented at an international colloquium entitled "The Cousin and Policy: Alliances with Jokes and Policy in Africa", Paris, France October, 2005: 27 – 28.

[4] Sabally, Lamin. "Joking Relationships are Our Treasured National Pride", 2008.

[5] http://www. allgambian. net/NewsDetails. aspx id = 306 – 41k (accessed June 7, 2008).

[6] Brown, A. R. Radcliff. "The Andaman Islanders", 1922. http:// www. britannica. com /eb/topic – 23492/ (accessed May 16, 2008).

[7] Brown, A. R. Radcliff. "On Joking Relationship" Journal of the International African Institute, Vol. 13, No. 3 (Jul., 1940), pp. 195-210. doi: 10. 1207/1156093.

Cultural Analysis of Chinese and American Views on Charity

Liu Xiaoyuan

"Meat and wine rot in the vermilion gates, corpses and bones freeze out on the streets." These verses from a poem by Tang Dynastic poet Du Fu, describe the social injustice and the extreme disparity between the rich and poor of that period (around the 8th century). The Gini Index is the indicator for measuring these characteristics of contemporary society. According to Chinese official reports, the Chinese Gini Index has already arrived at the 0.45% threshold, which means the richest 10% of the population owns close to half of the nation's total assets while the poorest 10% has but 1.4%. Such a sharp gap is leading to a polarization of consumption and consequently social instability, which will have a direct impact on economic growth because only a few people have discretionary income to spend. In turn, this undermines the great objective realization of constructing a harmonious and sustainable socialist society. How to solve this problem becomes an urgent imperative.

It is generally held that the first distribution of public wealth is achieved through the market in the form of income, the second through government adjustment, and the third through individual contribution of disposable income motivated by habit and religious ethics①. Here the third distribution of wealth comes to be served by charity. However, the fact remains that Chinese charity is far behind not only the developed countries, but even some of the developing countries, which involves factors such as

① *Holy Bible* (*New Testament*), (Scarborough: Christian Communication Inc. of Canada, 2005), p. 248.

delays in law-and policy-making, public misconceptions and attitudes towards giving.

This paper is attempting to focus on the conceptual aspect and make a comparative study between Chinese and American ways of thinking concerning charity, because the Chinese charitable culture and social environment are still at the starting point in contrast with America's highly developed charitable undertakings which are cooperating in a parallel with its economy towards a positive cycle of a harmonious and sustainable society. Hopefully it will be able to contribute to the betterment of the current backward state of China's charity where the wealth gap is growing dangerously larger.

1. Manifestations of Sino-American Conceptions of Charity

1.1 In China, charitable organizations are developing on a small scale although the number increases rapidly. There are about 100 at present, most of which are affiliated with the government and working at low efficiency. In contrast, America has 1,400,000 non-profit charitable organizations. European countries, like Germany, the United Kingdom and Switzerland, have more than 10,000 foundations respectively.

1.2 The charitable funds raised each year account for a very small percentage of China's GDP due to the poor fundraising techniques and lack of trust in China. According to the statistics, these 100 or so organizations have altogether 0.1% worth of GDP. Among them, the China Charity Federation and China Legal Aid Foundation are the most influential and capable in fund-raising, but even their funds raised annually are no more than 80 million Chinese Yuan. In contrast, America's charitable organizations hold 8% ~9% of America's GDP.

1.3 The charitable concept has not been popularly accepted by Chinese people so far. Since the founding of the P. R. China, social welfare has been brought under the control of the planned economy so that charity has not got a chance to assume a role and consequently the general public has not cultivated the awareness of actively participating in charity. Investigation shows the majority of the public, including the wealthy, did not make any active donations. They expect the government to continue to assume responsibility for social welfare and poverty alleviation programs.

1.4 One more interesting point is the totally different rhetorical definitions of charity found in some of the authoritative Chinese and English encyclopedias. For example, according to Encyclopedia Chinese, charitable cause refers to a social cause which engages in helping the weak with money or articles and provides them with some other practical aid from compassion, pity or religious belief. With a heavy religious and superstitious implication, it aims for doing good and receiving good recompense. Usually donators regard charitable causes as a kind of almsgiving, which serves only as a temporal and negative aid to a small proportion of people. Controversy remains about its social effects①. In Americana Encyclopedia, philanthropy is "one of the most enduring societal traditions, and the effort to promote human welfare through donations of money or service."②

However, it is one thing to say that the charitable concept has not been established in China; it is quite another thing to say that Chinese people are not a helpful, caring or loving people. And the fact is that Chinese people are very considerate of their compatriots.

According to historical data, Chinese charitable history traces back to as early as the Spring and Autumn Period (770 – 476 BC) and Warring States (475 – 221 BC) when The Book of Rites put forward the idea of Great Harmony, which means that because people are sincere in their words and deeds and live in peace and harmony, men do not love only their relatives; nor do they treat as children only their own sons and daughters; the aged should be supported till their death; the able-bodied should be given chances to demonstrate their abilities; the young should be cared for and tended to, and the widowed, the orphaned, the childless and the disabled all secure provisions③. Mencius, one of the greatest thinkers after Confucius, also suggested that people help each other like neighbors do so as to live harmoniously. It is thus clear that Chinese charitable ideas emerged at an early time, taking a different form though, and they demanded that people should not only care for their own families

---

① 引自 http://www.sina.com.cn.《南方周末》2005 年 10 月 6 日。

② Kathleen D. McCarthy, *The Encyclopedia Americana*, *International Edition* (Danbury: Grolier Incorporated, 1998), p. 874.

③ 王昌坤译:《礼记》,齐鲁书社 2006 年版,第 21 ~ 22 页。

and relatives but also love all others in the society, so that all the weak, including widowers, widows, orphans, childless couples and the disabled could be cared for and looked after. During the Tang Dynasty (618–907 AD), charitable causes supported by monasteries developed rapidly. In the Song Dynasty (960–1279 AD), nongovernmental charity was brought under government control so that governmental charitable organizations were set up. At the same time, nongovernmental charitable propagation and private charitable activities prospered.

Then why does contemporary charity in China develop so slowly and lag far behind? Before making any exploration on the causes, it's necessary to distinguish three important terms first: charity, philanthropy and benevolence. According to on-line Wikipedia, "although giving to those nearly connected to oneself is sometimes called charity, normally charity denotes giving to those not related.. The need of a large financial commitment creates a distinction between philanthropy and charitable giving. Charitablc giving typically plays a supporting role in a charitable organization initiated by someone else. Thus, the conventional usage of philanthropy applies mainly to wealthy persons, and sometimes to a trust created by a wealthy person with a particular cause or objective targeted." ... "Many non-wealthy persons have dedicated-thus, donated-substantial portions of their time, effort and wealth to charitable causes. These people are not typically described as philanthropists because individual effort alone is seldom recognized as instigating significant change."① This encyclopedia gives the term benevolence two definitions: 1. charitable kindness; 2. altruistic gift or act②. Here I'd like to claim that when I'm arguing China has a long charitable history, I mean it more benevolently. Chinese people have never been mean in helping and caring about others or the poor by spending time, or donating materials like food and clothes, which is what is implied in Confucianism's benevolence.

① http://www. wikipedia. com.

② Ibid.

2. Cultural Reasons for the Existence of Sino – American Different Conceptions on Charity

2.1 Benevolence and Charity

2.1.1 The core of Confucianism is "benevolence", which as a concept extends immediately from the blood relationship within the family. Therefore, familial love is the most immediate and primary love for a human being. Anybody, after being born, finds the most immediate people are his family members and therefore naturally cherishes a deep love for his relatives. One of Confucius' disciples You Ruo took filial piety to parents and revering elder brothers as the essence of benevolence: "And surely proper behavior towards parents and elder brothers is the trunk of Goodness". ① Later on, the Confucian School accepted "loving your relatives and respecting the elderly" as the fundamental meaning of benevolence, according to which one person can extend his love to others only when he loves his own family members first. Adam Smith raises exactly this point in his *Theory of Moral Sentiment*. Benevolent love is first of all deeply rooted in familial blood relations and then extends to others as "extending your respect for your aged parents to all the aged, and extending your love for your own children to all children"②. Therefore, Chinese traditional charitable culture originates from the family as a basic unit, maintaining that benevolent love moves from "educating his family, to ruling his state, to governing the world well". Within the traditional ethical framework of Chinese people, the familial relationship is the most immediate. Since "the core of benevolence is to be filial to one's parents"③, most Chinese people without exception leave or prefer to leave their property to their descendants. Thus, Confucian benevolent love is layered from family to relatives to friends and ultimately to society.

2.1.2 Compared with the Chinese concept of charity, America has a long history with religious brotherly love as its essence, which goes through the whole Bible.

① Arthur Waley 译:《论语》,外语教学与研究出版社 2005 年版,第 3 页。

② 蔡希勤编著,何祚康、郁苓英译:《孟子格言录》,华语教学出版社 2003 年版,第 250 页。

③ 蔡希勤编著,何祚康、郁苓英译:《孟子格言录》,华语教学出版社 2003 年版,第 222 页。

Jesus summarizes the Jewish law when he says, "Love your neighbor as yourself."① This attitude colors all Christian thinking. This charitable conception originated from its religious doctrine of "brotherly love". Christianity holds that we human beings are born sinful, which is contrary to Confucian doctrine that "man's nature is good at birth". This sin implicates later generations and becomes the origin of human suffering, but Christians are redeemed by believing in Jesus and empowered to love in a new way because they are confident Jesus loves them. Thus, Christian benevolence teaches Christians to abandon the seeking for external materialistic world and to care more about the internal spiritual one, to be specific, "to love others as much as you love yourself." In contrast with Confucius layered structure of benevolent love, Christian love is a brotherly universal love on the basis of equality. Only when universal love is aspired to, can unselfishness, service and even sacrifice be available to promote charitable spirit among the general public. Therefore, charity in the name of universal fraternity, being essentially a special personality derived from the belief in God and Jesus, is taken by Christianity as the means of getting closer to God by behaving like Jesus.

2.2 State and Community

2.2.1 The Influence of the Concept of the Benevolent Rule of State

Benevolent government stood in the way of nongovernmental charitable development in Chinese history. In accordance with the traditional political ideology, government was supposed to be the main and even the only provider for social welfare. Once when intending to help the poor with his own property, Confucius' disciple Zi Lu was stopped by Confucius explaining that relieving the poor with individual property implied the immorality and incapability of the government, and would be a great shame to one who was always claiming to be benevolent and meanwhile keen on face-saving. Recuperative centers in the Tang Dynasty, set up to help the poor and the ill by Buddhism temples and later abolished by the authority, had much to do with the above-mentioned idea of the rule of state, which directly brought then embryonic charitable consciousness to an end. This thought of the rule of state got intensified by the highly centralized state power in the mid-20th century, and its fierce criticism and attack a-

---

① *Holy Bible* (*New Testament*), (Scarborough: Christian Communication Inc. of Canada, 2005), p. 44.

gainst humanitarianism buried the nongovernmental charity as well as the feudal system completely. The consequence is that whenever Chinese people are in trouble, the government is the first place they would like to turn to. This stereotype has blocked the formation of charitable consciousness in Chinese people's minds.

2.2.2 Mutually-Helping Culture

Americans' active participation in charitable causes also lies in its long history of a mutual helping culture. It is well-known that under British colonial rule, Americans did not have any social security. The government had not been empowered with the imposition of tax and therefore couldn't provide the citizens with any social welfare before the Federal Constitution was passed. Consequently the public was forced to get associated and help each other. Therefore, in America, mutually-helping activities have been common and often organized in the name of community which, in contrast, is a pretty new concept to Chinese people. Benjamin Franklin, one of America's earliest philanthropists, contributed his large property to helping better the community he was living in and founded local citizen organizations such as a Volunteer Fire Brigade and other public facilities. America's philanthropic tradition thus started to prosper. This is why America has got a "small government and big society" image.

2.3 Wealth

2.3.1 The Concept of Wealth

America's "being rich is sinful" culture which is totally different from what Chinese people generally refer to ever as "hating the richness" culture, originates from the Christian concept of "rich man's original sin". Early Christianity blamed, resented and even denied entirely secular wealth, people's material desires, rich men and their business conduct. It was generally held that businessman who bought and sold at low prices were committing crimes severer than stealing, and commerce and trade fostered people's avariciousness for a secular world so as to abandon God-seeking. Consequently in early Christian societies, Christians ought never to work as businessmen. Christians were discouraged from lending money at interest. Thus, Jews who had no such limitation became the first bankers in the Middle Ages. Christians are expected to help each other and take care of the poor, widows and orphans. Steel magnate Andrew Carnegie, one of the great founders of American nongovernmental philanthropic companies, published in 1889 an article entitled "The Gospel of Wealth", which is regarded as the masterpiece of modern American philanthropic causes, and from which we can see how deeply the doctrine of rich men's original sin is rooted in Americans' minds. In his article he wrote, "It was held that public sentiment would soon say of one who died possessed of available wealth which he was free to administer: 'The man who dies thus rich dies disgraced'. "① Another founder, petroleum big shot John Davison Rockefeller, having sincerely believed in Christianity since childhood, declared his aversion to wealth many times and lived what Christianity upholds as a very plain life. What's more, he contributed the vast majority of his property before passing away. It is generally agreed that it is the doctrine that "the rich is innately sinful" that keeps reminding these Christian wealthy people of contributing their money.

Another important factor which helped the emergence of modern American charitable culture is Protestant ideas, according to which rich men serve more as the social manager of wealth than its owner. That is, legally speaking, wealth is privately owned, but the part exceeding what is needed for making a living belongs to society in terms of ethnics and value. Carnegie in his "The Gospel of Wealth" made this idea very clear. To him, the wisdom to find ways of contributing extra wealth, to make it benefit society is as important as that needed for making money. The objective of making profit is supposed not only to satisfy one's material demand but also to help out those in poor situations by contribution. Rich people in their life time should make a good arrangement for their wealth so that it can maximally benefit the public. This Protestant doctrine manifested itself in the 19th century American literary works such as Catharine Sedgwick's *The Poor Rich Man* and Eliza Follen's *Sketches of Married Life*. The wealthy families in these novels tried to "unite the economic and the domestic... through a project that is centered on the welfare of others", and "prospered, in part, through improving the lives of the poor and, in turn, reinvest their

① Andrew Carnegie, *The Gospel of Wealth* (Cambridge Mass.: Belknap Press of Harvard University Press, 1962), p. 30.

profits in a continuous cycle of benevolence"①. This model of public and private immersion turned out to be the embryonic form of American modern philanthropic company.

2. 3. 2 Social Status of Businessmen

2. 3. 2. 1 Mainstay of American Businessmen

Under the influence of the Christian "sinful richness culture", American rich men's philanthropic donation has a long history. The term businessman originated from the USA in the 1830s. These businessmen comprised unique creators and leaders of American public associations. They had an intense interest in public beneficial undertakings. Many American universities, hospitals, museums, concert halls and railroads were sponsored or established by these businessmen. Their ideal belief is the prosperous cooperation between the public and individual. The future of the public associations means their own future, so in the USA businessmen are always addressed as "social sponsors". Such a tradition is inherited and passed down to later generations of businessmen who expand it further. Bill Gates, who has more than $40 billion, has donated more than half so far. His explanation for his warmhearted philanthropy turns out to have come from the teaching of his parents.

2. 3. 2. 2 Discrimination against Chinese Businessmen

The ruling class adopted the policy of highly valuing agriculture while belittling business in Chinese feudalist society so that the small-scale agricultural production lagged too far behind to relieve the stress from the population, war and natural disasters. Those who were satisfied with their farming lives and unwilling to leave their homeland were regarded as law-abiding people while commercial activities were strictly forbidden, and those engaged in them were looked down upon as idlers. Shang Yang Reform in 359 BC tried different ways to reward cultivation while devaluing business, which resulted directly in the recruitment of businessmen into armies when the emperor Qin Shi Huang went on a punitive expedition afterwards to unite six countries. Early Han Dynastic businessmen were allowed only to wear coarse clothes

① Jill Bergman and Debra Bernardi, *Our Sisters' Keepers* (Tuscaloosa: The University of Alabama Press, 2005), p. 95.

instead of luxurious ones as brocade and their children were deprived of the right to become government officials. What's more, the Emperor Wudi of Han dynasty (156 – 87 BC) imposed much heavier tax on businessmen, causing most of these middle class businessmen to go bankrupt. It can be seen that the early commerce was belittled as the humblest job, whose significance was not given a full play, and businessmen were situated in the low class. Commerce developed faster later on, which called attention to its significance, but the fact remained that people conducting it were still looked down upon as snobs for attending to trifles to the neglect of essentials, although as a profession it began to be valued as a necessary element of national development. In his "Song of the Lute Player", Tang Dynastic poet Bai Juyi when describing the singing girl's miserable life, expressed his pity for her marriage to a businessman, because he held that businessmen cared more about interests than about affection, and that this behavior was against Confucianism's emphasis on righteousness while neglecting benefits. This poet's thought is typical literati opinion on the personality of businessmen in Chinesc history.

After the founding of P. R. China, class struggle became the guiding principle which means capitalist class was the main enemy of the public and must be cracked down on, so this revolutionary consciousness negated capitalism represented by businessmen as a whole, holding that being rich was being merciless. Therefore, the wealthy people in Chinese history have never been provided with any chance to cultivate a strong sense of social responsibility in helping the nation solve social problems. They haven't cultivated a sense of social identification in helping voluntarily maintain the normal operation and continuity of the whole society, which is quite different from American tradition.

2.4 Value System

2.4.1 Collectivism Orientation

Chinese people are collectivism-orientated. Under such an influence groups like family, society and nation have got the priority, and individual interest can be neglected or even sacrificed if necessary, just as a Chinese saying goes, "To be the first to show concern and the last to enjoy oneself."

In dealing with the relationship between individuals and groups or the environment, people get accustomed to avoiding "failing to show restraint", because of the ideas in idioms such as "shooting the bird which takes the lead", "one who wants to be ahead of others will get into trouble". Individualism is looked upon as disobedience to parents, monarch and friends and an evil conduct against which strict precautions must be taken. This is partly why wealthy Chinese are unwilling to participate publicly in charitable causes.

2.4.2 Individualism Orientation

American culture belongs to an individualism-orientated culture, in which everybody is an autonomous and independent entity. They do not rely on anyone else, even their parents, which would be a disgrace otherwise. To Winston Churchill, what he owns does not come from inheritance but from hard work①.

In terms of the relationship between individuals and groups or the environment, Americans advocate small government, big society, putting emphasis on individual priority over the government, which is embodied in two aspects as far as charity is concerned. One is the disbelief in the government. The public suspect that there is a widespread inefficiency and corruption among government officials, so they prefer to be more devoted to private charity. The other is the individual sense of responsibility. They think charitable donation is the duty of being a good citizen.

Conclusion

Evidently, compared with the advanced American charitable culture, what China is deficient in is not only material conditions, but more important some spiritual elements such as cultural and belief traditions, in addition to systematic factors like systems, laws and ideology. Traditional concepts like benevolent love, the rule of state and discrimination against businessmen have had much negative influence on the cultivation of the Chinese charitable consciousness. However, China is a nation with a long charitable history and benevolent love like a two-edged sword also makes Chinese a helpful, caring or loving people, which help contemporary Chinese charitable

① 引自贾玉新著:《跨文化交际学》,上海外语教育出版社 1997 年版,第 63 页。

cause towards a new beginning. Recently Charities Act has been incorporated into the legislative plannings of both NPC and the State Council. The spring of China's charitable cause is coming soon.

References:

[1] Bergman, Jill and Debra Bernardi. *Our Sisters' Keepers*. Tuscaloosa: The University of Alabama Press, 2005.

[2] Carnegie, Andrew. *The Gospel of Wealth*. Cambridge Mass.: Belknap Press of Harvard University Press, 1962.

[3] McCarthy, Kathleen D. *The Encyclopedia Americana*, *International Edition*. Danbury: Grolier Incorporated, 1998.

[4] *Holy Bible* (*New Testament*). Scarborough: Christian Communication Inc. of Canada, 2005.

[5]蔡希勤. 孟子格言录[M]. 北京:华语教学出版社,2003.

[6]贾玉新. 跨文化交际学[M]. 上海:上海外语教育出版社,1997.

[7]礼记[Z]. 王昌坤,译. 济南:齐鲁书社,2006.

[8]论语[Z]. Arthur Waley,译. 北京:外语教学与研究出版社,2005.

态度、知识、技能并重，培养跨文化交际能力

周真　马玲

外语学习的最终目的是得体地运用语言进行有效的跨文化交际。2000 年国家教委颁布的《高等学校英语专业教学大纲》包含了学生跨文化交际能力的培养目标，明确提出："除了强调培养学生运用语言的准确性外，还要培养对文化差异的敏感性、宽容性以及处理文化差异的灵活性，以适应日益广泛的国际交流的需要。"我们从 1997 年开始，就为英语专业本科三年级学生开设了"跨文化交际"课程。2003 年，根据学生要求又将此课提前到了二年级。目前，主要使用三种教材和参考书进行互补：理论框架和学科概念来自北大出版社引进的《跨文化交流》第 5 版，应用语境和课堂实践采用暨南大学的《文化与交际》，课外阅读和交流体验用《体验跨文化》。在教学中，我们坚持态度、知识、技能并重，综合地提高学生的跨文化交际的意识和能力，帮助学生进一步增长知识、扩大视野，了解和理解不同的文化，学习对母语文化和目的语文化进行比较，对交际体验中的态度、行为、效果进行反思，获得跨文化交际的基本概念和能力。从学生的自我评价、课内外的表现、问卷调查和测试的结果来看，学生的跨文化交际能力得到了有效的提高。

我们采用美国跨文化心理学家 C. Kelley 和 J. Meyers 设计的"跨文化适应能力调查问卷"。该问卷的内容涉及四个方面的跨文化适应力，即情绪调节能力（共 18 题，总计 108 分）、灵活性和开放性（共 15 题，总计 90 分）、感知敏锐度（共 10 题，总计 60 分）、自制力（共 7 题，总计 42 分）。我们在课程开始时进行前测试，要求学生根据测试结果对自己的跨文化适应能力进行分析，写出行动计划，并找一位同学督促和帮助自己实施计划。在课程结束时用同样的问卷再作一次后测试，对修课前、后学生的跨文化适应能力的变化进行

调查、比较和评估，从一个侧面反映课程教学效果。分别调查的结果表明，由于课程的介入，学生各方面的能力均有所提高（见“04 级学生跨文化适应能力测试分析报告”）。

著名语言教育家 H. D. Brown 指出：“语言的最高境界不是掌握语言形式，而是掌握语言形式以完成语言的交际功能。”英语专业二年级学生已经具备了一定的英语语言知识和听、说、读、写技能，但是运用目的语得体地进行交际却始终是英语学习中的一根“软肋”。正如何自然所指出的，英语作为外语的语用能力，不会随着学生的英语能力（语法词汇能力）的提高而自然提高。调查表明，二年级学生普遍认为自己的交际能力弱，多以“紧张”、“没话可说”或“词不达意”描述自己用英语进行沟通的过程，并表示迫切希望通过跨文化交际课了解不同的文化和提高交际能力。

情感态度是学习和发展的内动力。孔子早在两千多年前就提出了情感态度在学习中的重要性。他说:“知之者，不如好之者；好之者，不如乐之者。”培养跨文化交际能力的一个重要方面是培养学生积极的情感态度，引导他们的好奇心和求知欲，主动探究文化的差异和共性，尽量克服以本文化中心的态度去评价其他文化的倾向。学生在理论上可以认同各种文化的形成和发展都与特定的地域、历史、社会、民族、宗教有关，都有其存在的合理性，都值得我们尊重和学习。然而，以本文化为坐标来看待其他文化的态度却是长期形成的。正如张鸿雁指出的：“每一个民族和文化群体对另外一种文化都有某种程度的文化偏见，而这些偏见除了政治原因以外，就是这样两个原因：一是价值观的不同；二是对另外一种文化的不了解。价值观的不同是可以通过文化交流来取得某种认同的，而对另外一种文化不了解，这才是文化发展的最大障碍，不了解就没有文化认同的前提，就会有偏见。”① 学生对目的语文化的了解比较肤浅，或带有一些偏见和刻板印象，同时对母语文化也不明就里，在描述不同文化时，常会用到一些诸如 strange，good，bad，advanced，backward 等价值判断词。在学生阅读课程参考书《体验跨文化》的读书报告里，一个同学写道：“I'm not sure why in Western culture there're so many taboos concerning privacy. However, I have to admit that it's good to give everyone a space to live in. But I appreciate the Chinese way. Having too many taboos, people cannot communicate with each other thoroughly.”我们把这样的语句提出来供全班同学一起思考。此句在语言

① 张鸿雁：《民族偏见与文化偏见——中西文化比较新论》，辽宁教育出版社 1993 年版，第 2 页。

层面上并无不妥，但是经过适当引导，问他们“How many is too many?”“By whose standard?”“Is the purpose of cultural comparison to tell good from bad?”学生会用学过的概念分析其中以本文化为中心的态度和比较方式，以及由此而来的价值判断倾向。讨论式的课堂气氛有助于激发学生思维和求知欲，鼓励他们探寻语言背后的文化内涵，反思自己无意识的情感态度，在运用中加深理解，在学习和运用的过程中体验跨文化交际中多元文化的碰撞，使自己的思维从封闭到开放，增强跨文化的意识和沟通能力。一定的反思可以帮助学生从点到面、从已知到未知逐步构建新的知识系统，加深对诸如 mindfulness，suspend judgments，ethnocentrism，cultural relativism 这样一些概念的理解。孔子说：“不患人之不己知，患不知人也。”这就是要求我们首先要了解别人，在跨文化交际中采取文化相对主义态度，在了解的基础上理解和包容别的文化，丰富和发展我们自己的文化。自觉地实践“在文化交流中，应该首先看到其他文化的合理性、存在的客观性，并抱着向另外一种文化学习的认识观来研究文化”①。

社会心理学认为，人们的态度决定他们的行为。成功的跨文化交际在很大程度上取决于我们是否愿意了解和理解不同的文化，认真倾听和观察、学习。为了树立学生对外来文化的积极态度和激发进一步了解其他文化的求知欲，我们（在课文阅读和讨论之外）还观看了电影《西洋镜》和《刮痧》，并着重讨论影片中不同人物对待文化冲突的态度、文化差异的价值根源，沟通和了解在处理矛盾中的作用。学生以各自不同的文化背景和认知角度表达他们的感受。通过合作学习，他们能够超越自己的认识，更全面地理解事物，调整原有的知识、经验系统，建构新的认知结构。用英语开设选修课使单纯的语言教学转向将语言教学与内容教学相结合，语言既是文化的一部分又是交流的工具，用它来学习主题内容而不仅仅作为直接的学习目标。学生以往的学习主要集中在语言本身，而很少思考文化对语言运用的影响。在跨文化交际课上用英语学习一些新的学科概念，他们感到既新奇又有一定难度。我们既注重 culture specific 层面，也使用 culture general approach。用 E. T. Hall 关于 high/low context 和 direct/indirect 交际模式分析和比较英、汉语言现象。用实例讲解语言、交际与文化之间的关系和它们之间的相互影响。我们认为，Hofstede 提出的四个衡量价值观的尺度（categories of central values—individualism/collectivism，power distance，uncertainty avoidance，masculinity/femininity）对帮助学生进行文化

① 张鸿雁：《民族偏见与文化偏见——中西文化比较新论》，辽宁教育出版社 1993 年版，第 7 页。

比较很有价值。同时，我们也注意引导学生避免用文化定型代替客观的观察与描述，认识自我和他人既是各自文化的产物又是独立的个体。来自相同文化背景的人有着各自不同的性格与经历、话语与行为方式，而不是能用简单、机械的模式可以概括的。

学期中，我们要求每个学生理论联系实际，以“我与跨文化交际 + 自拟小标题”为主题作3~4分钟的主题发言。多数同学能够用课程中所学的知识对自己过去的一些成功的或失败的交际经验进行反思，分享自己在适应新的文化环境和与来自不同文化背景的人沟通的过程和心得。每个同学发言完毕都会得到全班同学的掌声鼓励，他们在交流中互相学习，取得了较好的效果。

我们在各个教学环节都坚持态度、知识、技能并重的做法，强调学以致用，着重培养语境意识和适应能力，培养在不同社交语境中自然地开始、继续和结束谈话，引进、发展、转换话题，得体应对和捕捉非言语信息的能力。对于有一定难度的概念，如 values，empathy，difference between individualism and selfishness 等，我们常采用角色扮演或讨论案例的方法来帮助学生理解。例如，在讲解“己所不欲，勿施于人”、“己之所欲，施之于人”、“人之所欲，施之于人”等三种待人处世的态度和原则的过程中，学生不但进行了比较和讨论，还在我们设计的各种语境中作角色扮演，并讨论所用原则以便加深理解。为了使学生体会在不同语境下汉、英语言的不同表达方式，我们把 addressing and greeting，meeting and introducing，inviting people，receiving guests and showing hospitality，giving and receiving compliment，presenting and receiving gifts，apologizing，making a phone call，telling good/bad news 等日常交际行为作为任务布置给学习小组，要求学生在课外活动中设计语境和对话。他们必须先用汉语自编对话，然后直译成英语，再尽量修改成得体的英语。要求同学在语言转换过程当中进行对比，体会两种语言在不同语境中的语用差异和文化异同，然后在课堂上交流他们的体会，最后把文字稿交给老师作进一步修改。经过几个步骤的反复琢磨，学生加深了对不同语言与文化的理解。

在不断改进教学方法，努力培养学生的跨文化交际能力的过程中，态度、知识、技能相辅相成可以取得较好的效果。学生的自我评价、主题发言的表现、问卷调查结果和考试成绩表明，通过课程的介入，他们的跨文化交际的综合能力得到了一定的提高。学生普遍认为这门课生动有趣，知识性和实用性都比较强，大量的语言材料和丰富的文化知识相结合，能够培养他们对跨文化交际的兴趣和能力，提高他们对中外文化差异的敏感力和包容度，提高与他人相处和沟通的能力。升入三年级后，在选修“人际沟通理论与实践”课程的学生当中，学习过跨文化交际课和没有选修过此课程的同学相比，前者在学习积极性、知识面、对语境和文化因素的敏感度、语言应用能力等方面较后者有明显优势。

参考文献：

[1] Brinton, D., Snow, M. A. & Wesche, M. B.. *Content-Based Second Language Instruction*[M]. Boston: Heinle & Heinle Publishers, 1989.

[2] Brown, H. D.. *Teaching By Principles: An Interactive Approach to Language Pedagogy*[M]. Prentice-Hall, 1994.

[3] Krashen, S.. *Principles and Practice in Second Language Acquisition*[M]. Oxford: Pergamon, 1982.

[4] Savignon, Sandra J. *Communicative Competence: Theory and Classroom Practice*[M]. Addison-Wesley Publishing Company, 1983.

[5] Wang, Ge, Zhou, Zhen. Intercultural Language Education in China: Problems and Prospect[J]. *Journal of Communication Practices Volume* 2/2, 2005.

[6] Widdowson, H.. *Teaching Languages as Communication*[M]. Oxford: Oxford University Press, 1996.

[7] Larry A. Samovar & Richard E. Porter. *Communication Between Cultures, fifth edition*[M]. Beijing: Beijing University Press, 2006.

[8] 胡穗鄂．文化与交际——新编实用英语教程[M]．广州：暨南大学出版社，2005.

[9] 周真，David R. Knapp. 体验跨文化[M]．昆明：云南人民出版社，2007.

[10] 高一虹．跨文化交际能力的培养："跨越"与"超越"[J]．外语与外语教学，2002(10).

[11] 胡文仲．跨越文化的屏障[M]．北京：外语教学与研究出版社，2004.

[12] 何自然．语用学习与英语学习[M]．上海：上海外语教育出版社，1997.

[13] 张鸿雁．民族偏见与文化偏见——中西文化比较新论[M]．沈阳：辽宁教育出版社，1993.

女歌人小野小町

张丽花

「小町（こまち）」一词在近代以前的日本，和中国的「西施」一样，是家喻户晓的美女的代名词。比如，吉备古国的美女也许会被誉为「吉备小町」，而浅草一带的美女也许便会被叫做「下町小町」。「小町」一词源于日本历史上有名的美女「小野小町（おののこまち）」，这在日本恐怕无人不晓。即便如此，这位著名美女的真实面貌至今却仍覆盖着一层神秘的面纱。她是何时、何地为何人所生的？如何长大的？又是在何地如何逝去的？都无从考证。她的存在仅凭『古今集』中收录的和歌及一些民间传说得到证实。

纪贯之（きのつらゆき）（868？—946）在『古今集』的假名序中描述道：「小町は古（いにしえ）の衣通姫（そとおりひめ）の流なり。」在此，小町被喻为传说中的美女衣通姫（そとおりひめ）。据『日本書紀』记载，衣通姫（そとおりひめ）是允恭（いんぎょう）帝的一个妃子，玉肤晶莹剔透，隔衣可见，美艳无比，且精于和歌。和歌山县的玉津岛神社自古以来就是把衣通姫（そとおりひめ）作为和歌神来供奉的。显然，后来小町的知名度远远地超越了衣通姬。当然，纪贯之（きのつらゆき）的一句赞誉不会有如此大的社会效应，小町的名气更源于她的才华和有关她的各种戏剧性或者说悲剧性的传说。

日本全国有很多名曰「小野」的地方，且都有关于小野的传说。据『世界大百科事典』记载，小野生卒年月不明，出生于出羽国，即今秋田县雄勝町的小野村。父亲是出羽国的郡司小野良实（よしむね）。小野9岁时随任期已满的父亲回到京都。成人后的小野小町美丽且具教养，进宫为仕，成为仁明天皇的后宫，深得宠爱。后由于藤原氏的阴谋而被疏远。因此，宫内生活并不快乐。仁明天皇殁后，对故乡的眷恋促使她回到了小野村。在这里，她建庵而居，静心咏歌度日。许多男子慕其美貌与才华，纷纭来访，留下了很多故事。其中，关于她与深草（京都市伏見区）少将的悲恋流传最广。

少将倾慕小町的美丽，申请了郡代职，离开京都追随小町来到小野，并传书表达了相思之意。小町却提出了苛刻的条件，即每日一枝植百株芍药。少将接信，立即从山上挖取野芍药种植，开始了表达爱情的百日之旅。然而不幸的是，在他精心种植芍药第 100 天的时候，无情的暴雨冲垮了木桥。桥毁人亡的惨剧撕碎了小町的浪漫。悲痛欲绝的小町将少将埋葬后，在旁另建一冢，言已身故后必葬于此。这就是两人的比翼冢，有名的「二ッ森」。

而『京都伏見歴史紀行』中也有类似的记叙。面对少将热烈的追求，小町令他「百夜通い」。

于是，少将每晚从自己居住的「欣淨寺（ごんじょうじ）」去拜访五六公里外「随心院」的小野。在第 100 天的晚上遭遇暴风雪，受冻身亡。现「欣淨寺（ごんじょうじ）」境内还有少将和小野的墓冢，及「墨染（すみぞめ）の井戸」。现京都「欣（ごん）淨（じょう）寺（じ）」就有名曰「墨（すみ）染（ぞめ）」的电车站和街道。据说，那口井中永不枯竭、源源不断流淌出的是少将思念的泪水。著名诗人西条八十为此咏道：

通う深草百夜の情け
小町恋しい涙の水は
今も湧きます欣淨寺

至于深草少将，『京都伏見歴史紀行』认为与他最接近的人物是和歌作家僧正遍昭（そうじょうへんしょう）（816—890）。一般认为，他是大纳言良峰冬嗣（よしみねのふゆつぐ）之子，平安京营造者桓武天皇之孙。曾官拜左卫少将，故传说中被称为“深草少将”。在宫中深得仁明天皇的喜爱。天皇殁后，悲痛之下出家为僧，曰遍昭（へんしょう）。是著名的六歌仙之一。据『欣淨寺（ごんじょうじ）略記』记载，「欣淨寺（ごんじょうじ）」就是遍昭为祭奠仁明天皇而建的。下面收录在『小倉百人一首』中他的这首歌被认为描述了他与小野的邂逅。

○ 天（あま）つ風雲の通（かよ）ひ路（ちふ）吹きとぢよ

乙女(をとめ)の姿しばしとどめむ

——空を吹く風よ、雲の中を通って天帰る道を吹いて遮っておくれ。

天女の姿をもうしばらくここに止めておきたいものだ。

此歌描述了宫廷「新嘗祭(にいなめさい)」① 或「大嘗祭(だいじょうさい)」② 翌日举行的「五節(こせち)の舞(まい)」的情景和歌者欲托风留住这美好场景的心情。其中的「乙女」被认为就是小野。

在日本，有关他与小野小町的爱情逸闻不胜枚举。他们的浪漫恋情从下面的『後選和歌集』收录的一唱一和的两首和歌中似乎也可以得到佐证。

○ いはのうへに旅寝をすればいとさむし

苔(こけ)の衣(ころも)を我(われ)にかさなむ

——石上ならぬ岩の上に旅寝をすれば肌寒くなりませんか。あなたの苔の衣を貸してください。

参诣奈良县天理市石上(いそのかみ)寺的小野小町听说遍昭也行到此，便以「心見む」为题致歌一首。歌中的「いわのうへ」是和歌的修辞法「洒落(しゃれ)」。它既指「岩の上」，又喻指石上(いそのかみ)寺。而「苔の衣」则兼指生于岩石上的「苔衣」和和尚的「僧衣」。遍昭戏答道：

○ 世をそむく苔の衣はただひとへかさねば

うとしいざ二人ねむ

——法衣(ほうえ)はたった一重、寒さを凌げないでしょう。

かと言って貸さなければ冷淡だ。さあ、二人で肌を寄せて寝ましょう。

这首「心見む」很显然不是在考验遍昭的向佛之心，而是在试探出家后

---

① 新嘗祭：每年收割季节由天皇主持举行的一种祭祀活动。用新收割的五谷祭拜以天照大神为中心的天地诸神。

② 大嘗祭：天皇即位后主持的第一次新嘗祭。是一代一度的大祭。

的他是否失去了风流心。

而『古今集』第十二卷开头收录的她的三首歌则把孤夜寂寞的女子对恋人的切切思念表现得淋漓尽致。当然，不可避免地它们都被与遍昭联系在了一起。

① 思ひつつ寐ればや人の見えつらん
夢と知りせば覚めざらましを　　（『古今集』552）
——恋しく思いながら寝入ったので、その人が現れたのだろうか
夢だと知っていたら、目覚めたくはなかったのに

② うたた寐に恋しき人を見てしより
夢てふものは頼みそめてき　　（『古今集』553）
——不意に落ちたうたた寝に恋しい人を見た その時から
夢という頼りないはずのものを頼みに思うようになってしまった。

③ とせめて恋しき時はむだたまの
夜の衣をかへしてぞ着る　　（『古今集』554）
——どうしようもなくあの人が恋しいときは
夢で会える呪いで寝間着を裏返して着るの

日本有一种俗信，认为把「夜の衣」翻过来穿着睡，就可以在梦中见到恋人。歌中反映了等待与异性的幽会和担心恋人移情别恋的焦灼、寂寞的心情。

除此以外，她与其他和歌家之间的对答情歌也很有名。由此，小野小町风流多情的文学真实便也由此产生了。然而，历史的真实究竟如何却无从考证。但是可以肯定的是，她的歌中充满了男性本位的社会性别差异意识。即便是拥有美貌与才情，同时身为贵族的小野小町也无法超越习惯的社会性别意识。因此，对青春与美貌的关注必然地在她的歌中占了很大的比重。她在『百人一首』著名的一首中流露出自己为众多男子所倾倒的花容月貌，在不知不觉中逝去的悲哀与无奈。

○ 花の色はうつりにけりな徒（いたづら）に

わが身世にふるながめせし間（ま）に　　『小倉百人一首』

——桜の花は色褪せてしまったなあ。我が身を徒にこの世に置き、むなしく時を経るばかりの、物思いをしていた間、空からは春の長雨が降り続けていたその間に

「世」有男女关系之意，这里指为恋人耗费了人生。不难读出其中所蕴涵的「この世は空虚だ」的佛教无常观。

而另一首歌则表达了因自己容颜衰老而情人变心的幽怨之情。

○ 今はとてわが身時雨にふりぬれば

言の葉さへに移ろひにけり　　（『古今集』782）

——私は老けてしまったので、あなたの言うことまでも変わってしまいましたね。

あんなに愛の言葉をかけてくださったのに

即便是美丽的才女，失去了昔日的光艳，其命运当然也是凄惨不堪的。于是，传说中的小町便有了一个落魄的晚年。歌谣「卒塔婆（そとば）小町」中她便成了满脸皱纹、弓腰驼背、一身污秽的乞丐婆。据『国語大辞典』记载，「卒塔婆（そとば）」是梵文的音译，译为高显处、方坟、圆冢、灵庙等。是为安放和供养佛舍利而搭建的土石或木结构的塔。它随着舍利信仰的发展被大型化，成为五重塔。「卒塔婆（そとば）」是五重塔的简化形式。在日本为 1 ~ 2 米的木板，竖立墓后，上刻梵文，作供养之用。9 世纪后期，日本原有的血秽观念与佛教的「女人（にょにん）罪業観（ざいごうかん）」相结合，形成女人「不净（ふじょう）」观，进而产生了禁止女性进入的「女人結界（にょにんけっかい）」。「女人結界（にょにんけっかい）」多为佛教圣地等。百岁的小町坐在「卒塔婆（そとば）」上休息，显然打破了「女人結界（にょにんけっかい）」的禁忌。路过的僧人企图劝说她离开。小町从救济的平等性出发，驳斥了女人禁制的不合理性。僧人诚服，并感叹道：「悟れる非人なり」。

『玉造小町子壮衰書（たまつくりこまちこそうすいしょ）』中晚年的小町脖子上挂着维系生命的粟豆袋，背负沾满污垢和油脂的布包，肘挂竹篮，随身带着破蓑笠。这是日本中世典型

的「非人」的打扮。「非人」是日本中世、近世身份制度中贱民身份的一种，是被村町共同体竭力排斥的存在，大多是流落外乡的乞丐、下层「遊女(ゆうじょ)」等社会最底层的人们。小町的晚年落魄传说把被社会家庭关系排斥在外的女性的悲惨境遇描述到了极致。显然，她的晚年传说里也反映了传统社会中家族或家庭对个人的社会保障或福利功能的重要性。同时，更重要的是它反映了女性价值取向和心理的时代特征，那便是容貌的价值比重于女性的重要性。

关于小野小町，没有切实的记载，仅有的画像也不能反映她的真实面貌。她的美丽便留给了人们以想象。但是，她的才华却是有凭有据的。她留下的众多和歌令她当之无愧地拥有了「三十六歌仙」之一席。

高桥认为，小町并非她的真名。在她生活的平安时代（794—1190），「~町」是后宫女子的称呼。一般认为「小町」即数名姐妹中的「小妹妹」之意。而从其姓氏可推测她是小野一族的女性。小野氏族系最早的遣唐使小野妹子的家族，自古以来便是京都市左京区上高野一带的名门望族。继妹子之后，历代皆被选为遣唐使，为中日文化的交流作出了很大贡献。其中，小野被任命为最后的遣唐使副使。其孙小野好古(よしふる)是天慶(てんぎょう)之乱的中坚分子。小野道風(みちかぜ)则是书家高人。奈良时代（710—784）到平安时代之间，小野一族在文武两方面皆功绩卓著。小野小町有可能是这名门望族的一员，拥有优越的生活，受到良好的教育。与传说相反，也许她还有一个与歌为伴的恬静、安详的晚年呢。

另据 NHK『歴史発見——小野小町伝説より』考证，小野有可能是仁明天皇的「更衣(こうい)」小野吉子。「更衣(こうい)」是天皇嫔妃的一种称谓，地位比「女御(にょうご)」低。「更衣(こうい)」可以在被称为「常寧殿」的建筑物中拥有一个自己的房间。那个被割开的四方形的空间就叫做「町」。顾名思义，「小町」之名便源于此。没找到确切的证据，但也许高桥的「小妹妹」之说也源于此呢。但是，如果小町确系「更衣(こうい)」，即便下一代天皇即位被赶出皇宫，她也应该有「更衣田」为生，不会像传说那样有一个落魄的晚年吧？

众所周知，小野小町生活的平安时代是日本所谓「国風文化」的形成时代。随着中国唐朝的衰落，日本停止了遣唐使的派遣。9 世纪后期，日本进入消化、吸收并融合唐文化的时期。平安中期，掀起了一股文化的国风化运动。当时，高尚的汉文学是贵族男子的必须教养。专为贵族子弟设置的大学、大学别曹等教育设施是不允许女性涉足的。为了满足自己对知识的渴求，贵族女性在宫中游戏「歌合(うたあわせ)」中找到了机会。于是，最能表达女性纤细的感性的仮名文字（主要是平仮名）迅速普及，并引起了日本语言文学的巨大变革。古典名著『源氏物語』（紫式部）、『枕草子』（清少納言）、『土佐日記』（紀貫之）等便是那时产生的。小野小町在这样的文化氛围中造就了自己的文学才能。

紀貫之关于她的歌风评道：「あはれなるようにて、強からず。いはば、よき女の悩めるところに似たり。強からぬは女の歌なればなるべし。」与她缠绵柔弱的歌风相比，在『歴史発見——小野小町伝説より』中，她却具有坚毅、清傲的一面。「更衣」小町尽管没有得到仁明天皇的多少宠爱，但在他殁后，她却为他坚守贞节，拒绝了所有倾慕者的追求。而她那些充满哀怨和眷恋的和歌都成了她对那位天皇不朽爱情的反映。而这种假说竟与下面的传说有一脉相承之感。

江户后期著名的纪行家、随笔家菅江真澄（1754—1829）曾访问小野村，在『菅江真澄遊覧記』中，以「小野の古里」为题，记录了一些当地的小町传说。其中有一则是关于近亲相奸的。

> 一位绝世无双的美貌女子，来到了小町父亲良实的身边。于是，小町诞生了。不久，此女子显出鹿身，入山而去。年幼的小町被拐到宫古。在宫古一带出落得美丽无比的小町与伟岸的父亲相遇，彼此为对方的魅力所吸引，竟结为姻缘。后小町得知对方实为自己的亲生父亲，她悲叹自己的罪孽之深，发誓从此不再与任何男子结缘。

这有些类似希腊神话爱狄普斯的传说。如果如学者所言，前者预示着男性宿命的话，那么后者是否可以说是东方女性所谓红颜薄命宿命观的反映呢？

不管怎么说，像中国的「西施」、「杨贵妃」一样，「小野小町」作为美女的代名词已深深地扎根于日本文化中，成为一个被提炼、抽象了的理想模型。而那些想象丰富、寓意深刻的传说叙述着人们对人生与社会的理解。通过有限的记载，和对小野和歌的诠释，人们把一个个的历史残像拼合在一起，描绘出了平安时代一位美女和歌作家的生活轨迹。在人们的意识中，小町的和歌与她的人生重合为一体。据此，我们是否可以窥见日本女性观冰山之一角呢？

今天，在传说的小野的出生地秋田县雄勝町，每年6月的第二个星期天，还在举行「小町祭」，选7名少女进行和歌咏读。自1998年起，他们的选美范围扩大到了全国各地，并命名曰「小町峰会」。一千多年后的今天，人们对女性的评价标准有了多少变化，又没有多少变化呢？

参考文献：

[1] 竹西寛子. 古今集 [M]. [出版地不详]：岩波書店，1997.
[2] 宇治谷孟. 日本書紀 [M]. [出版地不详]：講談社，1988.
[3] 片桐洋一. 後選和歌集 [M]. [出版地不详]：岩波書店，1990.
[4] 菅江真澄. 菅江真澄遊覧記 [M]. [出版地不详]：平凡社，2000.
[5] 高橋ちはや. 歴史を動かした女たち [M]. [出版地不详]：中央公論社，1997.
[6] 大隈和雄等. 日本史 [M]. [出版地不详]：清水書院，1984.
[7] 加藤道里等編. 新編常用国語便覧 [M]. [出版地不详]：浜島書店，1991.
[8] 峰岸純夫編. 家族と女性——中世を読む [M]. [出版地不详]：吉川弘文館，1992.
[9] [作者不详]. 国語大辞典 [Z]. [出版地不详]：小学館，1996.
[10] [作者不详]. 世界百科大事典 [Z]. [出版地不详]：平凡社，1980.
[11] 山本眞嗣. 京都伏見歴史紀行 [M]. [出版地不详]：山川出版社.
[12] NHK BOOK. 歴史発見——小野小町伝説より [M]. [出版地不详]：角川書房，1995.

浅议阿拉伯书法艺术

马利章

阿拉伯书法艺术是一座璀璨的宝库。对阿拉伯书法艺术进行深入研究，会给我们提供理解不同文化的途径，消除中、阿两大民族文化上的陌生感。阿拉伯书法家在书法领域的天赋表现得淋漓尽致。这门艺术令他们引以为豪。在阿拉伯国家的各种建筑物上，各种颜色的石头巧妙地镶嵌在一起，构成精美的书法艺术。

阿拉伯书法家把他们的内在感受和外部经历融合在一起，借助饱含感情的笔画，把各自的感情淋漓尽致地呈现在书法中。一个书法家心灵和内外世界的结合，往往导致个性化的字体的产生，当然这和长期的知识积累是分不开的。一种字体的发展常常体现了书法家独特的个性，书法也被认为是个人自我修养的体现。

阿拉伯书法艺术起源于手抄本的《古兰经》。伊斯兰教的第一部经典，就是用阿拉伯文写成的。在穆斯林们看来，文字和语言一样是促成人和真主之间交流思想的一种媒介和手段，这就使阿拉伯文字蒙上了一层玄妙神圣的色彩。为了表示对真主的虔诚和尊敬，阿拉伯书法家不仅创造了各种形式优美的字体，而且聘请第一流的书法家抄写经文。这些书法家在当时也必然享有崇高的社会地位。

阿拉伯字母让研究者着迷。有些人甚至认为，这些字母是只有安拉才知道的符号；有的人则根据自己的理解来揣测含义。毫无疑问，这些字母有象征意义，促使穆斯林不断求知、研究、探索。字母传达词义，词义表明思想。

阿拉伯书法家对阿拉伯字母从细节到整体都很重视。阿拉伯字母出现在建筑物上，起到装饰、美化建筑物的作用。阿拉伯书法家根据几何原理，研究各种书法的结构，在书法艺术的创造与组合方面挥洒自如，以便保持字母间的连续性。阿拉伯书法艺术是文明的象征，优美的书法使道理更加明白，是精神上、视觉上美的享受。

一、发展过程

阿拉伯书法艺术是阿拉伯艺术园地中的一朵璀璨的奇葩。经过 1 400 余年的发展，其技法、造型和艺术表现力都达到了完美的境地，充分体现了阿拉伯民族的审美情趣，极大地丰富了阿拉伯人的精神生活。

伊斯兰第四任哈里发阿里（600—661）说过："一手好字使真理熠熠生辉。"由此可知，阿拉伯书法艺术的诞生是和人们的需要息息相关的。《古兰经》标准本产生后，各地誊写者为使自己的抄本更加光彩夺目，各施其技。在传统书法的基础上，又创造出许多带有地方色彩和书法家个人风格的艺术体。到了伍麦叶（661—750）时代，随着阿拉伯帝国的日益昌盛，书法艺术也有了很大发展。到阿拔斯（750—1258）时代，帝国国势鼎盛，中国造纸术的传入促进了阿拉伯书法艺术的繁荣和普及，出现了百家争鸣的局面。当时，最杰出的书法大师是有"书法三杰"之称的伊本·穆格莱（886—940）、伊本·白瓦勃（1022 年卒）和古特·穆斯台绥姆（1298 年卒）。他们既效法古人，又善于创新，不仅为阿拉伯书法艺术归纳、总结了各种字体的规范笔法，制定了书法艺术的基本规则，还融合各种字体的长处，创造了一些新的字体。

阿拉伯字母无论是手写或者印刷都可以连写，具有高度的简洁性。语言简洁成为一种修辞，也使得音符和语法更加简洁、明白。用同样大小的铅字以阿拉伯文和拉丁文印刷同一个句子就可以看出阿拉伯语的简洁程度。

土耳其伊斯坦布尔大学东方学教授、东方语言专家利塔尔说："在卡玛尔运动前，学生们做讲座笔记速度很快，因为阿拉伯文字母简略，但今天他们不得不要求将句子重复好几次，他们解释说因为拉丁字母无法简缩，阿拉伯文书写是世界上最容易、最清楚的书写。"①

阿拉伯字母可根据位置、距离、面积的不同而变化，具有弹性，因此在书写时，可以根据情况不同而灵活驾驭它，无论字母连写或分写都能准确记载内容，尽管字母书写变化无穷，但并不影响内容的表达。

阿拉伯字母优于其他字母的一大特点是形式多样。字母的每一形状都有自己的位置和用途，以适应需要，在书写时可繁、可简。

---

① 引自阿拉伯文期刊《埃及》第 25 期。

二、阿拉伯书法的种类

阿拉伯艺术家非常重视书法，创造了各种各样的形式，直到今日，还在不断探索、改进。阿拉伯书法种类繁多，各种书法都有自己的特点。随着历史的推移，阿拉伯书法在发展的历程中日渐丰富。它大致分为6种：

（1）库法体：以伊拉克的库法城命名，又称为“棱角体”。其特点是：字体古朴方正，强调纵向笔画，线条笔直、棱角清晰，带有明显的装饰性，相当于中国的金石文或隶篆体。因其具有几何图形的美感，用于美化建筑物及雕刻在工艺品上，或者作为碑碣、墓石、金属货币的文字。

（2）纳斯赫体：该体书写清楚、端正、庄严，容易辨认，便于手写。纳斯赫（al-Naskhi）阿拉伯文是“抄写”之意，故又称做“誊抄体”、“手抄体”。其字母大小均有严格规定，适用于日常生活的记录、通信。该体广泛用于抄写《古兰经》，几乎成了《古兰经》的专用体而沿用至今。

（3）迪瓦尼体：该体字形委婉多变，洒脱大方。迪瓦尼（al-Diwani）阿拉伯文是“文书”、“宫廷”之意，故这种字体又称为“公文体”或“宫廷体”。书写时，其字母的形状大都要用圆弓形予以表现，且不加音标和装饰符号，使其整体有如浮云滚滚、波浪起伏，令人赏心悦目。常用于书写文告、贺词和文章标题。

（4）波斯体：该字体的发明者是波斯著名阿拉伯文书法家米尔·阿里·大不里士（1360—1420），并使该体成为波斯历代相传的一种书写体。其特点是字母大小、长短悬殊，词句间隔松紧不等。其中曲线笔画较为突出，书写时要随时变换笔头，以随势运笔。该体由纳斯赫体演化而来，笔画流畅，字体优美，字体由上而下向左倾斜。流行于伊朗、阿富汗、巴基斯坦等地①。

（5）苏勒斯体：该字体具有端庄、高雅、华丽等特点。书写时字与字盘曲在一起，造型成花卉、水果等形状，字形复杂，字体雍容华贵，有“阿拉伯书法之母”之称。“苏勒斯”（al-Thulthi）一词系阿拉伯语音译，意为“三分之一”，故译为“三一体”、“三分体”。该体多用于书写中堂、条幅、匾额、书名和标题，以及建筑物上的装饰性文字。

（6）卢格阿体：该体的特点是手写自然、简洁明快。书写时用笔尖完成字母的构形，是一种简便易写的大众化的字体，多用于撰写著作、信札、笔

① 宛耀宾主编：《中国伊斯兰百科全书》，四川辞书出版社1999年版，第100页。

记。“卢格阿”（al-Ruqi）一词系阿拉伯语音译，意即“行书”。这种字能连笔草书，因其较适应现代节奏而日益普及。

三、装帧与装饰

阿拉伯书法的装饰艺术构成一个多姿多彩的艺术世界，在世界艺术史上享有盛誉。随着时代的进步和发展，阿拉伯书法家不断探索字母的内涵，摸索出适用于装饰的字体，产生了装饰书法。

阿拉伯书法家在书写形式上用形式多样的几何图形构成字母，有直线、方形、长方形、圆形、椭圆形、菱形、圆锥形、半圆形、多边形、螺旋形和波纹形，或单用一种，或数种套用，或与植物图案结合使用。以后又在简单的几何图形的基础上发展出星形和格子形。

这是阿拉伯书法视觉上的延伸，它首先能吸引人的目光，引导人们从一种形式想到另一种形式，从一个意境到达另外一个意境。这种书写的目的在于将意识引向思考。

阿拉伯书法家在书写《古兰经》经文时，进行装饰上的创造和深化，用各种精美的形式来书写。推动他们进行创造的动力是信仰。经文的每一章节的开头，更是用极其精美的书法来表现。因为圣训说：“任何工作未用‘奉至仁至慈的真主之名’开始的都是不完整的。”

阿拉伯书法家以创造性的思维和丰富的想象力，对书籍进行精美的装帧，无论是美妙的图形，还是树木花草的植物画都装帧得相映成趣。植物图案，以植物的花叶为基本形式，使树叶、花卉、攀缘植物、藤条植物互相缠绕，创造出或工整对称，或夸张变形的无数图案。书籍装帧是推动阿拉伯装饰艺术发展的主要因素之一。至于手写的书籍，书法家对每一页都要精心装帧，尤其是开始的章节，更是装帧得妙不可言。有的用精细美丽的树叶图案、花叶等装帧书籍。每章标题和结尾部分都要绘画装饰性框边。即一打开书，就令人肃然起敬。

阿拉伯字母除用于装帧书籍外，还用于其他的装饰。阿拉伯字母形状各异，加以夸张变形，就能变化出无数的独具魅力的图形。文字装饰的图案被认为是阿拉伯装饰艺术的点睛之作。阿拉伯装饰艺术处处可见。首先是宗教场所——清真寺。其壁龛上刻着各种花纹和图案，地毯上编织着精美的花边图案，墙壁上镶着各种色彩的天然石块构成的图案，艺术化的文字饰带悬挂在大厅内，随风飘动。这一切构成了一个美的世界。各种图案的文字还被编织进挂毯或地毯中，烧在陶器上，装饰在各种建筑物的墙壁和门窗上，雕刻在水晶或玻璃制品上，镶嵌在工艺品上。这些装饰构图完美、结构精巧。这是阿拉伯装饰艺术的特点。一件手工艺品往往就是一件精美的艺术品。

权威与可信：中、英学者学术语篇中的人际附加语

田有飞

一、引　言

中国英语语言学研究者与英国同行相比是如何表达立场的？或者说，这两个分属不同地域的群体如何就所述内容传达自己的判断、意见和责任度等人际意义的？该问题从根本上说涉及怎样认识学术语篇这一特定的语类；对其作专门探讨可在理论上为深入研究此领域增添新的信息。从现实角度看，国内英语语言学研究队伍在学术活动不断国际化的进程中日益壮大；越来越多的研究者用英文撰写论文，与英国等国的同行交流。探讨他们相比于后者如何表达立场对英文论文撰写者来说无疑具有直接的参考价值。

本研究的原动力来自于对学术写作本质的认识。学术写作本质上是一个社会过程。这是 Hyland（1997，1998，1999，2000，2002）一直以来坚持的学术写作的社会学观点。他认为，写作不是简单地考察自然，而是创造一种世界观；现实的构建离不开社会过程，故文本不是世界的精确表述，而是作者从自己所处的学术团体的视角出发，经过选择、突出、象征等行为对世界进行“过滤”后的结果。这样的看法跟认知科学的世界上不存在纯粹客观的真理性认识的研究成果（Vygotsky，1987）一脉相承。被 Van Dijk 尊称为“政治语言学教父”的 Chilton（2004：58）也指出，人们生产语篇时以“自我”（即“我”或“我们”）为指示中心，沿时间、空间和情态三条轴线确定实体的相对位置，从而有可能将千变万化的实体结构概念化；而情态轴线表达的是“自我”，不止是“此在”（here）和“现在”（now），同时还是真实性认识（epistemic true）和正当道义（deontic right）的原点的总体思想。Hyland 强调

的社会过程和 Chilton 论述的情态轴线都表明：确立合理立场、由此建立互动关系和评价系统是学术写作的一项重要内容；其最终目的是增强论文的说服力。笔者认为，增强说服力意味着作者要按学科规范构建一个包含权威和可信这两个基本元素的“作者自我形象”；“权威”指作者对命题的自信，而“可信”则指能让读者信服。而通过合理的人际语言制衡权威与可信则是成功投射作者形象和表达立场的关键。

表达立场的语言手段绝不局限于传统语法所热衷的情态动词，而是多种多样。这其中就包括本研究要考察的似乎跟主语一样普遍的人际附加语(Thompson, 2004: 151)。这里的人际附加语是指原则上不能作主语、而又给小句添加人际意义的语言结构：其典型形式是副词词组和某些介词短语①；但这样的结构不时也以小句形式出现，从而形成一个词组—小句连续体②。近年来，不少学者以不同标签对此类语言现象作不同程度的探讨。Hyland（1999）就将立场划分为证据性（evidentiality）、情感（affect）和关系（relation）三要素，并由此建立了一个框架来描写哲学、微生物学等八门学科各自论文中立场的基本语言特征。该框架经 Hewings & Hewings（2004）适当调整，用来分析伯明翰大学 MBA 专业母语非英语的学生的毕业论文与该领域期刊中英文论文在运用“先行 it 句型”表非个人化立场上的不同。此外，Conrad & Biber（2000）考察了口头语、新闻报道和学术语篇中立场的副词标示语，指出：三类语篇的副词标示语在语义类型、语法形式和位置上的不同倾向与语篇的交际目的和生产环境有关。另外，McEnery & Kifle（2002）对厄立特里亚的大学二年级学生同英国高中生论文中认识型情态的使用情况所作的对比分析一定程度上也涉及人际附加语。这些研究都有助于了解作者如何定位自己跟主题和读者的关系。

但是，副词词组/介词短语与相应的小句结构在语篇中执行的功能会因级阶等因素的变化而有所不同，从而创造不同的立场意义。上述诸研究的一个严重不足正在于未区分这一点：Hewings & Hewings 和 McEnery & Kifle 分别排除了副词词组和情态小句；Hyland 跟 Conrad & Biber 均未区分诸如 obviously 和 It is obvious 的级阶，而是将它们笼统归类。这些处理方式都不利于整体把握人际附加语在学术语篇中的分布特征和作用。本文对中、英英语语言学研究论文中的人际附加语作描写分析，正是希望在一定程度上弥补该项研究的不足和为

---

① 参见 North, 2004: ix; Thompson, 2004: 62.

② 参见 Halliday & Matthiessen, 2004: 43-46.

如何建立互动关系、有效表达立场提供一些帮助。

二、语料与分类

本研究以中国、英国学者两个语料库为基础。鉴于中国的英语语言学研究主要是应用语言学的，本研究随机抽取的语料都限定在最近几年公开发表的、直接讨论应用语言学话题的论文。中国学者语料库（以下简称C库）包含32篇论文，涉及40名作者；这些论文均来自国内出版的Teaching English in China，US-China Foreign Language和Sino-US English Teaching等学术期刊。英国学者语料库（以下简称B库）包括12篇论文，涉及14名英国作者；12篇论文都取自著名的Applied Linguistics学刊。两个语料库中的每篇论文都排除了图表和注释两部分；经扫描统计，最后形成了各约为92 300个英文单词的语料库。两个语料库相近的语场使它们具备了较大的可比性，从而确保研究过程和研究结果的可信度①。

基于C、B语料库，笔者建立了一个描写框架。其中的分类和相互关系如下图所示：

- 人际附加语
  - 情态类
    - 隐性
    - 显性
      - 主观
      - 客观
  - 非情态类
    - 强调
      - 隐性
      - 显性
    - 态度
      - 隐性
      - 显性

情态类人际附加语是指表达作者在肯定与否定两个极性之间的语义区域就命题或信息的可信度作出或高、或中、或低的价值判断的人际附加语。如：always，plausibly，I believe，It seems likely等。这类用语传达的是作者对命题的责任度。always和plausibly为隐性附加语，即以副词词组形式嵌入承载命题或

① 本研究采用手工方式而非语言学软件对人际附加语作统计分析。原因有二：本研究涉及句法结构，但目前尚无成熟的用于句法结构分析的软件；意义是语篇分析的核心问题，而游离性是其基本特征。对某些附加语，手工分析能依据它们出现的具体位置确定其传递的究竟是语篇的还是人际的意义（参见Martin & Rose，2003：272）。

信息的小句中；而单独以小句形式出现的 I believe 和 It seems likely 则是显性的附加语。情态类显性附加语又有主、客观之分：诸如 I believe 这类小句是主观的，其典型的体现形式是心理过程和某些言语过程；而类似于 It seems likely 的小句是客观的，往往体现为关系过程。

非情态类人际附加语包括强调和态度两种。体现强调功能的附加语传达作者对信息或命题力的肯定：作者表明某一命题是真实的，或当前条件下可作出某一推理或结论，如 clearly, evidently, It is true, It follows 等；或者作者强烈提醒读者注意某一点，如 exclusively, It should be noted, We should note, It is essential to understand 等。态度领域的非情态类人际附加语表达的是作者的情感或评价，如 hopefully, interestingly, paradoxically, surprisingly, It would be foolish, It is safe, It is a common fault, It is surprising，等等。必须承认，态度和强调之间的非情态类人际附加语的区分不是绝对的，带有较大的主观色彩。非情态类人际附加语也可按情态类的标准作隐性、显性划分，但显性的非情态类附加语基本上是客观的。这可能跟学术语篇的客观性性质有关。

三、发现与讨论

（一）总体情况

中、英学者在人际附加语的使用上存在明显差别。其基本情况见表 1。

表 1　中、英学者使用人际附加语的总体情况

语料库	人际附加语总次数	情态类附加语总次数	非情态类附加语总次数	每 1 000 个词中的频率
C	633	195	438	6.86
B	1 190	360	830	12.90

表 1 显示，中国学者使用人际附加语的次数远不及英国学者的高，在各项指标中仅占英国同行的 50% 略高一点；两国学者使用情态类人际附加语的次数远低于非情态类附加语的次数：前者相比于后者似乎是一种受限的表达方式。而两国学者每 1 000 个词中使用的人际附加语的频率差异表明英国学者更倾向于把命题或信息置于个人判断和评价的框架之中。下面将从不同方面对这一总体情况加以讨论。

（二）情态类人际附加语

1. 隐性情态附加语

C、B两个语料库显示，中、英学者在“是”与“非”之间的语义区域对命题或信息的可信度作出各种程度的可能性判断时都使用到了隐性的和显性的附加语；两国学者使用隐性附加语的比率都远高于显性附加语的比率。基本情况见表2。

表2　中、英学者使用情态附加语的基本情况

语料库	情态附加语总数	隐性附加语	显性附加语	隐、显性之比
C	195	152	43	77%；23%
B	360	255	105	71%；29%

但上述数据并不能说明中、英学者在使用情态类人际附加语上没有除数量之外的其他明显的不同。表3统计的是中、英学者采用隐性视角表达对命题的立场时各自使用的最频繁的10个隐性附加语（频率相同的并列）。

表3　中、英学者使用的隐性情态附加语

中国学者	英国学者
often（31）	often（73）
usually（22）	always（21）
always（15）	usually（19）
sometimes（13）	frequently（17）
never（13）	perhaps（16）
frequently（12）	sometimes（15）
probably（9）	normally（12）
certainly（6）	probably（11）

续 表

中国学者	英国学者
commonly (5)	certainly (10)
possibly (3)	never (10)
maybe (3)	
normally (3)	
seldom (3)	
(共138处，约占隐性情态附加语的91%)	(共 204 处，占隐性情态附加语的80%)

表3表明，中、英学者各自使用的最频繁的10个隐性附加语词汇和频率似乎相差不多。然而，这种相似背后却存在两点明显的不同。首先是C库中没有出现就陈述或意见表达较低可信度的perhaps，而该词在B库中出现的次数却较多：笔者发现，尽管perhaps在传统的使用观念中主要是口头的，但或许正因为如此，英国学者用在论文中表达立场时就显得自然、亲切①。如：

①In example [30], it is *perhaps* fear which is dominant. (B库)

②Indeed, in cases such as [82], [13] and [14], it is *perhaps* more appropriate to talk of "delegated averral", since the reporter is stating his or her own view but indicating that it is shared by, or originates from someone else. (B库)

③... the assignment takes on some of the qualities of a presonal narrative or diary: she writes for herself *perhaps* more than for others. (B库)

其次，虽然中、英学者使用的词汇及其频率相似，但连同它们的加强成分(intensifiers)一起考虑时，就出现了较大区别。作为一类语法词汇，加强成分的基本功能是增强或减弱立场或态度的力量（volume of force)。而英语中增强

① 类似的作用在语篇功能范畴中同样存在。如传统上小句复合体内部的结构连词but和so近年来已突破了传统写作的束缚，逐渐取代了however和therefore这两个连接附加语的位置，在小句复合体之间分别执行差异性配比和衔接功能。这些情况在Halliday & Matthiessen (2004) 以及Widdowson (2004) 的行文中是比较普遍的。该转变表面上是语篇衔接的，但同时也是人际的，如使论述更加接近口头讨论场合。相似阐述详见Thompson & Zhou (2000)。

成分（如 extremely，sharply）似乎远比减弱成分（如 fairly，somewhat）多，使用得也更频繁[①]。不过，B 库显示，英国学者除使用增强成分外，也使用了相当多数量的减弱成分，其中最突出的是对 fairly 一词的使用。换言之，英国学者在增强和减弱两个等级上对加强成分这一语言资源有着合理的挖掘和运用。相反，C 库中的学者似乎走向了一个极端：其中只有增强成分的运用，却不见减弱成分的影子。比较以下几个典型的例子（加强成分为黑体，隐性附加语为斜体）：

④The data revealed that spatial prepositions do not mostly occur as adjuncts, as they are commonly taught in textbooks, but are **more** *often* used to introduce post-modifying phrases ...（B 库）

⑤... but this may not always be desirable—for example, repeated use within an essay will **almost** *certainly* become counterproductive.（B 库）

⑥...（mental processes reporting verbs in academic papers typically refer **fairly** *unambiguously* to other written texts in which those thoughts have been expressed-see Thompson and Ye, 1991）.（B 库）

⑦ For example, certain genres, such as instructional leaflets（Al-Sharief, 1996）and direct sales letters（Frank, 1989）, exploit this option **fairly** *frequently* in the form of questions 'from the reader' which the writer then answers.（B 库）

⑧In China and the US, important positions are **most** *often* held by men instead of by women.（C 库）

⑨Both groups employ attribution shields **most** *frequently* and plausibility shields **least** *frequently*.（C 库）

C、B 语料库表明，英国学者即便用表高值的隐性附加语对命题或信息作可能性判断时，往往都会用 fairly，somewhat，almost 等减弱成分加以限制，而中国学者在类似情况下却趋向于以 most，very，quite 等予以加强，使得可能性判断近乎于定言判断。

2. 显性情态附加语

如表 2 所示，中、英学术语篇中均使用了相当多数量的显性情态附加语。这佐证着 Biber et al.（1999）有关英语学术语篇的一个显著特征是以“先行 It

① Martin & Rose, 2003: 38.

句型”为代表的显性表达法的出现率要远比在新闻报道和对话等语域中高得多的调查结果。显性的情态表达法是系统功能语言学中人际语法隐喻的一个重要内容：它拓展着情态语义域，使得原本为隐性附加语表述的人际成分以小句形式获得了命题的地位，即把情态意义与真正的命题内容在小句层面相互分离，将人际评判从简单小句中的副词词组或介词短语级阶提升到小句连续体中的一个小句级阶①。C、B 语料库中该策略的普遍存在表明：中、英学者都能遵从学术语篇的这一基本特征，以有关及物性（心理、言语、关系）过程小句作人际投射，对命题或信息进行情态判断。他们使用的显性主、客观的情态附加语的情况见表4。

表4 中、英学者使用的显性主、客观情态附加语

语料库	显性主观及比例	显性客观及比例
C	22；51%	21；49%
B	37；35%	68；65%

表中显性主、客观情态附加语的比例对比说明，中、英学者都注意到“科学客观性”是学术语篇的必备特征②：他们创造客观判断视角的场合要远比突出主观视角的场合多。

但这绝不是说两国学者就没有不同之处。表 5 所列的是笔者将 Thompson（1996）有关文本声音的五类划分融合为三类，以及中、英学者使用最频繁的几个显性主观附加语结构的情况（括号内为出现次数）。

表5 文本声音及中、英学者使用最频繁的几个显性主观附加语结构

中国学者	英国学者
作者自我声音	作者自我声音
I think（2）	I argue（10）
We think（1）	I believe（3）

① 参见 Halliday & Matthiessen，2004：626.

② Markkanen & Schroder，1997.

续 表

中国学者	英国学者
The authors think (2)	We believe (3)
This paper believes (1)	I would suggest (2)
The authors believe (1)	
他者声音	他者声音
They think (1)	They (Collin, Sinclair, etc.) argue (5)
They (Bailey, Halliday, etc.) believe (8)	Others believe (1)
	This suggests (1)
	She assumes (1)
	Some have claimed (1)
文本内读者声音	文本内读者声音
It is believed (3)	It might/could be argued (5)
It is assumed (2)	It has been argued (3)
It is presumed (1)	It is expected (1)
It is supposed (1)	It is held (1)

从表5中表情态意义的动词来看，中、英学者的一个最大区别是前者使用believe的次数最多（13次），而中国学者根本没有使用的argue则是英国学者使用得最频繁的（23次）。这一明显不同值得注意。believe和argue虽然按Thompson（2001）所区分的假设—真实和让步这两类学术语篇语境来看都主要出现于前者，但严格照及物性系统来看，believe是心理过程，而argue是将心理过程believe延伸并外化的言语过程。这或许是argue更容易让读者体会到文本声音的缘故。当然，文本声音有着不同的来源。就中国学者的believe而言，其主要表现为他者声音和文本内读者声音。而英国学者的argue则不同：它较集中地以作者自我声音出现，并且与其他两类声音保持某种平衡。有趣的是，中国学者不时地以The author/This paper believes/thinks这类显性主观情态附加语小句传递作者自我声音。这明显是受到汉语写作语境的影响：作者似乎

出于谦卑，有意不以 I 或 we 作为感受者或说话者，以减轻潜在的面子威胁行为①，而英国学者却无类似情况。换句话说，中国学者从汉语语境嫁接来的这类附加语策略是不为英语写作语境所接受的。总之，中、英学者的学术语篇虽然都反映着 Kristeva（Moi，1986）基于 Bakhtin（1981）强调的语言使用的对话本质提出的语篇多声（heteroglossia）的思想，但彼此又有所不同：中国学者的显性主观情态附加语尽管比例不低，但语篇声音似乎主要是他者或文本内读者的，而英国学者却在兼顾这两者的同时强化自己的声音，其手段则是 I/we argue 等的多次使用。

中、英学者在显性客观情态附加语上也存在着明显差别。表 6 反映的是他们使用显性客观情态附加语的基本情况。

表 6　中、英学者使用的显性客观情态附加语结构

中国学者	英国学者
It seems（6）	It is possible（23）
It is common（4）	It seems（11）
It is impossible（3）	It may be（7）
It is likely（1）	It appears that（5）
It is possible（1）	It would（4）
	It might（3）
	It is impossible（3）
	It could（2）
	It can（1）
	It is plausible（1）
	It is feasible（1）
	It is probable（1）
	It is usual（1）

① FTA，见 Brown & Levinson，1987.

表6中一个最直接的区别是中国学者采用显性的客观视角来判断命题的确实性的手段远不及英国学者的丰富多样。前者有限的语言策略极易使他们在构建“自我形象”和确立人际意义上走向纯粹客观的极端。而这一点使我们注意到中、英学者的又一个且更为本质的区别：正如 argue 一词在显性主观情态附加语策略中不受中国学者青睐却为英国学者频繁使用一样，情态动词（modal operators）在显性客观情态附加语结构里未被中国学者运用但却成为英国学者表达立场的又一重要资源。为直观起见，笔者将表6中含情态动词的结构集中如下：

It may be (7)
It would (4)
It might (3)
It could (2)
It can (1)

其中的情态动词除 would 表中值判断外，其余的均表低值判断[①]。它们在显性客观附加语结构中的意义是：取代了 be 或 do 在语气部分的限定成分（Finite）位置，即将情态小句中有关（伪装的）命题的可信度的肯定或否定的极性判断改换为不定判断。试比较：

⑩Within the limits of this, **it is impossible** to present a detailed report on the test but the result indicates that... （C 库）

⑪... **it would seem impossible** for the subject to fragment. （B 库）

上述两句的黑体部分虽然都表达着隐性附加语 impossibly 所含的人际意义，但区别是⑩将该意义伪装成命题时是以 it is impossible 这一肯定判断形式出现的，而同样的过程在⑪中则因 would 占据了 does 的限定成分位置而复加了一层人际意义，即 would impossibly。B 库中，would 和 might 等低值主观情态动词在显性客观情态附加语结构中的使用提出的问题是作者为什么对命题本身或命题的归属是不确定的[②]。在笔者看来，这种不确定性是积极的而非消极的：

① Halliday & Matthiessen, 2004: 624.
② 参见 Thompson, 2001.

一方面，它拓展着命题的可能性：作者意识到其他声音存在的可能，故具有弹性的提法为进一步发展自己的观点留有余地；另一方面，既然任何一个情态符号都是作者陈述个人观点而非客观事实以及表达礼貌的常用策略①，那么B库中显性客观结构中的复式情态则传达着作者婉转的语气，呈现出客观理性的态度。而这一点是C库中没有的。

（三）非情态附加语

情态类附加语涉及的是中、英学者就命题的可信度表达何种判断或责任度从而确立自己的立场的。而非情态类附加语则与作者对命题或信息的评价有关，是作者确立立场的又一重要资源。这种语言手段的出现次数如表1所示远比情态类的多。但统计发现，就隐性的非情态附加语而言，中、英学者的区别主要是数量上的；本质的区别则表现在显性的非情态附加语上，故这是本节讨论的重点。

1. 隐性的非情态附加语

表7表明，中、英学者的隐性非情态附加语同他们的隐性情态附加语一样在数量上远超过显性的附加语结构。

表7　B、C语料库中的隐性非情态附加语

语料库	非情态附加语总数	隐性附加语	显性附加语	隐、显性之比
C	438	322	116	74%；26%
B	830	728	108	87%；13%

从强调和态度两个分类看，中、英学者的一个共同特点是强调类的隐性非情态附加语次数要远比态度类的多。就态度而言，中国学者只有少得可怜的4次，仅限于 surprisingly（2），superficially（1）和 fundamentally（1）这三个词；英国学者的28次，为 unfortunately（7），admittedly（3），fortunately（2），potentially（2）等16个词体现。可以说，尽管两国学者表态度的隐性用语都不及表强调的多，但英国学者的用词还是要比中国学者的丰富。

① Thompson，2004：73.

表 8 是 C、B 语料库中两国学者各自使用最频繁的 10 个强调类隐性非情态附加语及次数:

表 8 C、B 语料库中两国学者各自使用最频繁的 10 个强调类隐性情态附加语及次数

中国学者	英国学者
only (65)	only (64)
mainly (22)	clearly (53)
generally (20)	partly (50)
quite (17)	in fact (29)
clearly (13)	typically (26)
fully (11)	simply (26)
of course (10)	of course (21)
naturally (8)	already (21)
simply (8)	fairly (17)
in fact (7)	necessarily (15)

这一模式表明，中、英学者使用的非情态强调附加语有着某些相似之处。如，only 是他们使用得最频繁的一个词；还有几个词虽频率排位不同，但都是双方学者使用的。不同的是，英国学者没像中国学者那样频繁地使用 quite 这一表增强意义的词 [见三（二）1]；该词在 B 库中只出现过 5 次。而中国学者也没像英国同行那样习惯性地使用 fairly [见三（二）1]，typically，necessarily 等词（后两个词在 C 库中都只出现 2 次）。这里的 3 个词同情态附加语中的 perhaps 在英国学者的语篇中似乎有着独特的地位：它们表明却又不刻意夸大作者的立场。如：

⑫As Table 6. 3 shows, only the articles in philosophy, which *typically* consist of long narratives engaging the arguments of other writers, consistently included the cited author in the reporting sentence.（B 库）

⑬Although the most frequent words in a text (prominent) are not *necessarily* stylistically significant (salient), they provide a good way into a text. (B 库)

2. 显性的非情态附加语

这类附加语结构理论上也可作主、客观之分，但或许是 C、B 语料库还不够大的缘故，其中没有发现表态度的主观结构，且表强调的主观结构也很少。稀罕的主观结构似乎暗示作者强调知识生产的非个人性，从而不愿将自己的身份明显投射到文本中①。C 库中唯一的主观强调结构为仅出现过 2 次的 I would like to；而 B 库中的类似结构有 3 个，但都只出现过 1 次：we should note，we do not need，I propose to assign. 很明显，这几个结构的作用是引导读者注意新的命题或信息。但它们在 C、B 语料库中的有限数量使得主、客观之分失去了实际意义，因而下面主要讨论显性客观结构。

（1）态度类显性非情态附加语

C、B 语料库显示，中、英学者用以表态度的显性非情态附加语分别为 53 次和 54 次。与同类的隐性非情态附加语相比，它们所占比例分别为 93% 和 66%。这说明中国学者更加倾向于使用显性的非情态结构来表达态度。两国学者常用的态度类显性非情态结构及频率如表 9 所示。

表 9　中、英学者常用的态度类显性非情态附加语及次数

中国学者	英国学者
It is difficult (10)	It is difficult (13)
It is important (10)	It is important (5)
It is easy (6)	It is useful (5)
It is significant (3)	It is appropriate (4)
It is better (2)	It is surprising (3)
It is understandable (2)	It is easy (3)
	It is effective (2)
	It is desirable (2)

① 参见 Hyland, 1999.

跟隐性的态度用语一样，中、英学者的显性态度用语有着相似的一面：各自使用频率最高的两个形容词都是 difficult 和 important；其他未列入表 9 的形容词数量也大致相当：中国学者除几个名词外，使用了 11 个形容词，而英国学者的全部是形容词，为 12 个。

然而，有一个不同点不容忽视：中国学者在显性的态度用语结构中使用的形容词有几个是英国学者那里根本找不到的；它们各自出现的次数尽管只有 1 次，但在学术语篇中却显得极不协调：

⑭It is *imperative* that these plans are practical ...（C 库）

⑮It is *requisite* for each leaner to have a study plan ...（C 库）

⑯It is *discouraging* for the students to have an EFL teacher whose command of the language is far from adequate ...（C 库）

⑰It is *strange* to require them to draw on self-questioning sheets to ...（C 库）

⑱It is *amazing* to have a native speaker communicate while writing.（C 库）

这一问题 Hewings A. & Hewings M.（2004）也注意到了，但未说明原因。或许这些用语之所以不协调是因为它们在很大程度上违背了文本是学术团体中享有同等地位的作者、读者的共同产品的学术常规；中国学者以此力推己见的做法难免在一定程度上破坏了语篇中“读者友好”的氛围。

（2）强调类显性非情态附加语

中、英学者用于表强调的显性附加语的次数分别为 63 次和 54 次；与同类隐性的用语相比，所占比例各为 16.5% 和 7.2%。综合上一小节的数据来看，中国学者相比于英国同行更多地用以“先行 It 句型”为代表的显性结构来表达对命题的评价。两国学者常用的强调类显性非情态结构及次数如表 10 所示。

表 10　中、英学者常用的强调类显性非情态附加语及次数

中国学者	英国学者
It is necessary（17；含 3 处 unnecessary）	It is clear（15）
It is hard（7）	It is necessary（7）
It is clear（3）	It is worth noting（7）
It is essential（3）	It is true（5）

续 表

中国学者	英国学者
It is evident（2）	It is evident（2）
It is natural（2）	

表10显示，虽然中国学者使用显性客观结构表强调的比率要比英国学者的高，但常用结构有不少相同之处，尽管频率有所不同；中、英学者所用的形容词clear，necessary，evident等都有着表达深信不疑的命题的意味①。

⑲It is *clear* for example that many people would regard privileged knowledge essentially as a manifestation of a power struggle within society.（B库）

⑳It is *necessary* to have a clear definition of the goal of language teaching.（C库）

但他们之间差别还是不小。笔者发现，在这种高估命题的模式中，中国学者却缺少英国同行善于使用的It is worth noting这一结构。如：

㉑*It is worth noting* that this draft, and others like it that I have collected, lend themselves well to discussion using the type of grid above, and can be exploited as the basis for awareness training with groups working on academic writing.（B库）

㉒*It is worth noting* that ... options here are not necessarily fixed by the initial choice...（B库）

It is worth noting结构与其说是强调的，倒不如说是亲和的；其表达着作者诱发读者参与的意图。换句话说，常用强调结构并不被英国学者一味地用来表达强调或自信，他们同时还注意到读者的存在与参与。相比之下，中国学者却过分自信地强调命题，很少留心与读者的互动。

中国学者的这种倾向同样存在于表10之外的其他强调用语中；这些用语是B库中类似结构里所没有的。如：

---

① Hewings A. & Hewings M., 2004.

㉓It is a new *reality* that today's English, even the spoken British English, is already a mass of hybrid forms. （C库）

㉔It is no *wonder* that most of the English teachers in rural areas are not capable of practicing. . . （C库）

㉕It is *incredible* that an organism can learn the language structure without any knowledge of language essence. （C库）

这些用词似乎要说服读者必须接受后面的命题，但这些命题实际上是一些可信度不用怀疑的信息，因而对具备一定背景知识的读者而言，这种策略显得多余而武断。

相比于中国学者生硬的强调结构，英国学者在类似结构上同对待显性客观情态附加语结构一样，会不时地以低值情态动词加以限制。这在一定程度上制衡着他们的自信或强调语气。如：

㉖Yet it *may be necessary* to construct an integrated research program ... （B库）

可以说，中、英学者使用的显性客观强调结构虽有共同之处，但具体的分析表明：中国学者似乎倾向于一味强调（overstate），而英国学者却有折中，不忘弱言陈述（understate）。

四、结 语

树立权威且可信的“自我形象”是作者从事学术论文写作的两个基本诉求，是如何确立立场的中心内容，也是增强论文说服力的重要因素。而所有这一切都要通过相应的语言策略才能实现。就人际附加语而言，中、英英语语言学研究者有着明显的不同。从量上说，中国学者使用的该类语言手段远不及英国学者的多。这可能是前者的论文中有着大量定言（categorical）判断的一个直接原因，而这就使得中国学者笔下的人际空间变得相对封闭和狭窄。从质上讲，中国学者在语篇生产过程中所作的人际“闯入”相比于英国同行是直率的：他们就命题无论是作可信度判断，还是传达自己的感受或评价，都有着就“高”不就“低”的严重倾向。从“心”、“行”合一的行为主义观点看，中国学者似乎在借此建立一个权威的作者形象：自己认为有意义的也是读者看重的，而读者看重的正是自己要着力肯定的。然而，由此树立的权威形象是单边的，故未必是可信的，因为它不是在英国学者那种通过保持强、弱人际附加语的合理平衡使得对命题的陈述留有余地的条件下产生的。

造成中国学者在人际附加语运用上的匮乏和错位的一个可能的重要原因是他们对英语学术语篇的认识存在偏差。中国学者倾向于将学术写作视为个人对事实作非个人化的描述的过程；他们尽管也强调客观科学性，但却是个人眼里的客观科学性。实际上，学术语篇有着母语学术团体认可和共享的交际目的，这是其作为特定语类存在的理据；这样的理据不但限制着语篇的图式结构，而且还影响和遏制着对内容和语言的选择①。这就是说，学术写作不是个人行为，而是基于团体视角表达团体利益的活动。中国学者的不少人际附加语之所以显得生硬，可以说是没有充分考虑团体因素的结果。从这个意义上讲，中国英语语言学研究者在本体研究过程中，有必要留意英国学者对包括人际附加语在内的人际语言系统的运用，以便撰写出符合英语写作语境的论文，做到有效交流。

参考文献：

[1] Bakhtin, M. M.. The *Dialogic Imagination*, trans. Emerson, C. and Holquist, M. Austin: University of Texas Press, 1981.

[2] Biber, D. Johansson, S., Leech, G., Conrad, S. and Finegan, E.. *Longman Grammar of Spoken and Written English.* Harlow: Longman, 1999.

[3] Brown, P. and Levinson, S.. *Politeness: Some Universals in Language Usage.* Cambridge: Cambridge University Press, 1987.

[4] Chilton, P.. *Analysing Political Discourse*: Theory and Practice. London and New York: Routledge, 2004.

[5] Conrad, S. and Biber, D.. Adverbial marking of stance in speech and writing. In: Hunston, S. and Thompson, G. (ed.). *Evaluation in Text: Authorial Stance and the Construction of* Discourse. Oxford: Oxford University Press, 2000:57-73.

[6] Halliday, M. A. K. and Matthiessen, C. M. I. M.. *An Introduction to Functional Grammar* (3rd edition). London: Hodder Arnold, 2004.

---

① 参见 Swales, 1990: 58.

[7] Hewings A. and Hewings M.. Impersonalizing stance: a study of anticipatory "it" in student and published academic writing. In: Coffin, C., Hewings A. and O'halloran, K. (ed.), *Applying English Grammar: Functional and Corpus Approaches*. London: Arnold, 2004:101 - 116.

[8] Hyland, K.. Scientific claims and community values: articulating an academic culture. In: *Language and Communication*, 1997, 16 (1): 19 - 23.

[9] Hyland, K.. *Hedging in Scientific Research Articles*. Amsterdam: John Benjamins, 1998.

[10] Hyland, K.. Disciplinary discourses: writer stance in research articles. In: Candlin, C. N. and Hyland, K. (ed.). *Writing: Texts, Processes and practices*. London and New York: Longman, 1999:99 - 122.

[11] Hyland, K.. *Disciplinary Discourses: Social Interactions in Academic Writing*. London: Longman, 2000.

[12] Hyland, K.. Genre: language, context and literacy. In: *Annual Review of Applied Linguistics*, 2002(22):113 - 135.

[13] Markkanen, R. and Schroder, H.. *Hedging and Discourse: Approaches to the Analysis of a Pragmatic Phenomenon in Academic Texts*. Berlin: de Gruyter, 1997.

[14] Martin, J. R. and Rose, D.. *Working with Discourse: Meaning beyond the Clause*. London: Continuum, 2003.

[15] McEnery, T. and Kife, N. M.. Epistemic modality in argumentative essays of second-language writers. In: Flowerdew, J. (ed.), *Academic Discourse*. London: Pearson Education Limited, 2002.

[16] Moi, T. (ed.). *The Kristeva Reader*. New York: Columbia University Press, 1986.

[17] North, S.. Glossary for Coffin, C., Hewings A. and O'halloran, K. (ed.), *Applying English Grammar: Functional and Corpus Approaches*. London: Arnold, 2004:ix - xxiii.

[18] Swales, J.. *Genre Analysis: English in Academic and Research Settings*. Cambridge: Cambridge University Press, 1990.

[19] Thompson, G.. Voices in the text: discourse perspectives on language reports. In: *Applied Linguistics*, 1996, 17 (4): 501 - 530.

[20] Thompson, G.. Interaction in academic writing: learning to argue with the

reader. In: *Applied Linguistics*, 2001, 22 (1): 58 – 78.

[21] Thompson, G.. *Introducing Functional Grammar* (2nd edition). London: Arnold, 2004.

[22] Thompson, G. and Zhou, J.. Evaluation and organization in text: the structuring role of evaluative disjuncts. In: Hunston, S. and Thompson, G. (ed.). *Evaluation in Text: Authorial Stance and the Construction of Discourse.* Oxford: Oxford University Press, 2000: 57 – 73.

[23] Vygotsky, L.. Problems of *General Psychology*, trans. N. Minick. New York: Plenum Press, 1987.

[24] Widdowson, H. G.. *Text, Context, Pretext: Critical Issues in Discourse Analysis.* London: Blackwell Publishing, 2004.

日本战争题材电影对战争责任的概念偷换

赵毅达

日本政界右翼对于法西斯侵略战争罪行的事实从来都积极粉饰和妄图篡改，这对于世界已不是什么新鲜的话题了。在日本，除去右翼政客们公开的妄言叫嚣和见诸于文字的黑白颠倒的教科书篡改记录和政治语境之外，对于日本侵略战争的原罪性认识似乎已被搁置了。特别需要指出：相比于生硬晦涩的政治话语，生动活泼的艺术媒体所能偷换概念的本领远超出一般人的想象，尤其是20世纪的主要娱乐传媒手段——电影。

当今大众对于外界的认识日益依赖于视觉和听觉的饕餮盛宴。毋庸置疑，电影在当今以至于将来对受众的价值取向和认识方式的影响必然是深远和长久的。电影，作为世界性的文化传播载体能通过生动的影像和声音，潜移默化人们的价值观和认识。“艺术为政治服务”是个永远也无法被否认的跨国界的命题，而且将会是一个永久性的论断。自然，电影作为艺术的一个鲜活的表达手段肯定毫不犹豫地与本国的政治气候同气相求。但如果这个载体所承载的就是是非颠倒的内容，不难想象，它所传达的日本政治的观点就难以如同日本政治家一样为世人所认清其本来面目。

以下就日本电影（战后）的一些常见的偷换概念的手法进行浅析。

一、悲情武器

随着日本战后的经济重新崛起，电影的生产也纳入到了文化发展的快车道。日本先后成立了“东宝”、“松竹映画”等一批制作力量雄厚的电影厂和公司，也涌现出了诸如黑泽明、小津安二郎等这样的国际电影大师。尤其在当时，亚洲很多国家大多忙于建设经济而疏于对电影产业的关注，世界电影市场中来自日本的电影可以说是亚洲的生力军。日本电影的题材中一项重要内容就是拍摄战争。除去古代、近代历史片外，镜头很多都对准了第二次世界大战。

大凡看过日本战争影片的人都会对电影中描写的战争产生一种深深的悲伤。这并非完全来源于战争本身的残酷性，而是刻意地描述片中主人公所身处的绝境，在观众的心理上制造出悲戚共振，巧妙地把注意力转到了对某个个人的命运关注上，战争被简单地置换成了某个具体的人的生存和幸福的敌人。在这个强大的敌人面前，个体的生命都是那么的脆弱和不堪一击，同“战争”这个抽象而强悍的对象相比而言，影片中的人物理所当然地充当了弱势群体，全是受害者。

很多中国观众所熟悉的著名动画片《萤火虫之墓》改编自日本作家野坂昭如的同名小说，再经由动画大师宫崎骏的工作室制作完成。被冠以反战影片“经典”的评价。它描写的是战争后期日本普通人的生活悲剧。主人公是两个未成年的孩子。由于父亲战死、母亲病故，家也在空袭中被毁，失去生活来源的兄妹俩备受亲戚们的冷眼，不得已只好栖身于山洞内。由于长期营养不良，年幼的妹妹在饥饿和颠沛流离中渐渐地衰弱，最终病重夭折了。影片除了动用大场面描述战争的涂炭生灵（如美国飞机用燃烧弹进行大规模空袭），更加注重日本民族特有的“从小处下工夫”的描写手法。片中那个妹妹临死前还念念不忘的空糖盒，荒凉的山野里漂荡在空中的点点萤火，无不营造出一个让人泪流满面的氛围。这样一个超级“催泪弹”连同它的原著一块儿成了反战体裁作品的代表之作。然而请注意：作品耗费大量笔墨所刻画的是日本被轰炸后的遍地瓦砾、人员流离失所。战争被虚化成一个没有起因、超级抽象的悲惨背景，而在这背景前挣扎的众生所呈现出的苦难都是由这个从天而降的意外灾难带来的。看着一幅幅惨不忍睹的画面，观众的情绪当然会自动发生转移，偏向片中受难者一方。内心的怜悯会蒙蔽——至少是暂时地——追问“这一切是为什么”的理性。

拍摄于20世纪90年代初的《肉弹》，也就是选取了一个文弱的学生“眼镜”为主人公。他被强征去驾驶人操鱼雷，漂浮在茫茫大海上，守株待兔式地等待着美国军舰撞上门来。片中用了大量镜头拍摄“眼镜”在海上的非人生活。与此相映成趣的则是使用了很多插入式叙事镜头来讲述之前他与女孩“兔子”在战火中邂逅并爆发出的感情。那编织而成的一个美丽的背景与观众眼前的事实形成了强烈的反差，因而轻易地就博取了观众的同情。最后，在战争结束后多年，仍旧保持坐在漂浮桶上的姿势、已变成一具骷髅的“眼镜”

被海浪冲回到一个海滨浴场而引起了人们的恐慌和骚动的一场戏则把悲剧的色彩推到了高峰。恐怖中携带着悲情重重地撞击着每一个观众的心。——战争是多么的可憎啊！—— 一声叹息中，对历史真实的探寻，对战争责任的拷问，对战争主流受害者们冤屈的愤懑，都统统变成了对“战争”——这一被抽象了的词汇的憎恨了。日本电影在观众们泪眼蒙眬中完美地转换了战争问责的对象。

同时我们注意到，日本“二战”题材的影片几乎都把镜头对准“普通百姓”，所寄予同情的也都是普通平民所遭受的痛苦和无奈。片中的人们都被描写成“被卷入”战争，都处于“受动”状态。可以说，日本战争题材电影是一种“个人悲剧”或是“个人苦难”的陈述。基于这样的平台，就很难说日本战争题材电影具有真正意义上的反战性，因为首先是对战争的起源和性质作了刻意的缺省，如同一道只有作料而始终未见主菜的料理。只有“理”（精心地加工，甚至是粉饰）而没有“料”，看起来色泽光鲜，细品之下就乏善可陈。它没有清算战争的责任，没有对战争参与者进行鞭挞和对其灵魂进行拷问。除了如祥林嫂一般一遍又一遍地诉说“痛苦”、显示“伤痕”外，在片中鲜有对发动战争的忏悔和反省。

这一类型的电影之尤者莫过于描述广岛和长崎的“原爆”题材了。日本近代作家井伏尊二的名著《黑雨》被改编成了同名电影，曾经获得东京电影节大奖，也夺魁柏林电影节。影片整个的主体色调始终是昏暗和肮脏的。主人公是一位在广岛原子弹轰炸中的幸存者，但同样遭到了核辐射。与她同时登场的都是些在原子弹爆炸中受伤和濒临死亡的人。故事在一种沉重的气氛中展开，看着开头就知道结尾。无非是痛苦、死亡。加上一场点题的黑色的雨描绘了遭受原子弹袭击后如同人间地狱的广岛。又是一次悲情的重演，又是一次向世界表达“我是受害者”的叨念。在日本战后电影中，“原爆”被日本文化界定义为一个悲怆的符号，凡属“二战”题材的影片几乎不能免俗地祭起这面大旗。经过它的包装，发动战争的原罪和加害者的嘴脸就显得不那么刺眼。

二、激情武器

2006 年的新片《男人们的大和》，则着重凸显了日本战争题材电影的另一偷换概念的手法——激情主义。

在此专门解释一下：此说乃是突出个人或集团所表现出的激昂奋进的精神力量，它同上述的悲情主义看似相反的路线，但绝非南辕北辙，而恰恰是殊途同归。常用词“悲壮”的“壮”即是此意。历史上占日本文化重要一环的“武士道”可以说就是以此为核心的。

《男人们的大和》运用倒叙手法：战争中被炸沉的日本战列舰“大和”号上的幸存者以及他们的后人在“大和”号沉没60周年时到沉没的海域凭吊，以此开始追忆往昔的故事。在这艘本名就为“大和”的战舰上，编导着力地把这艘船刻画成日本（大和民族）的精神的载体。片中浓墨重彩地宣扬的是战友情、民族情、对国家和民族的忠诚以及对亲人的挚爱和责任，面对即将来犯之敌的同仇敌忾使这部电影看起来更像一首祖国保卫者之歌。为侵略而建造起来的“大和”号战列舰俨然被美化成力挽民族危难的中流砥柱。而战舰上的水兵们在镜头前都成了一群为了保卫国家而大义凛然、慷慨赴死的勇士。通过电影我们不难看出，武士道的熏陶在这个民族是如何地根深蒂固。导演熟练地运用电影语言塑造出一个个生动鲜活的20世纪40年代日本军人的形象：脸上没有战争带来的沧桑，全都洋溢着青春的豪迈和冲动，满腔豪情地准备和“来犯”的美军作殊死搏斗。电影一扫《黑雨》般沉闷晦暗的色彩，取而代之的是明快鲜亮的画面、整齐的军容、帅气的面孔，朝气蓬勃的精神面貌丝毫看不出处于战败前期的日本人内心的彷徨和困惑。经历了激烈的战斗，“大和”号被击沉，它没有成为日本在战败前垂死挣扎的救命稻草，而是可笑且可耻地葬身海底。三千多官兵一同被它带入了地狱。如果那些日本士兵真的是无辜的，那么他们应当诅咒这艘载他们驶向万劫不复的地狱的鬼船，应该去痛恨那些命令他们白白送死的国家领袖。遗憾！在电影中并没有看到这样的元素。观众看到的是不折不扣地执行命令的战争机器，听到的是“为了亲人和天皇而战”的豪言壮语。通过战前对士兵们与各自亲人的慷慨诀别和义无反顾地登上“大和”号出征的铺垫描写。特别是对一名在此前战斗中一只眼睛已经失明的军士仍然偷偷上舰加入这一有去无回的孤舰出征的那场戏的刻画，更加重了“壮志豪情”的感染色彩。影片接着过渡到了“大和”号的最后一战。这一场戏成了全片的高潮：“大和”号独自在海面上迎战蜂拥而来的美国战机编队，士兵们人人奋勇，个个当先。血肉横飞的场面没能让他们退缩，直到战斗到最后一息。对于必死的结果表现出了无畏的果敢。正如武士道所宣扬的：生如樱花灿烂，死如樱花悲壮。这样的场景确实是把激情和悲壮突出到了极致。该片的结尾也颇耐人寻味——模仿了美国大片《泰坦尼克号》的场景，画面是沉没在水下的“大和”号残骸，画面随着摄影角度的转动缓缓绕战舰一周，同时主题歌在悠缓、深情地唱道：“如果我能再次回归，将继续守护在你的身旁……”据统计，该影片在日本电影市场的排名目前位于第三。报道还称很多日本人边流泪边看……

日本著名的历史学家家永三郎曾说过，战争是“总战争”，发动战争不能只是追究上层阶级的责任，人民也在其中起到了推波助澜的作用，至少是表现出了默许……所以完全有理由反对那种把战争责任和老百姓完全脱钩的中庸、调和的话语。《男人们的大和》恰好是对这种语境的一种嘲弄。绝大多数日本人对日本的战败投降，对世界上已成定论的关于战争的性质并不能心悦诚服地接受，仍旧抱有“虽死犹荣”的观念，起码也是一种“胜王败寇”式的讥讽心态。所以在日本的电影中，在虚幻的世界里，日本的编导们一次又一次地弘扬“豪情”、表现“精神”，力图达到的目的无非就是：让观众在这些豪迈的煽情表演面前，产生出心灵的共鸣，对于那些可爱的电影中“英雄”的死引发出惋惜、同情，进而完全忘却这些银幕上的“皇军”曾经如何地犯下禽兽不如的罪行，从而一批又一批地把走出电影院的不懂得历史的日本人从真诚的忏悔中拉回来，转而助长一种负面、狭隘的民族情感。

类似的电影还不得不提一提《我愿为你赴死》。之所以这样，是因为日本右翼的干将——东京都知事石原慎太郎亲自为这部电影题词：“谨以此片，献给所有日本人。”这是一部取材于日本神风特攻队的影片，有真实的原型。这使得该片在欧美市场上更有了受关注的理由。不妨看看西方媒体对此的评论：

西方媒体对此片的不良苗头也很警惕。英国路透社2月23日在报道中就直接把石原称为“民族主义者”。《苏格兰人报》的题目也很能说明一切：《日本电影颂扬神风特攻队》。

美联社2月24日发出的一篇报道，其态度更为直接。文章称：“日本总有一些人，以卡通或者其他形式来改变世人眼中的战争形象，这就是他们的如意算盘……一些日本漫画作者将‘二战’期间的盟国领袖设计成胆小鬼或令人生厌的恶魔；还有一些人干脆继承了日本‘二战’时的军事宣传手段，把日本士兵打扮成胜利归来的样子，与家人幸福地拥抱、接吻，与邻居分享喜悦。其中一个叫小林义则的漫画家在他的作品中直言日本在‘二战’的形象是正面的，进行的战争是光荣和正义的。”文章对此的评价是“极其荒谬”。

较之于《我愿为你赴死》，拍摄得更早的一部反映神风式自杀的影片《萤火虫》也是通过描写队员们的普通生活来煽情的。首先使观众觉得他们和自己是一样的普通人，有着对美好生活的憧憬，并运用大量插入的蒙太奇式画面来讲述片中人物的往昔生活和对未来的期待。当然，爱情也是常用的手法之一。尤其是迸发于使命与人性冲突之际、绽开在生离死别关头的爱情故事，越发地抓住了观众的情感神经。在一切美好都似乎触手可及的一瞬间——命令下达了！生命即将永远地逝去，希望只能成为无法实现的梦想……在这种艰难抉择之中，影片中的队员人人都表现得义无反顾。送别场面：一杯水酒；一条印有日本太阳旗的白毛巾被每个队员郑重地扎在额头前；队友间的拥抱，互拍肩膀；请不出击的人转寄写好的家信，或是爱情的信物；日本人特有的鞠躬，再鞠躬；雄壮的音乐响起，队员登机出征。而后，画面就转到驾机冲向敌舰，慷慨赴死。一系列近乎于脸谱化的表演和公式化的场景都是为营造出"风萧萧兮易水寒，壮士一去兮不复还"的豪气。在高呼"天皇万岁"的口号声中，战争中正义与非正义的原则又一次被歪曲。

无论如何，清醒的人总还是有的。《朝日新闻》的主编渡边恒雄就曾说过：说队员勇敢赴死，并在死前高喊"天皇万岁"，这完全是个谎言。然而，普通百姓是很缺乏辨别力的，如果希特勒的"谎言重复一百遍也会变成真理"的逻辑是成立的话，后果堪忧！

三、"伪盲摸象"

盲人摸象，《汉语成语词典》的解释为："比喻看问题片面，以偏代全。"日本战争电影除了善于利用上述的两种情感武器来抓住观众的心理、达到偷换概念的目的外，在对战争事实（战例）的选取上也是"匠心独到"。表现为对战争全过程链条式的因果关系进行有目的的截取和掩盖。乍看之下，如同盲人摸象，突出了某个局部，这当然可以用电影时间上先天性限制来搪塞，但无可否认的是日本电影的"盲人摸象"却绝对不是看不到问题的全面和本质，乃有意为之。

大凡日本所拍摄的战争片几乎都以"二战"后期，尤其是以太平洋战争后期为主要取材对象（不包括与他国合拍的影片）。也有少量的是描写日军在东南亚作战的影片（如《野火》）。但无论是上述的哪一类型影片，其中出现的敌人都是美国！几乎闭口不谈同其他反法西斯国家的作战（如中国）。因为同中国的作战被搬上银幕的话，必然不可避免地涉及日军的攻城略地、日军的野蛮屠杀……这些都会触及日本上下非常敏感的神经，是属于"禁区"的话题。所以，"二战"题材的电影差不多都是"日美大战"，可谓"匠心独到"。

首先，在太平洋战争后期，日本已经丧失了进攻能力而转为守势。日本帝国不可一世的气运一路走低。随着在太平洋中途岛、瓜达尔卡纳尔群岛作战的失败，日本已一步步迈向覆灭的深渊……而盟国，尤其是美军，在太平洋战场上势如破竹，通过逐岛争夺的“蛙跳”作战，一天天向日本本土逼进。此时的日本帝国已是被打掉牙的恶狼，犹作困兽之斗。取材此时的战事呈现给观众的是日本军队乃至于日本整个民族都处于前有强敌、后无退路的绝境中。弹尽粮绝的士兵如何艰难地支撑，用生命的代价迟滞着美军向日本本土推进的速度。战争初期所拍摄的那些日军耀武扬威的“胜利”场面的影片，那些对被侵略国人民犯下滔天罪行的胶片都被战后电影编导“巧妙”地隐去了，就连那段时期的历史事实也被有效地“遗漏”了。战后的战争电影往往是：炮火连天中尽显男儿忠勇，残垣断壁下唯听妇人啜泣。

其次，电影编导在选择片中的“敌人”方面也煞费苦心。在本文提到的几部电影中，日本都是在同美国作战。此外，还有很多本文中没有一一详述的影片，诸如《野火》，描述东南亚丛林中日本士兵在穷途末路的情况下竟然发生人吃人的惨剧。本片也改编自同名小说。作者大冈升平曾参与作战后被俘。作为反战小说，一经出版便引起广泛的关注，也奠定了作者中坚作家的地位。如果说小说源于作者自身的经历的话，那么数量众多的电影就绝不是个人的原因而出现前述的雷同，除非有意为之。

面对强大的美军，本已是江河日下的日本就越发显得势单力孤，这样就为“败战”成为理所当然埋下了伏笔。也就是说，日本是在同空前强大的美军交手中力所不支才失败的。同时，通过电影光、影、音的综合运用，极力渲染美军的攻击力。我们可以从很多的影片中看到这样的场景：成群的美军轰炸机黑云压城般地飞临日本，把死亡投向“无辜”平民，到处是大火，到处是哭喊（本文所述的“悲情手段”）。或者就是处于明显劣势的日军仍然保持高昂的气概，奋不顾身地同破坏自己家园的美军作“玉碎”式的自杀式决战（本文所述的“激情手段”）。一石数鸟，既抹杀了日本因为发动非正义的侵略战争而在反法西斯盟国的共同打击下土崩瓦解的历史必然性，又可以借机宣扬“武士道”精神，助长狭隘的民族情绪，于潜移默化中改变日本人对战争的正确认识。可以说是因果倒置、是非混淆的极佳范例。

最后，在这种故意闭着眼睛摸大象的过程中，日本战争电影还极力把战争中对垒的另一方抽象化、机械化（非人化），以衬托己方的形象丰满、富于人情味。日本的战争片中，美军上镜的形象几乎就停留在各种战斗机器上：飞机、坦克、军舰。日本似乎就是在同这些机器作战，就算是出现美军身影的画面都作了长程、广角镜头处理：一群头戴钢盔、穿着咔叽布作战服的人在宽阔的背景画面上缓缓而行……而且大多使用的还是纪录片所截取的片段。战争片的另外一方被彻底剥夺了“露脸”的机会，镜头全都对准了日本军人！观众在被屏蔽了能正确了解一方情感、思想的机会的影片中当然只会把感情全部地倾注在被塑造得丰满生动的另一方。日本战争电影的“伪盲摸象”的手段给普通观众带来的是局部化、被改头换面的战争形象，是日本文化界在潜流中迎合政治右翼势力的掩耳盗铃。

四、结语

如前所述，当今电影语言能够在很大程度上决定受众的判断，影响他们的评判话语。在年青一代对政治言论的关注程度日益减低的日本社会，通过电影等影音媒体获取认知和传承文化信息已是一个重要的潜移默化的方式。非但日本，这种趋势在未来世界范围内都将广泛存在。正因为如此，我们对电影这个载体上所承载的“货物”如不进行认真的甄别，势必会默许很多非主流的不正确文化因素流入受众的价值观中。

日本战后所拍摄的战争题材电影无一例外地都烙有“反战”的印记。内容形式上也进行了新的加工，镜头前表现个人的生活与思想的剧情成为主流；似乎很能体现“以人为本”。然而通过以上几个层面的简单分析就能看到，日本对于发动战争的原罪依旧极不愿意承认。在面对世界上多数由于他们发动战争而受害的国家和受害者的目光时，“顾左右而言他”，从中很容易看出日本民族的狭隘和自恋情结。日本在电影这一民众娱乐传媒的大舞台上粉饰战争、掩盖战争的责任追究问题，把日本等同于其他受害国，抹杀原则性地申请“一视同仁”的同情，甚至是颠倒是非，在对战争原罪的追究上一再含糊其辞地歪曲战争的正义性与非正义的对决，与政治上的右翼势力沆瀣一气，在“反战”的论调下为日本军国主义设坛招魂。这不能不引起我们的警惕。

（注：引自 http://www. sdhh. gov. cn/news/Article_Print. asp? ArticleID = 14405）

参考文献：

[1]塚田，義房．常用国語便览[M].[出版地不详]：浜島書店，[出版年不详].

[2]日本学刊，2006(5)、(6).

第四部分　翻译研究

现代旅游宣传对中国古典文学翻译的影响浅析

——以美秀博物馆《桃花源记》译本为例

董丹萍

一、引　言

现代旅游宣传资料与中国古典文学，尤其是与诗歌、散文之间有着千丝万缕的联系。旅游目的地的魅力有很大一部分就来自于古代诗歌的不朽与增色。例如，苏州城外的寒山寺就由于《枫桥夜泊》而名扬天下。日本的美秀博物馆则和陶渊明的《桃花源记》有着深刻的渊源。很多的旅游宣传资料都会包含有古典诗句与散文、对联，等等。

古典文学是现代旅游文化资源之一，具有特殊的神奇力量，是旅游目的地核心的吸引元素之一。但是，古典文学作为旅游宣传资料的一部分，却对其本身的翻译产生了很有趣的影响。其中，游客身份的代入，使得古典文学中的历史甚至国别因素、情感，还有审美因素，遭受了某种程度的过滤。

二、美秀博物馆《桃花源记》

美秀博物馆是华裔建筑大师贝聿铭的杰作。据说，他第一次看到日本京都滋贺县丰富完整的自然景色时，就赞叹其为世外桃源，并成功地以桃花源的概念建造了美秀美术馆（Miho Museum），并获取了很多国际大奖。

美秀博物馆的景观介绍中，专门有一个精美的网页，上有《桃花源记》及其英文译本，并在译文下补充了一段：

Only after taking a gently sloping path lined with verdant cherry trees, passing through a tunnel and crossing a bridge can the Miho Museum be found. It was conceived as a paradise on earth by its architect, I. M. Pei, whose concept of the museum was based on this Chinese classical poem, "Peach Blossom Valley". Upon his first visit to the site on which the museum now stands, he was moved to declare, "This is Shangri-La."①

而游客的赞美也使得此地特别令人向往：想象落英缤纷、春光明媚的时节，沿着樱花盛开的路径前行，一种期待的心情隐隐酝酿着。然后，走进一座隧道，隧道内凉意袭人，弯弯的隧道无法一眼望穿。转个弯再往前行，出了隧道，过一座桥，白色合掌型的美秀博物馆端正地立于前方②。

（一）游客身份的代入

现代游客寻求更多的是一种体验，要么是历史，要么是文化，要么是冒险，要么是民族风情，等等，或者说在旅游中寻求更多的是参与感。那么旅游宣传资料中除了最基本的地理位置、风景、活动、门票等之外，最重要的是要让读者产生一种亲临其境的感觉，并且积极感受这个地方的魅力。

那么，游客身份的代入就成了古典文学翻译中一个不易察觉的手段。所谓游客身份的代入，就是使游客在阅读中国古典文本时，能感觉到这个故事似乎就是在描述自己的经历，或者说就是自己期待中的旅游经历。

以日本美秀博物馆网上宣传资料中《桃花源记》的翻译为例。桃花源的理念就是一个很大的吸引元素。游客在参观美秀美术馆时，体验到的第一个感受，或者说他们期待的旅游体验，很可能就是理想的桃花源圣境。那么，在宣传资料中，中文的《桃花源记》吸引的自然是中国文化的承袭者和爱好者，那么英文译本的《桃花源记》吸引的自然也是爱好中国文化、憧憬理想圣境的人，或者说游客。

但是，这两个身份——文化的追寻者和游客，是有某种冲突的，虽然更多时候，它们是相辅相成的。为了吸引更多的游客，英文的《桃花源记》，或者说，在翻译《桃花源记》时，就使用了很微妙的翻译策略和手段。其中最明

① http://www. miho. jp/english/landscap/landscap. html.

② http://www. wretch. cc/blog/CafedeRiver&article_id=2766556.

显的策略，就是游客身份的代入。

为了使古代中国的文本适应现代旅游业的需要，在汉译英的过程中，采取了很多的翻译策略。

1. 消除时间的模糊性，而给予具体的时日

譬如，美秀版本的《桃花源记》英译，就给原文中似乎永恒的渔人追寻世外桃源的形象，加入了更多、更为细致的时间坐标。

晋太元中，武陵人捕鱼为业；缘溪行，忘路之远近。（19 个汉字）

美秀版本：

Once upon a time there lived a fisherman in Wuling, Eastern China in the Taiyuan Period of the Jin Dynasty. One day, as he was rowing up a mountain stream daydreaming, he was unaware of the distance he had traveled.（40 个单词）

大家比较一下戴维斯（A. R. Davis）的译本：

戴维斯版本：

During the Taiyuan period（376—396）of Jin a man of Wuling, who made his living as a fisherman, ascended a stream, forgetful of the distance he traveled.（28 个单词）

戴维斯严格遵照原文的句式特征，特别是遵照句子的顺序来翻译。“晋太元中”对应 During the Taiyuan period of Jin，“武陵人”对应 a man of Wuling，“捕鱼为业”对应 who made his living as a fisherman，“缘溪行”对应 ascended a stream，“忘路之远近”对应 forgetful of the distance he traveled。

陶渊明描写了一个大致的历史年代、一个大致的地名、一个渔人，接着就马上开始讲述故事。这一点很类似寓言的讲述，其重点在于故事本身，而非故事的地点和时间。戴维斯也严格按照原文进行翻译，几乎一口气不停地在第一句就将故事叙述了一半。但是美秀博物馆的宣传资料则并非如此。相比较而言，美秀版本 A 的译文行文舒缓，它分为两句，并在每句开头都加上了时间的提示：Once upon a time，one day。这加强了游客的好奇心和时间意识。此

外，美秀版本还加上了地理位置的确切指示“Eastern China”和历史感“Taiyuan period of the Jin Dynasty”。

2. 将主人公的身份确定下来

在戴维斯版本中，严格按照陶渊明对“武陵人”身份的模糊处理，以“捕鱼为业”：

A man of Wuling, who made his living as a fisherman.

之所以如此说，是因为陶渊明本人就是以务农为业，但他同时又是诗人和哲学家。这位武陵人捕鱼为业，也说明这位渔人很可能也是一位不满现实却无力改变现实的归隐者，他也才可能在维持生计的当口上，却“缘溪行，忘路之远近”：

ascended a stream, forgetful of the distance he traveled.

用了 forgetful 这个词，其逃离现实的心态，就相当明显了。

但是在美秀版本中，首先就确定了古代中国生活着一个渔人：

Once upon a time there lived a fisherman in Wuling, Eastern China in the Taiyuan Period of the Jin Dynasty.

但他不是痛苦思索、急欲隐世的哲人，而是童话故事中一个心情愉快的打鱼者。为什么如此说呢？因为句型 once upon a time there lived ... 类似于童话故事的开头。童话的开头一般是这样的：

Once upon a time there was a widow who had two daughters...

Once upon a time there was a dear little girl who was loved by everyone who looked at her...

There was once a miller who had one beautiful daughter...

There was once a cook named Gretel...

There was once a very old man, whose eyes had become dim...

There was once upon a time a woman who was a real witch and had two daughters, one ugly and wicked...

There was once upon a time a queen to whom God had given no children...

A long time ago there lived a king who was famed for his wisdom through all the land.

Long, long ago, some two thousand years or so, there lived a rich man with a good and beautiful wife...

Long before you or I were born, there reigned, in a country a great way off, a king who had three sons...

如此，美秀译文的开头语气舒缓、基调明朗。读者（游客）的阅读和审美期待也从追随隐士、哲人的探寻一下子变为童话中一个渔人的神奇之旅。

3. 将写意的历史画卷加以清晰化，加上了更多的细节

在这个过程中添加了某些信息，将愁苦探寻的隐士偷换成了愉悦、探险的游客。

One day, as he was rowing up a mountain stream daydreaming, he was unaware of the distance he had traveled.

他在划船，而小溪沿着大山的山脉静静流淌。在静谧的环境中，渔人居然做起了白日梦，完全没有意识到他已经沿溪行了多远的距离。

便舍船从口入。

美秀译本如下：

The fisherman jumped out of his boat and entered the opening.

再对照戴维斯译本：

So he left his boat and went in through the opening.

“jump”这个动作的加入，给渔人的情绪染上了兴奋雀跃的色彩。

<u>初极狭，才通人</u>。复行数十步，豁然开朗。

美秀译本：

Once inside, he found himself on a narrow road, but traveling deeper, a splendid view suddenly opened before him.

戴维斯译本：

At first it was very narrow, barely allowing a man to pass, but as he went on for some tens of paces, it came out into the open air...

这个在狭窄的山缝间爬行的过程，肯定充满了恐惧。但是美秀译本就完全舍弃了这个意象和经历，反而把它描述成了一个充满了惊奇和期待的旅游经验：Once inside, he found himself on a narrow road。狭窄的山缝变成了道路，并且忽略了对这种可怕的狭窄的描述：barely allowing a man to pass。因为美秀博物馆重建的肯定不会是原始的只容一人爬行的山口，而是铺就的道路，以适合游客旅行。

接着，渔人“复行数十步”。美秀译本也舍弃了这个“数十步”的细节，而换成了另外一个细节：but traveling deeper，将 traveling 这个词替代原先的较为模糊的“行”。而用戴维斯的翻译，就是“as he went on for some tens of paces”。这就真的在字面上进行了“身份”的明显转换：渔人变成了游客；探险追寻变成了探奇旅行。

再接着，“豁然开朗”。戴维斯译本“it came out into the open air...”按照渔人的经历，渔人的注意力肯定是在山口上：这条山缝会不会是条死路？还有多长？前面是什么？这是比较符合原文的。但是美秀译本就不同了：“a splendid view suddenly opened before him”，却是更符合游客的期待，游客的注意力一直是在美景上。所以，他们向前旅行不久，就看到一个美妙绝伦的景色。

（二）旅游目的地的代入

在美秀译本中，桃花源在下意识中被替换成了美秀博物馆。这可以从许多的细节看出来。

(1) 忽逢桃花林。夹岸数百步，中无杂树，芳草鲜美，落英缤纷。(22 个

汉字）

美秀译文：

All at once he came across a grove of peach trees in full bloom. On either bank there was nothing but peach trees as far as the eyes could see. Their flowers were fragrant, delicate and lovely to the eye. The air itself was filled with drifting peach blossom petals.（50 个单词）

戴维斯译文：

Suddenly he came upon a grove of peach trees in blossom. They lined the banks for several hundred paces: among them were no other kinds of tree. The fragrant herbage was fresh and beautiful; fallen blossom lay in profusion.（39 个单词）

“夹岸数百步，中无杂树”这个细节在戴维斯译本中得到了忠实的翻译。戴维斯用了 16 个单词很严格地按照原文 9 个汉字的顺序翻译。但是美秀译本却融化了原文中的句式，更突出了桃林的一望无际。

芳草鲜美，落英缤纷。

The fragrant herbage was fresh and beautiful; fallen blossom lay in profusion.

戴维斯的译本完全对照原文，尤其是芳草一词，翻译成了 herbage，指的是地上的小草，和落花相映成趣。而美秀译本故意忽略了“芳草”一词，将注意力完全集中于桃花上。

Their flowers were fragrant, delicate and lovely to the eye. The air itself was filled with drifting peach blossom petals。

在翻译中加入了译者的想象，并且毫不吝啬溢美之词，也不顾虑译文的忠实，细心描绘桃花的芳香、柔和、美丽，而对“落英缤纷”的翻译更是突出了桃花下落过程中的曼妙舞姿，强调了桃花盛开到极致的、令人惊艳的美，更是突出了此地的静谧。

（2）初极狭，才通人。

美秀译本：Once inside, he found himself on a narrow road... 戴维斯译本：At first it was very narrow, barely allowing a man to pass... 美秀译本将“山缝”偷换成了“道路”，这一点以上已有说明。

接着描述桃源人家：“土地平旷，屋舍俨然，有良田、美池、桑竹之属。”戴维斯译本：... upon lands level and wide with houses of a stately appearance. There were fine fields and beautiful pools, clumps of mulberries and bamboos. 而 Miho 译本为：Imposing houses stood among rich fields and pleasant crystal-clear ponds all set with mulberries, willows and bamboos. 美秀译本舍弃了“土地平旷”的意象，接着将“美池”加以细节化，“beautiful pool”变成了“pleasant crystal-clear ponds”，水池变成了精心修筑的池塘，而池水也变成了悦人耳目的清澈的泉水。不仅如此，还精心搭配上了桑树、柳树和竹林。注意：柳树在原文中并不存在。而且，在原文中“有良田、美池、桑竹之属”，这些是农业社区必备的生活来源。但是到了美秀译本中，这些桑树、柳树、竹林，都被额外“set”（精心设置）成为良田和美池的点缀。也就是说，成为供人欣赏的人为的美景，成了园艺布局，而非原先陶渊明所描绘的理想的农业社会。

（3）桃花源批判现实意义的核心，就在于介绍桃花源人的来历以及外界战乱不断、人民生活困苦的状况：“村中闻有其人，咸来问讯。自云先世避秦时乱，率妻子、邑人来此绝境，不复出焉，遂与外人间隔。问今是何世，乃不知有汉，无论魏晋。此人一一为具言所闻，皆叹惋。余人各复延至其家，皆出酒食。”而美秀译本完全舍弃这一部分，因为它和景点无重要联系。

“太守即遣人随其往。”美秀译本也完全舍弃了这一点，而是加上了另一个细节：Awhile later he decided to pay another visit to the idyllic village with the governor。由太守派遣，变成了渔人自己决定再去寻访那个美丽的村庄。于是，在此过程中忽略了中国古代文化的某些细节，如渔人究竟有无自主权以及渔人告发并再次带人寻找那个村庄的动机等，而偷换成了现代游人的心态：决定再次游览那个美丽的村庄。

（4）南阳刘子骥，高士也。闻之，欣然规往，未果，寻病终。后遂无问津者。

美秀译本也完全舍弃了这一段。

而译文最重要的一部分，即译文的标题，也足以说明现代旅游业对古典文学翻译的影响。美秀译文的标题是："Peach Blossom Valley."而与戴维斯译文的标题"Peach Blossom Spring"相比，则将桃花源变成了桃花谷。因为美秀博物馆以两座山为基地，前山为接待处和餐厅，后山才是博物馆，两者以桥梁和隧道连接。

三、结　论

中国古典文学作品和现代旅游宣传可以说是相得益彰。但是在国际化旅游的趋势下，古典文学的翻译就变成了一个重要而艰巨的任务。要么完全舍弃不用，要么草草地以散文形式进行阐释，要么引用已有翻译。但是，所有这些都对中国景点的介绍有所损害，至少不够圆满，使得古典文学作为景点的核心魅力而遭到过滤，从而不能很好地发挥旅游景点的历史和文化优势。这是我们都不愿意看到的。所以，需要对这一现象进行观察、总结，并研究出必要的对策。

翻译并不仅仅是文本间的对应和转换，而且还受到其他许多因素的影响，譬如政治、宗教、文化，等等。以此为参考框架，本文对日本美秀博物馆网上宣传资料中《桃花源记》的英文翻译策略进行了仔细地分析，并阐明这些策略对旅游宣传目的的实现有着积极的作用。

旅游宣传资料中，中国古典文学的翻译是一个值得研究的课题。为了宣传目的的实现而采取增删、改变等翻译策略的合法性、实效性研究将引导我们对这个领域获得更多的认识和掌握。

参考文献：

[1] http://www.thehumanaught.com/blog/2006/09/28/maple-bridge-%E6%9E%AB%E6%A1%A5/(accessed 28/09/2006).

[2] http://www.cctv.com/english/TouchChina/School/Culture/20020301/100076.html(accessed 01/03/2002).

[3] http://www.chinese-forums.com/archive/index.php/t-178.html(accessed 09/10/2006).

[4] http://www.chinahighlights.com/suzhou/attractions/hanshan-temple.html(ac-

cessed 10/05/2007).

[5] http://www. miho. jp/english/landscap/landscap. html(accessed 15/06/2006).

[6] http://www. wretch. cc/blog/CafedeRiver&article_id = 2766556 (accessed 14/05/2007).

[7] 2006a. Translation and conflict: A Narrative Account. London & New York: Routledge.

[8] Baker, Mona. Reframing Conflict through Translation, published on *Social Semiotics*, V17, N.2, June 2007.

[9] Huang, Yunte. *Transpacific Displacement: Ethnography, Translation, and Intertextual Travel in Twentieth-century American Literature.* Berkeley, London: Berkeley University of California Press, 2002.

宗教词汇翻译：准确理解与灵活变通

——对 witness，sect（cult）和 ministry 译法的探讨

尹可秀

两千多年以来，基督教一直影响着西方国家乃至全世界。翻译基督教材料，可以帮助人们了解基督教，全面理解西方文化。为了达到这个目的，译者必须准确传达原文信息，才能为读者提供内容清晰、明白的译文。在实践过程中，笔者曾碰到几个难以翻译的常见词：witness（v.，n.），sect（cult）和 ministry。国内几乎没有专门的宗教英汉词典可供查询，而在一般书籍资料中也查不到相应的译法，所以必须根据上下文以及相关材料进行词义推究，在此对它们的译法进行探讨，拙漏之处，恳请读者给予指正。

一、witness 的译法

witness 一词，既可以当动词，又可以作名词，基本含义为"见证（上帝存在）"。

（一）witness 用作动词

（1）Those involved were convinced that by their vigorous Christianity they could eliminate such evils, send more missionaries to foreign lands, witness in the cities, and achieve personal holiness[①].

---

① 选自 Church History. New York：International Communication College，2001. 以下例句如无特别说明，均选自该书，其中文译文为笔者所作。

这个句子里的witness显然可以理解为“见证上帝存在”。整句译为：

(1)a 参与者相信，通过基督教的力量，他们可以消灭这些丑恶现象，向国外派遣更多的传教士，在国内城市见证上帝存在，获得个人圣洁。

事实上，这句话可以处理得更为清晰、工整一些。根据基督教的发展历史，19世纪至20世纪期间，城市的飞速发展给社会生活带来了一系列负面影响。针对社会不良现象，不同教会之间经常合作，在城市内共同举办传教活动。结合此句中向国外派遣传教士以及国内城市见证的情况，可以肯定国内城市的传教力度。因此，可以尝试将“传教”加入witness的含义中，译为：

(1)b 运动参与者相信，通过基督教的力量，他们可以消灭这些丑恶现象，向国外派遣更多的传教士，在国内城市传教，见证上帝存在，获得个人圣洁。

补充词义之后，国内、国外的对比情况更为清楚和完整，而原文语意基本没有改变。但是“传教”与“见证”的含义相差较大，这样的改动是否可行？笔者查阅了介绍基督教的其他书籍，以确认“传教”的译法是否可行，结果发现了类似的用法：

(2) “Witnessing” (is) a form of evangelism in which Christians seek to communicate their faith to others through their life and words①.

这句话对witnessing解释得非常清楚，将其定义为“福音派传教方式之一，教徒通过自己的生活和言谈，向他人传播信仰”。由此看来，witnessing的确带有“传教”的含义，并且可以更具体地译为“身体力行”。同样的例句还有：

(3) Witnessing is as much about showing people Christianity in the way we live as it is about explaining Christianity by the things that we say②.

---

① Coutin, *The Culture Of Protest*. Oxford: Westview Press, 1993: 126.

② from BNC: C8N/497.

该句的 witnessing 指“通过我们自己的生活方式和言语来向别人传播基督教”。这个含义与例句（2）对 witnessing 的定义如出一辙。查阅《英汉辞海》①，发现 witness 的动词项下有这样一条释义：“（如用言谈和行为）使他人知道某人所受过的宗教上的经历或某人所信奉的宗教道理：给某人的宗教信仰作见证。”虽然《英汉辞海》没有提供例句，也没有提出该词的具体译法，但至此可以肯定，在上述例句中，将 witness（witnessing）理解为“传教”或“身体力行”是有根据的，能够准确表达该词的含义。

（二）witness 用作名词

witness 不仅可以用作动词，还可以用作名词。例如：

（1）Many African Christians have suffered because of their witness for Christ.

（2）Consequently, they are willing to consider a biblical witness, and some followers of Islam are being converted to Christ.

许多词典将名词 witness 解释为“见证人/物”。在这两个句子中，witness 显然不能沿用这一解释。它所代表的应当是“信仰”：

（1）非洲有许多人由于信仰基督教而受到排挤。

（2）因而，他们愿意考虑接受基督教，有的伊斯兰教徒甚至改信了基督教。

从上述分析可见，动词 witness 除了表示“见证（上帝存在）”外，还可视情况译为“传教”、“身体力行”；名词 witness 除了“见证人/物”这类常见含义外，还可以表示“信仰”。

二、sect（cult）的译法

与 witness 一样，对 sect（cult）的翻译也需要根据其基本含义进行灵活变通。普通情况下，sect 指“宗教中的派别”，cult 和 pagan 是近义词，指“原始的膜拜、迷信”。而在有的句子里，sect 和 cult 是同义词。例如：

① 王同忆主编：《英汉辞海》，国防工业出版社 1990 年版。

(1) The nineteenth century witnessed the creation of a number of semi-Christian or sub-Christian groups that are often called sects or cults.

将该句的 sect 和 cult 译为“教派”或“派别”，似乎显得不够准确，因为原文旨在体现这些派别“半基督教”（semi-Christian）的性质，它们与路德教、圣公会等教派不同。在译文中应当怎样体现这种区别呢？笔者认为，可以参照同书中与之相关的一段文字来理解：

(2) In recent years, some Seventh-Day Adventist leaders have began to question Ellen G. White's prophecies and have leaned toward a more biblical understanding of justification by faith. Because of this, a few evangelical leader now tend to include Seventh-Day Adventists as part of the orthodox church.

在这本书中，守安息日复临派属于 sect 的范围。从这段话的最后一句可以看出，sect 通常是不被列入正统（orthodox）教派范畴的。因此，可以试着用“非正统教派”来翻译 sect 和 cult，以体现 sect 和 cult 的特点。例句（1）、（2）可以译为：

（1）19 世纪期间，许多半基督教性质的，或者说基督教新的分支建立起来了。人们一般将之称为“基督教非正统教派”。

（2）近年来，该教派的一些领导者开始质疑艾伦·G. 怀特的预言。他们的观点更符合《圣经》教义，认为最后审判将以人们的信仰为依据。因此，福音派新教的少数领导者将守安息日复临派归入了基督教正统教派。

将正统性引入对 sect 和 cult 的理解，译为“非正统教派”，这是建立在一定上下文理解基础之上的。毛荣贵教授指出，翻译有时不得不靠“猜”，因为某些词很难通过查阅词典去弄明它的含义，但是可以在上下文中理解①。为了检验这种译法是否可取，笔者参阅了其他材料中关于 sect 和 cult 的用法：

(3) Following Cromwell's leadership... practically every one has now free to

① 毛荣贵、范武邱编著：《英汉翻译技巧示例》，上海交通大学出版社 2003 年版，第 67 页。

use whatever gifts he had for attracting listeners eager to hear that Christ was at hand, that no matter what the learned or the well-placed might say to the contrary, they were his chosen ones, his true church. Sects under such conditions multiplied and flourished as never before①.

这段材料表明，sects 宣扬的教义可能与基督教学者（the learned）和领导者（the well-placed）所持的观点相悖，但是它们的教义仍与基督教有关。正如例句（1）所描述的那样，它们带有“半基督教”的性质。这说明，例句（2）对 sects（cults）所下的定义是适用的。例句（3）的大意是：

（3）在克伦威尔的统治下，人们有权自由传教。他们各施所长，无视基督教的正统理论，宣扬耶稣即将复临，声称他们的教派才是真正的基督教，他们的信徒才是上帝的选民。在这种情况下，基督教许多非正统教派成立了，并且获得了前所未有的发展。

下面这段材料进一步说明了 sect 的特点：

（4）Churches（are）large, stable, mature, socially accepted religious organization... Sects, in contrast to churches, are relatively small, are alienated from the surrounding world, and may not have the bureaucratic social structure characteristic of churches②.

虽然从字面意思来看，socially accepted 不等于例句（2）中的 orthodox，但是作为一个具有两千多年历史的世界性宗教，基督教的正统教派无疑已经获得了社会的承认和接受。从这个意义上来说，用例句（2）的 orthodox 来理解该段 churches 的特点是可行的。与 churches 相对的 sects 自然就该译为“非正统教派”。这样一来，译文就可以做成：

（4）正统教派是具有较大规模、稳定、成熟、为社会所接受的宗教组织。

---

① William, Haller. *Liberty and Reformation in the Puritan Revolution.* New York: Columbia University Press, 1955: 229.

② Anthony, F. C, Wallace. *Religion* New York: Random House, 1966: 84.

与之相比，非正统教派的规模较小，自我封闭，不一定具备正统教派的管理组织。

通过对上述例句的分析，可以确定，当 sect（cult）表示与传统的基督教派存在较大差别，而又具有半基督教性质的教派时，可以将之译为“（基督教）非正统教派”。

三、ministry 的译法

除了 witness 和 sect（cult）以外，在有的句子中，ministry 也会给翻译工作带来困难。ministry 的基本含义是“服务”。这个含义非常宽泛，包括多种服务，例如常规宗教服务、慈善活动、委派牧师履行神职等。而在这些服务类别之中，我们又可以进行更具体的分类。例如，牧师履行的神职包括主持宗教仪式、传教以及与别的牧区进行交流等。如果忽视这些具体差异，一概将 ministry 译为“服务”，译文未免显得粗糙，不利于读者准确理解原文的意思。笔者认为，除了采用“服务”这个含义较广的词语来翻译 ministry 以外，在一些情况下，对 ministry 的翻译应当具体化。这里列举三种情况以供讨论。

（一）第一种情况

先来看两个例句：

（1）All of these social changes made a profound impact on the religious character of American. The more dynamic churches responded to the realities and established many ministries to reach settlers on the frontier and immigrants in the cities.

（2）The Second Great Awakening resulted in marvelous ministries both to the cultured city people of the East and the pioneers on the Western frontier.

在这两个句子中，教会的活动面向国内的未信教者和教徒，以传教或为教徒提供服务为主要目的。由于这种服务与宗教直接相关，因此可以理解为“宗教服务”或“宗教活动”。这两个句子可以译为：

（1）这些社会变化对美国的基督教产生了深远的影响。结合当时的情况，教会积极提供了更多的宗教服务，以便与拓荒者和城市的移民保持联系。

(2) 在东部城市和西部拓荒区，第二次大觉醒运动促进了宗教活动的广泛开展。

(二) 第二种情况

教会除了提供“宗教服务”以外，还会在社会上开展一些活动，或者创立一些机构。例如：

(1) Social ministries. Other churches became “institutional” in an attempt to provide programs such as gymnasiums, libraries, clinics, and social rooms for all aspects of life. Still others changed their message and preached a “social gospel”.

(2) He promoted many ministries including schools, rescue missions, the publication of periodicals, the I. B. R. A. radio network, and a savings bank.

教会提供的这类服务一般包括开办学校、建立慈善机构等，目的不在于传教，而在于给人们提供帮助，体现教会对社会的关心。根据其目的和内容，这类服务应当称为“社会公益活动”。例句 (1)、(2) 可以这样翻译：

(1) 社会公益活动。其他教派开始热心于建立公共机构。例如，他们设立了体育馆、图书馆、诊所和向社会所有阶层开放的公众活动室。还有一些教派在传播“社会福音”，即社会公益事业。

(2) 他促进了许多公益活动的开展，包括建立学校、成立救济机构、创办期刊、建成国际读经协会广播站和开办储蓄银行。

(三) 第三种情况

第三种情况是 ministry 指代“教会委派牧师或信徒担任某项工作”这一含义。例如：

(1) Following a period of study, Finney started preaching, and he was licensed by the Presbyterian Church... His ministry took him twice to England.

这句话固然可以译为“……因牧师工作的需要，他两次前往英国”，但是由于文中没有交代他是否曾经受任神职，因此译文显得有点唐突和模糊。其实，这里的 ministry 和 preaching 是同义词，都表示“传教”，可以试着将其译为：

(1) 经过一段时间的学习，芬尼获得了长老会的许可，开始传教……他两次前往英国举办布道活动。

再看一个类似的例子：

(2) In fact, Du Plessis was a leader of that church for a decade before he resigned to assume a global ministry through the Pentecostal World Conference. He took this move because he believed that God had called him to a ministry that would be both ecumenical in nature and worldwide in scope.

如果用“履行神职”来翻译 ministry，那么在译文中，该词的含义会比较模糊。因此，对 ministry 的理解最好能够具体一些。和例句（1）一样，这个句子里的 ministry 主要是指“传教”。我们可以采用这个具体含义来进行翻译：

(2) 事实上，杜·普莱西斯辞职以前，曾经在这个教会担任了十年的领导。他感到上帝需要他去开展传教活动，并且这种活动应该是普世教会性质的，要在全世界进行。于是，他毅然辞去神职，通过世界五旬节主义大会的帮助，到世界各地去传教。

从上面的例句可以看出，对 ministry 的翻译应当准确而具体，除了采用“服务”、“神职”等译名以外，还可以视情况将之译为“宗教服务”、“社会公益活动”和“传教”。

四、小　结

Witness、sect（cult）和 ministry 是基督教材料中常见的词，类似的词还有 practice, concern 等。翻译这类词语时，首先要准确理解它们的基本含义，然后以这些含义为基础，进行灵活变通，这样才能够准确传达原文的内容。按照这种方法，笔者对 witness、sect（cult）和 ministry 的译法进行了思考，认为在与本文例句类似的文本中，可以将动词 witness 译为“传教”或“身体力行”，名词 witness 译为“信仰”，sect（cult）译为“非正统教派”，ministry 译为

"宗教服务"、"社会公益活动"或"传教"。由于笔者所见有限，不排除这几个词语带有其他含义的可能。正如联合国高级译员李长栓教授所说："我们经常遇到这样的情况：想尽了一切办法，到了交稿时，对某个词或句子的译法还是不满意，使我们感到终身遗憾。"① 笔者提出的上述观点和体会，旨在探讨新词、难词的翻译方法，难免挂一漏万，请各位读者指正。

参考文献：

[1]李长栓. 非文学翻译理论与实践[M]. 北京:中国对外翻译出版公司,2004.
[2]毛荣贵,范武邱. 英汉翻译技巧示例[M]. 上海:上海交通大学出版社,2003.
[3]王同忆. 英汉辞海[M]. 北京:国防工业出版社,1990.
[4]BNC (British National Corpus, C8N/497).
[5][作者不详]. *Church History*[M]. New York: International Communication College, 2001.
[6]Coutin, Susan Bilber. *The Culture of Protest*[M]. Oxford: Westview Press, 1993.
[7]Haller, William. *Liberty and Reformation in the Puritan Revolution*[M]. New York: Columbia University Press, 1955.
[8]Wallace, Anthony F. C.. *Religion*[M]. New York: Random House, 1966.

① 李长栓：《非文学翻译理论与实践》，中国对外翻译出版公司2004年版，第133页。

第五部分　外国语言研究

法庭交叉讯问中问句与权势的关系

——对法庭交叉讯问中问句的多层次批评性分析

王晋军

一、引 言

法庭的基本作用就是对每一个民事或刑事案件作出法律裁决。法庭交叉讯问作为法律裁定的必要程序，往往凸显着互动的权势层级关系，即法官和律师之间的关系以及法官、律师与被告、证人之间的关系。法官和律师被法庭这个机构赋予了提问以及选择和控制话题的权力，而被告和证人处于权势的底层，他们只能对问话作出回答。不少学者和专家对法庭交叉讯问作过研究。如O'Barr（1982），Ruth Wodak（1985），Paul Drew（1985）和Sandra Harris（1984）。但他们主要是对问句类型进行了语用分析。本文指出法庭交叉讯问中的问句作为表达权势的重要手段，不仅体现在问句比例以及不同问句的类型上，而且可以从语音层、词汇层、会话结构层和语类结构层来详尽揭示法庭交叉讯问中的问句与权势的关系。

二、问句与权势的自然结合

（一）关于权势与问句

权势是批评话语分析关注的中心。Fairclough 和 Van Dijk 把权势当做话语现象，自然产生于言语交际之中。Fairclough（1989：46）指出："话语权势就是有权势的参与者控制并限制无权势者的话语使用。"Van Dijk（2001）认为，社会权势就是控制。也就是说，有权势的团体能够控制其他团体的行为和思想。Watts 对权势作了更为具体的解释。他（1991：60）认为："拥有权势意味着他/她有实现其既定目标的行为自由，而不考虑为了实现有利于他/她的行为而把其愿望强加到另一个人的身上。”因此，权势是实现一个人目标的话语权力。在一些高度规约的言语交际（如法庭交叉讯问、医生与病人的对话等）机构会话中话语权势易于发现。相比较而言，日常会话中话语权势是隐藏的，需要细察才可以区分。

“问句是用于区分句子功能的术语，可以从语法和语义上来定义”（Crystal，1985：254）。Crystal（1985）认为，从语法上问句可分为是非疑问句、特殊疑问句和附加疑问句。从语义上问句寻求得到更多的信息，并要求听者给予回答。根据 Sacks（1995）对话轮转换机制的描述，一个人发问后，就占有了一个话轮或者说就有了一个选择和邀请受话人的机会。例如①一个人问“And that's what happened to you last year，isn't it?”这说明提问人期望受话人给予回答，同时要把话轮传递给受话人。Sacks（1995，ii）指出，问句期望答句使得问句和答句构成了典型的相邻对，而问句在某种程度上意味着下一个话轮必须作答。

（二）问句与权势的自然和内在的结合

问句的特点使其与权势有着自然和内在的联系。首先，问句期待受话人作出回答，这使得提问人将其意愿强加于受话人，从而明显地实施着控制。其次，一旦提出一个问题后，提问者就有优先权占有话轮、控制话轮并选择下一个说话者。这可以看做实现一个人目标的自由。Sacks（1995）认为提问是一种权势或控制力。他（1995，I：49－55）指出：“提问的人似乎有优先权根据回答进行操作。就是这种权力使得会话看起来像场竞争，人人都试图拥有‘提问者’的地位……一旦一个人占有了提问的位置，那么很大程度上他就控制了这个对话。”第三，三种主要问句限制、约束并核准了答句的话题——会话的指称内容。特殊疑问句通过疑问代词（如 why，what，when，where）选择并限定话题。选择疑问句通过所提供的两种选择来筛选话题。是非疑问句要求作出肯定或否定回答来确认并核准话题。第四，一些问句可看做威胁面子的言语行为。Tsui（1994：103）认为：“问句要么预测受话人的行为，从而给受话人施加压力。问句要么限制受话人行为的完成，从而侵害受话人实现其行为的自由。”一些问句（传统上称为“修辞问句”）传递着提问人的认知立场，它们可以看做断言。这些问句通常包含着“敌对的内容”（Heritage，2002：1427），或者可以看做一种“挑战”（Koshik，2003：51）。Heritage（2002）指出，一些以“isn't”，“don't you”和“shouldn't you”开头的否定疑问句能产生断言，因为这些问句不是寻求信息而是用于表达立场或观点。例如②Doctor：Don't you think it would be pretty careless for you to get pregnant while you haven't got a house or a job?（Heritage，2002：1432）一些特殊疑问句听起来像挑战，主要因为它们出现在已经确定的语境（如分歧、指控、抱怨等）中。如③Who cares?（I don't care）What difference does it make?（It makes no difference）

三、法庭交叉讯问中问句的多层次批评性分析

问句与权势具有自然和内在的联系。在机构话语特别是在法庭交叉讯问中，问句所表现出的权势尤为突出。在法庭交叉讯问中，只有法官和律师有权提问，证人和被告一般无权提问，除非被要求这样做。Linell（1990）注意到在法官和律师的话轮中问句占了80%。笔者根据收集语料所作的统计（即法官和律师的问句占了91.1%，而被告和证人的问句只占8.9%）也证明了法官和律师对提问的绝对控制。为了对法庭交叉讯问中的问句与权势关系作深层语言分析，本文根据系统功能语言学的多功能传统，欲从语音层、词汇层、会话结构层和语类结构层等四个层面对法庭交叉讯问中的问句进行批评性分析，从而详尽揭示法庭交叉讯问中的问句与权势的关系。

（一）语音层

语调是问句不可缺少的部分。Halliday（1970：21）指出，语调不是为了说起来好听，“语调的重要性在于它是表达不同事物的手段”。众所周知，语调是有意义的，一个句子的语调变化会导致句子意义的变化。英语的基本语调是升调和降调，尽管它们可以进一步再分为降升调和升降调。Halliday（1970）和O'Connor and Arnold（1973）探讨了一些问句语调与态度的表达。Halliday（1970）认为，带降调的特殊疑问句是中性的（neutral），而带升调的特殊疑问句意味着试探性的或顺从的；同样，带升调的是非问句是中性的，而带降调的是非问句则表示有说服力的或不耐烦的。O'Connor and Arnold（1973）发现，带降调的特殊疑问句表示平淡的、无同情心的甚至敌对的或事务性的。带降调的是非问句表示感兴趣的、吃惊的或敌对的。而带升调的特殊疑问句则表示吃惊的或试探性的，带升调的是非问句则表示感兴趣的或怀疑的。

Tench（1996）更进一步，他将问句的降调和升调与参与者的社会地位结合起来。Tench（1996：18）认为：“语调单位中包含主要信息的降调表示‘说话者的主导地位’，即说话者知道、告诉、命令、要求等。而同一语调单位中

的升调则表明‘说话者的顺从地位’：说话者不知道所以问，没有权威所以请求、哄劝等。”这样，Tench 就把问句的语调与参与者的社会地位联系在一起了。Tench 的观点也从神经心理学的角度得到了证实。Cook（2002）以神经心理学的实验分析为基础，提出并证实了他的假设即人类情感的编码和解码是与语调的编码和解码相关联的。根据音乐理论，大调常与喜悦、自信、庄严和胜利联系在一起，而小调则通常表达悲伤、害怕、不安和绝望。Cook（2002）通过实验证明乐调的变化表达了一系列的心理变化：小调很自然地与低微的社会地位和谦恭的心理相关，而大调与优越的社会地位相关。进而，他把音乐的旋律与语调相比较，认为人类的语调与音乐的旋律相似，即升调表达说话人的谦恭与顺从，而降调表达说话人的支配和优越地位。根据笔者对语料所作的语调标记，法官和律师作为权势的实施者，在他们的问句中倾向于使用降调来传达他们的权威和法律的神圣和不可侵犯。例如：

④JUDGE：Mr. Starlings，what is your position↓？

STARLINGS：I work for the National Security Agency.

JUDGE：Do you feel that your position in the government would make it difficult or impossible for you to do equal justice between the government and the defendants in this case↓？

STARLINGS：No，sir.①

法官的两个带降调的问句不是普通的寻求信息的问句，而是像命令，因而被告不可能拒绝回答。

（二）词汇层

词汇是人们表达不同态度和立场以及构建社会身份和地位的重要手段。从词汇层对法庭交叉讯问中的问句进行批评性分析，就是要揭示提问者和回答者的态度以及他们表达出的意识形态。可以从三个方面来揭示问句中的词汇表达与观点、态度及权势的关系，即评价词汇，情态表达和称呼语。

1. 词汇评价

根据 Martin（1997，2000）对评价系统的描述，评价词汇可分为情感、判断和欣赏。表情感的评价词汇有 sad，happy，fed up，satisfied 等；表判断的评

---

① 语料来自电影剧本 *The Trial of the Catonsville Nine.*

价词汇有 lucky, fortunate, odd, stupid 等；表欣赏的评价词汇有 fascinating, exciting, repulsive。如果一个参与者拥有较多的评价词汇，表明他/她拥有较强的评价能力，能够充分表达自己的态度和观点。下面一段法庭对话选自美国畅销电视剧Alley McBeal。评价词汇用下画线标出。

⑤Lawyer 2: Woosh! Jacob, truthfully, when you heard Mr. Stevens' broadcast, you already knew there was no Santa, didn't you?

Child: No, I did not!

Lawyer 2: No need to get loud, sweetheart. You thought Santa delivered presents to all over the world?

Child: On Christmas Eve.

Lawyer 2: So it takes a jet going 700 miles per hour, six hours just to fly across one country, and you thought eight tiny reindeer could lug this big sled all over the world in one night? Isn't that a little dopey to think that, Jacob?

Child: Well...

Lawyer 2: Can we talk about the size of Santa's bag? That little sack has enough toys for 300 million children? Are you retarded, Jacob? ①

律师的问话围绕着"不存在圣诞老人"的论点而展开。律师完全控制了评价的权力。而且在律师的问句中出现了一些否定评价词汇来评价孩子的观点。如 tiny reindeer, big sled, a little dopey, retarded 等。相反，孩子没有使用任何评价词汇来进行反驳。律师的评价词汇不仅使孩子相信根本不存在圣诞老人，而且也对孩子实施了权势。从评价词汇上可以看出，律师占有了绝对的权势，而孩子处于从属地位，也没有评价的能力。

2. 情态表达

问句中的情态表达是表达提问者观点和态度的突出手段。情态表达不仅反映礼貌的度，而且反映权势的层级。情态表达根据情态值分为高、中、低三种，如表1所示：

① *Crazy English*, Vol. 32, 2002: 87.

表1 情态表达分为高、中、低三种

情态值	情态表达
高值	must, have to, ought to, can't, couldn't, mightn't, certainly, always
中值	will, would, should, probable/usual
低值	can, may, could, might, possible, sometimes

情态值与礼貌的度紧密地结合在一起。一般来说，情态值越高，情态表达听起来就越肯定，因而也就不太礼貌；反之，情态值越低，情态表达听起来就越不肯定，因而也就越显得礼貌。情态值不仅反映礼貌的度，而且反映权势关系和参与者的社会关系。Hoey（1997：63）认为："情态涉及说话者或作者的权威，而不考虑其他特别的尺度。从字面上看权威与权势相关，个人或集体可对他人或另一集体实施权势。" Fairclough（1989：3）也指出："权势存在于各种情态之中。" 情态是一种有效的手段，通过它一些人可以对另一些人实施权势。在法庭交叉讯问中，由于存在多层级的权势关系，即法官处于权势的最高端，律师处于其次，证人和被告处于权势的最底层。因此，法官和律师所用问句中的情态表达往往会反映这种权势的层级关系。一般来说，法官在对律师和传讯员的问句中常使用中量值和高量值的情态表达，而律师和传讯员在对法官的问句中常使用中量值和低量值的情态表达。如：

⑥Counsel: My lord, <u>may</u> I very respectfully at this stage explain what this man did?[①]

律师使用了低量值的情态 may 来表达他对法官的尊重，同时表现出他的顺从和从属地位。

情态与权势相关。正如 Hodge & Kress（1993：122）所说的："情态总体上确定了一个语句的权威级别。换句话来说，通过使用情态表达，说话者把对自己权势地位的不确定转化为对自己话语的不确定。" 因此，可以说，问句中的情态表达不仅揭示了礼貌的层级，更主要的是反映了权势和社会距离的差异。

---

① Hoey, 1997: 131.

3. 称呼语

问句中的称呼语可以构建社会身份和社会距离。称呼语是在正式和非正式场合称呼一个人的用语。称呼语可分为好几种，其中包括爱称，如 darling，honey 等；昵称，如 red dog，boy 等；头衔加姓名，如 Mr. Graham，Ms. Morrissey 等，以及敬语，如 Sir，Madam 等。Levinson（1983）把称呼语作为社会指示语来识别参与者的社会身份或参与者间的社会关系。Hudson（1996：126）指出："名称的使用是不均等分布的。一个明显的趋势就是常用教名来称呼年轻人，而用表地位或职业的名字来称呼年长者。"一般而言，有权势的参与者可以在问句中使用名字来称呼对方，而无权势的参与者常用头衔加姓或敬语来称呼对方。如律师常用"your honor"和"my lord"来称呼法官，以示对法官的尊重。而拥有最大权势的法官却可以用不同的称呼语来称呼律师、传讯员和被告、证人等。如在例⑥中，律师自动遵照法庭的仪式在问句中用敬语"my lord"来称呼法官。再看以下的例子：

⑦Magistrate：Why haven't <u>you</u> been paying more than this?
What will <u>you</u> give us a reason?（to the defendant）
Magistrate：Is that right <u>Mr. -</u>（to the clerk）①

从法官的问句中我们可以看出地方法官用了不同的称呼语来称呼被告和传讯员。他用了普通的代词 you 来称呼被告，而用头衔加姓"Mr. -"来称呼他的同事以示尊重。尽管法官对传讯员可以实施权势，但法官用了不同的称呼语来区别对待传讯员和被告，以示权势差异。

（三）会话结构层

从会话结构层揭示法庭交叉讯问中的问句与权势的关系主要是分析问句所占有的话轮以及问句所充当的言语功能（speech function）或语步（move）。根据 Halliday（1984，1994）对会话的描述，一个话轮可以由两种基本语步即起始语步（initiating move）和回应语步（responding move）来实现。起始和回应言语功能又可以再细分（见表2）。

① Harris，1994：164.

表 2　起始和回应言语功能 ①

Speech roles	Initiating speech function	Responding speech functions	
		Responses expected (agreement)	Discretionary alternative (disagreement)
Giving goods-&-services	offer	acceptance	rejection
Demanding goods-&-services	command	undertaking	refusal
Giving information	statement	acknowledge	contradiction
Demanding information	question	answer	disclaimer

同时，一个话轮可以由一个或多个言语功能来体现。而且，语步或言语功能可以由不同的语气来体现。如，提问（question）的典型体现形式是疑问句，命令（command）的典型体现形式是祈使句，提供（offer）的典型体现形式是情态疑问句，陈述（statement）的典型体现形式是陈述句。

基于 Halliday（1984）的言语功能网络和 Eggins and Slide（1997）对日常会话所描绘的言语功能网络，笔者确定了法庭交叉讯问中问句和答句的言语功能网络（如下图所示）。

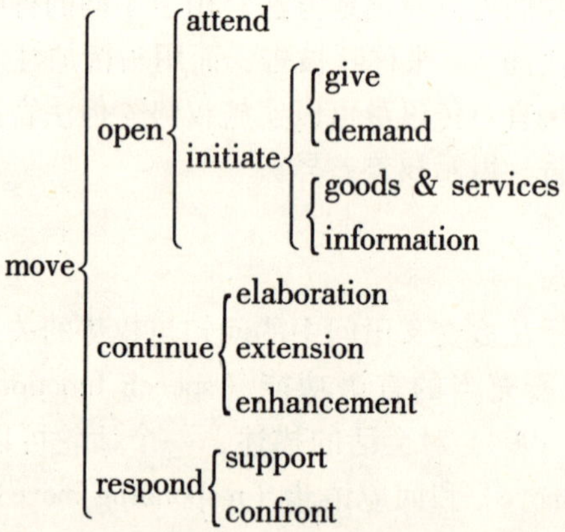

法庭交叉讯问中问句和答句的言语功能网络图

展开（opening）语步包括参与（attending）语步和起始（initiating）语步。

① Halliday，1994：69.

展开语步用于引出一系列的谈话，因此它具有一种控制权。换句话说，一个参与者使用了展开语步，就拥有了控制谈话的优先权。回应语步是对前一个语步或起始语步的应答。回应语步由支持和对抗两个语步构成。继续语步是指目前的说话者保持谈话状态的语步。根据 Halliday（1994）对小句的逻辑语义的描述，继续语步又可再分为详述（elaboration）、扩展（extension）和增强（enhancement）三种小类。

对法庭交叉讯问中的问句进行会话结构分析时，可首先标出参与者所占有的话轮，其次标出话轮的各个语步，然后统计出参与者所用的问句、占有的话轮数以及言语功能。最后，根据统计结果作对比分析。以下面一段法庭交叉讯问⑧为例作分析，其中 C 代表传讯员，D 代表被告，M 代表地方法官（见表 3）。

表 3 一段法庭交叉讯问

⑧Speaker	Turn/move	Conversational structure	Text
Information Gathering			
C	1a	O：I：attending	Thank you
	1b	O：I：question	is it correct that on 16th of June last year you were fined a total of ninety pounds in respect of three road traffic offences and also ordered to pay costs of four pounds ninety-two pence-making a total of ninety-four pounds ninety-two pence
	1c	O：I：question	is that correct
D	2	R：s：acknowledge	Yes sir — it is
C	3	O：I：question	and you were ordered to pay by weekly installments
D	4	R：s：acknowledge	Yes

续 表

M	5a	O：I：question	why haven't you been paying more than this
	5b	O：I：question	What will you give us a reason?
D	6a	R：S：statement	Well actually you worship like I've uh you know about a year and a half I fell out of-well my wife left me like
	6b	C：extension：statement	and I've been all—you know I just started drinking and that like and uh--go to the pub one night and seen her
	6c	C：extension：statement	and we've got back together again now so①

该段法庭交叉讯问所用的言语功能统计如表3：

表4 该段法庭交叉讯问所用的言语功能统计

Speech function	Clerk	Magistrate	Defendant
No. of turns No. of moves No. of interrogatives	2 4 3	1 2 2	3 5 0
Opening initiating move Attending Question	1 3	0 2	0 0
Continuing moves Extension：statement	0	0	2
Responding moves Support：acknowledge Support：statement	0 0	0 0	2 1

从统计结果可以看出，只有传讯员和地方法官使用了问句。其中，传讯员

① Harris，1994：164.

问了3个问句，法官问了2个。他们的问句充当了展开起始语步，从而控制了法庭讯问的主动权。相比较而言，被告没有使用一个起始语步，只使用了应答语步和继续语步。毫无疑问，被告处于被动的位置，只对法官和传讯员的问题作出回答，而且被告对所问的问题给予了肯定的回答，并对事实一一承认。此外，尽管传讯员使用的话轮、语步和问句比法官的略多一点，但通过展开参与语步，我们可以看出传讯员是在法官的许可下才进行问话的。通过对言语功能的对比分析，我们能够比较清晰地看出法官处于权势的最高层，传讯员次之，而被告处于权势的最底层。

（四）语类结构层

Sandra Harris（1988：102）把法庭交叉讯问的语类结构潜势（GSP）用公式总结为：

S^ SI^P^IG ^O^C^

S summoning

SI Swearing in

P Preliminary

IG Information Gathering ^ pause/break

O Ordering ^ fixed order

C Closing

根据Harris的描述，所有的成分（阶段）都是必要成分。而信息收集（Information Gathering）阶段是最引人注目的，因为该阶段存在法官、律师和被告之间互动的、多层权势关系。从语类结构层揭示法庭交叉讯问中的问句与权势的关系，可以借助对问句的会话结构分析，辨别出问句在各个必要成分中所起的作用。如果问句在必要成分中占据了主导地位并控制了必要成分，那么提问者就对受话人实施了权势。从例⑧可以看出，该语篇属于法庭交叉讯问的信息收集阶段。通过上述对例⑧所作的会话结构分析，不难看出法官和传讯员的问句控制了交叉讯问并占有了主动权，而被告处于从属和被支配的地位。因此，在语类结构层上法官和传讯员的问句占据了主导地位并控制了必要成分，因而对被告实施了权势。

四、结 语

从四个不同层面对法庭交叉讯问中的问句所作的分析为详尽揭示法庭交叉讯问中问句与权势的关系提供了多种手段。也就是说，可以从不同层面来反映法庭交叉讯问中问句与权势的关系。需要指出的是，法官、律师和传讯员所具有的提问权力不是与生俱来的，而是由法庭这个机构所赋予的。尽管被告可以对所问的问题采取抵制回答来蔑视法官和律师的权势，但他们始终处于被支配和从属的地位。

（注：由于不易得到真实的法庭交叉讯问的语料，基于剧本与真实生活的相似性，文中语料主要来源于两部电影剧本及其 VCD 影碟即 *Kramer vs Kramer* 和 *The Trial of the Catonsville Nine*。*Kramer vs Kramer* 的剧本来自 http：//www. godamongdirectors. com/scripts/ kramer. shtml，2004 – 01 – 08；*The Trial of the Catonsville Nine* 的剧本来自 http：//www. geocities. com/ Hollywood/Cinema/ 3761/catonsville9. html，2004 – 01 – 08；以及剧本 *Inherit the Wind*，by Shumlin and Jones. New York：Banton Book，1960）

参考文献：

[1] Cook，N. D.. *Tone of Voice and Mind* [M]. Amsterdam/Philadelphia：John Benjamins Publishing Company，2002.

[2] Crystal，D.. *A Dictionary of Linguistics and Phonetics* [Z]. London：Basil Blackwell，1985.

[3] Drew，P.. Analyzing the Use of language in Courtroom Interaction [C]//T. A. Van Dijk (ed.). *Handbook of Discourse Analysis*. Vol. 3. London：Academic Press INC. LTD，1985.

[4] Eggins，S. & D.. *Slide*，*Analyzing Casual Conversation* [M]. London & Washington：Cassell，1997.

[5] Fairclough，N.. *Language and Power* [M]. London：Longman，1989.

[6] Halliday，M. A. K. Language as Code and Language as Behavior：A Systematic Functional Interpretation of the Nature and Ontogenesis of Dialogue [C]//R. Fawcett，M. A. K Halliday，S. Lamb & A. Makkai (eds). *The Semiotics of Cul-*

ture and Language. Vol. 2: *Language and Other Semiotic Systems of Culture*. London: Pinter, 1984.

[7] Halliday, M. A. K.. *An Introduction to Functional Grammar* [M]. London: Edward Arnold, 1994.

[8] Halliday, M. A. K.. *A Course in Spoken English: Intonation* [M]. Oxford: Oxford University Press, 1970.

[9] Harris, S. Questions as a mode of control in magistrates' courts [J]. *International Journal of the Sociology of Language*, 1984(49): 5-27.

[10] Harris, S. Courtroom discourse as genre: some problems and issues [C]//In R. P. Fawcett and D. Young (ed.). *New Developments in Systemic Linguistics*. London and New York: Pinter Publishers, 1988.

[11] Heritage, J.. The Limits of Questions: Negative Interrogatives and Hostile Question Content [J]. *Journal of Pragmatics*, 2002 (34): 1427-1446.

[12] Hoye, L.. *Adverbs and Modality in English* [M]. London & New York: Longman, 1997.

[13] Hodge, R. & Kress, G.. *Language as Ideology* [M]. London & New York: Routledge, 1993.

[14] Hudson, R. A.. *Sociolinguistics* [M]. 2nd edition. Cambridge: Cambridge University Press, 1996.

[15] Koshik, I. Wh-questions used as challenges [J]. *Discourse & Society*, Vol. 5, 2003 (1): 51-77.

[16] Levinson, S. C.. *Pragmatics* [M]. Cambridge: Cambridge University Press, 1983.

[17] Linell, P.. The power of dialogue dynamics [C]//I. Markovά and K. Foppa (ed.). *The Dynamics of Dialogue*. London: Harvester Wheatsheaf, 1990.

[18] Martin, J. R.. Analyzing Genre: Functional Parameters [C]//F. Christie and J. R. Martin (eds.). *Genre and Institutions: Social Process in the Workplace and School*. London & Washington: Cassell, 1997.

[19] Martin, J. R.. Beyond exchange: Appraisal System in English [C]//S. Hunston and G. Thompson (ed.). *Evaluation in Text: Authorial Stance and the Construction of Discourse*. Oxford: Oxford University Press, 2000.

[20] O'Barr, W. M.. *Linguistic Evidence: Language, Power and Strategy in the Courtroom* [M]. New York: Academic Press, 1982.

[21] O'Connor, J. D.. and Arnold, G. F.. *Intonation of Colloquial English* [M].

London: Longman, 1973.

[22] Sacks, H.. *Lectures on Conversation* [C]. Vols. I. II. (G. Jefferson, ed.) Oxford: Blackwell, 1995.

[23] Tench, P.. *The Intonation Systems of English* [M]. London & New York: Cassell, 1996.

[24] Tsui, A.. A functional Description of Questions [C]//M. Coulthard (ed.). *Advances in Spoken Discourse Analysis*. London & New York: Routledge, 1992.

[25] Van Dijk, T. A.. Critical discourse analysis [C]//S. Deborah, D. Tannen & H. E. Hamilton (ed.). *The Handbook of Discourse Analysis*. Oxford: Blackwell, 2001.

[26] Watts, R. J.. *Power in FamilyDiscourse*[M]. Berlin: Mouton de Gruyter, 1991.

[27] Wodak, R.. *Disorders of Discourse*[M]. London and New York: Longman, 1996.

浅论阿拉伯语的若干特点

蔡春阳

阿拉伯语(اللغة العربية)是阿拉伯民族的共同语，属于闪含语系闪米特语族，共有 28 个字母，分为标准语和方言。阿拉伯语产生于阿拉伯半岛，最初是游牧民族的语言，随着公元 7 世纪伊斯兰教的产生，阿拉伯语迅速传播，成为西亚和北非 23 个阿拉伯国家和地区的官方语言，也是全世界穆斯林的宗教语言和联合国工作语言之一。由于自然环境、历史条件和宗教信仰等原因，阿拉伯语具有鲜明的个性特点。

一、阿拉伯语的民族性

斯大林说："自人类社会形成民族以后，语言就打上了民族的烙印。"[①]民族是"历史上形成的一个有共同语言、有共同地域、有共同经济生活以及有表现于共同文化上的共同心理状态的稳定的共同体。"[②]语言是人类交流和沟通的工具，是各民族在劳动实践中创造出来的，由于自然环境和历史条件不同，以及文化背景、宗教信仰、价值观念、风俗习惯和心理素质等诸多方面的差异，每种语言都有自身的、有别于其他语言的特点。阿拉伯语的特点就表现为它的民族性。

---

① 候健：《文学通论》，北京大学出版社 1886 年版，第 401 页。
② 《斯大林全集》第 2 卷，人民出版社 1953 年版，第 294 页。

丰富的词汇和修辞方法呈现出阿拉伯游牧民族的基本特征。不同语言的词汇不是一一对应的，它反映了使用这种语言的民族的基本特征。古代阿拉伯人以游牧民族为主，主要生活在荒凉的沙漠里，生活方式朴实简单，生存环境艰苦恶劣，能见到的就是炽热的太阳、一望无际的沙漠、成群的骆驼、寥寥无几的牧民。这样的自然环境和历史条件对阿拉伯语词汇的发展产生了深刻的影响，而阿拉伯语在词汇方面也呈现出阿拉伯游牧民族的基本特征。如，阿语中关于风的词汇很多：沙漠地区多风沙，不同的风对气候的影响很大，而不同的天气直接影响着放牧活动的进行，因而阿拉伯游牧人对风的观察十分细致，能分辨出各种不同的风，并一一予以命名。如：البليل（带有湿气的冷风）、الحاصبة（刮起石头的风）、الواقع（授粉的风）、العقيم（没有雨也不会折断树的风）、الهجوم（拔起帐篷的风）等。据德国人迪哈默统计，阿语中的骆驼及与骆驼有关的事物名称共有 5 644 个，这众多的名称可以区分骆驼的公母、年龄、品种、大小、强壮。如：جمل（四岁以上的公驼）、المتراح（奶易枯竭的母驼）、السلوف أو الدفون（带路的骆驼）、الذبول（用以驮物的骆驼）、القعود（当坐骑的骆驼），等等。"根据人类学的观点，某种事物或概念在一种文化中的地位越重要，有关它的词汇就越多，分类也就越细。"从阿拉伯民族对骆驼的分类情况来看，我们可以看出骆驼对于阿拉伯游牧民族社会生产和生活的重要性①。

此外，阿语 أهلا وسهلا（你好）原意为"来到平原，见到亲人"，反映出阿拉伯人长期生活在沙漠里，人烟稀少，很难见到过往的人，所以来到平原见到路人，就好像见到自己的亲人一般亲切温暖。这是游牧生活的真实写照，也是游牧民族生存环境的折射和产物。

修辞方法上，阿语通常用جمل（骆驼）比喻吃苦耐劳的人，因为骆驼对游牧民族的作用非常大，他们的日常生活和交通工具主要依靠骆驼。أسد（狮子）比喻勇敢的人，غزال（羚羊）形容身材娇好的女性，قمر（满月）形容容貌美丽的女性——游牧民族白天生活在炙热的太阳下，夜晚的月亮给他们带来凉爽宜人的感觉，在他们心中，晚上的满月是最美丽动人的。حمار（驴）比喻愚蠢和脾气暴躁的人，ببغاء（鹦鹉）比喻随声附和、人云亦云，بلبل（夜莺）形容动

① 朱立才：《游牧文化与农耕文化在阿汉词汇中的体现》，载《世界汉语教学》2004 年第 4 期。

人的歌喉，قنفذ ليل（夜刺猬）比喻挑拨离间者，حبة（蛇）比喻长命百岁。用这些沙漠中常见动物来描述客观事物，反映出游牧民族既古朴又原始的生活方式。

二、阿拉伯语的宗教性

众多的宗教用语和宗教术语渗透出阿拉伯民族对伊斯兰教的虔诚信仰。阿拉伯语是伊斯兰教经典《古兰经》的语言，伊斯兰教是阿拉伯民族的主要宗教信仰，阿拉伯语中有大量的宗教用语和宗教术语贯穿于阿拉伯民族生活的方方面面，这反映了阿拉伯语与伊斯兰教的密切关系、阿拉伯民族对伊斯兰教的虔诚信仰以及阿拉伯人对真主安拉的敬畏。

阿语中与真主安拉（الله）有关的用语比比皆是。如：بالله عليك（请看在真主面上），يا الله（主啊！）表示祈望、痛苦、悲伤和激怒，الله أعلم（真主知道得最清楚）表示谦虚，الله يسلمك（主使你顺利、平安）通常在外出平安归来时使用，ان شاء الله（但愿如此）、باسم الله رحمان رحيم（以大慈大悲的真主的名义）经常出现在阿拉伯人的口语和书面表达中——在阿拉伯人看来，他们的一切行为都必须服从真主的意愿，以真主的名义进行，因此阿拉伯人在会议、新闻广播、信函、谈判、文件等正式场合都要首先诵读这句话[①]。الحمد الله（赞美真主、真主至上）是阿拉伯人对美好事物表示感叹时的独特表达方式，他们把一切功劳和美名都归功于真主安拉，他们的命运掌握在安拉手中，日常生活的方方面面都受真主安拉的监视，赞美真主、祈求庇护成为日常心愿，这就使得语言与宗教相结合，受宗教感染并表现出强烈的宗教性。

阿拉伯人名与其他民族人名的最明显区别就是常把自己视做真主的奴仆和用伊斯兰教先知的美名作为自己的名字。如：عبد الله（阿卜杜拉）、حميد الله（哈米德拉），علي（阿里，先知穆罕默德堂弟、女婿、第四任正统哈里发的名字），محمد（穆罕默德，伊斯兰教先知的名字）。这些含有浓厚色彩的宗教名字在阿拉伯语中屡见不鲜。

此外，阿拉伯语中有大量的宗教术语。如：الصدقة（教法、教律）、غسل

① 朱立才：《阿拉伯人的交际用语》，载《世界宗教文化》2004年第3期。

（大净）、وضوء（小净）、لهام سماوي（天启）、عيد الأضحي（开斋节）和伊斯兰教的五功：الشهادتان（念）、الصلاة（礼拜）、لصوم（斋戒）、وكاة（天课）、الحج（朝觐），还有每日的五次礼拜：صلاة الصبح（晨礼）、صلاة الظهر（晌礼）、صلاة العصر（晡礼）、صلاة المغرب（昏礼）、صلاة العشاء（宵礼）等。以上的例子不难看出阿拉伯民族强烈的宗教性集中地反映在了它的语言上，而阿拉伯语也细致描绘出阿拉伯民族强烈的宗教信仰。

三、阿拉伯语的开放性

大量借用外来词表现出阿拉伯民族对外来文化的开放性和包容性。语言学家萨丕尔说："语言像文化一样，很少自给自足。交际的需要使说一种语言的人和说邻近语言的或说文化上占优势的语言的人发生直接或间接的接触。语言的接触实质上是文化的接触，这种接触导致外来词的产生。"外来词是从其他语言借用到本民族语言的词。世界上的任何语言都是在与其他语言进行交流和相互吸收的过程中生存和发展的。借用外来词是丰富本民族语言的主要途径和重要方法，世界上没借用过外来词的语言是不存在的，但阿拉伯语对大量外来词的借用也是历史上罕见的。这是由于阿拉伯世界一直处于东、西方文化的交汇处，历来承担着东、西方文化交流的纽带作用。阿拉伯世界复杂而丰富的历史，尤其是受到全球化浪潮的影响，使得阿拉伯语在历史发展中吸收了大量的外来词，因而也造就了阿拉伯语蔚为大观的开放性与包容性特征。

阿拉伯语吸收外来词的历史主要分为三个时期：（1）贾希里亚时期和伊斯兰教初期；（2）倭马亚朝和阿拔斯朝期间；（3）近代阿拉伯文化复兴运动和当代阿拉伯科学复兴运动（19 世纪末至今）。第一时期主要借用阿拉米语和波斯语词汇。第二时期以百年翻译运动为特色，大量借用外来词，尤其是波斯语和希腊语词汇。如：波斯语的 اليقوت（宝石）、البنفبج（紫罗兰）、الوسن（百合）、السيد（白面包）以及源于希腊语的 العردوس（天堂）、البطاق（标签）、القطل（水管）、الطبيعة(自然）等。第三时期主要从英语、法语、意大利语等西方语言中借用外来词，这个时期借用的外来词数量很大，涉及现代生活的各个领域，尤其是科技方面。如 piano—بيانو（钢琴）、autobus— اوتوبيس（公共汽车）、shampoo—شامبو （洗发水）、nicotine— نركودين （尼古丁）、radar—رادار （雷达）、soviet—سوفيات （苏维埃）、telephone— تلفون（电话）、television—تلفزيون（电视）、computer—كومبيوتر(计算机)等[①]。阿拉伯语对大量外来词的借用和吸收，追求自身语言的不断完善和发展，表现出阿拉伯民族对外来文化的开放性和包容性。

四、阿拉伯语的丰富性

阿拉伯国家西濒大西洋，东邻印度洋，北面隔地中海和欧洲相望，中间横贯红海，位于西亚、北非，紧靠欧洲，总面积约 1 400 万平方千米，比欧洲面积还大。阿拉伯民族主要包括阿拉伯人、贝都因人、柏柏尔人、索马里人、德鲁兹人和埃及人，还有库尔德人、土耳其人和黑人等少数民族。阿拉伯国家地形复杂，西部高、东部低，西部为山区、东部为台地，还有山脉、沙漠、河流等各种地形。这种广阔的地域、多样性的民族构成和复杂多变的地形造就了阿拉伯语的丰富性。

标准阿拉伯语起源于阿拉伯半岛的古莱什语，后来传播到阿拉伯半岛相邻的国家和地区。阿拔斯王朝著名的哲学家和思想家法拉比普说过：“古莱什民族是最善于选择最简明、最易上口、最动听而又最能表达内心情感的词句的阿拉伯人。”[②]由于历史条件和社会环境的影响，古莱什部落把演说和赛诗作为他们文体活动和表现自我的主要形式，在这种环境下，阿拉伯语不断发展成熟，阿拉伯人个个能言善辩，阿语成为使用最广泛、词汇最丰富、表达最精练的语言。

阿语中言简意赅的表达形式屡见不鲜，几个词的简单组合就寓意丰富了。如：عين بعين意为以眼还眼、以牙还牙，عين意为眼睛，三个简单的词组合在一起就形象地使读者明白其意，反映了阿拉伯人用词的精准。又如：ما فات فات意为生米煮成熟饭，فات意为错过，意思是错过的就错过了，无法改变，不可挽回。仅用两个相同的动词就展现出一种动态情景，可以看出阿拉伯人用词的

① 陈中耀：《阿拉伯语的词汇与词（三）》，载《阿拉伯世界》2000 年第 1 期。
② 刘开古：《阿拉伯语发展史》，上海外语教育出版社 1995 年版，第 247 页。

灵活。又如：صداقة كأسا وطاسا意为酒肉朋友，كأسا和طاسا都是酒杯的意思，صداقة是友谊的意思。还有بيضة الديك，意为异想天开，原意是公鸡蛋。通过这种最能表达事物特征的词和简单句式表达出丰富的内涵，表现了阿拉伯人用词的简练。

种类繁多的同义词描绘出阿拉伯民族丰富的情感。阿语词汇中有大量的同义词，阿拉伯人常用同义词或同一语的重复使用来加强语气，表达丰富的情感和细腻的内心世界。如：阿语中的زوجة（妻子）、حبيب（恋人）、عشيقة（情人）、خليلة（情妇），这四个词意思相近，属于同义词，但词的感情色彩不同，所表达的内心情感也完全不同。阿拉伯语同义词繁多，如“狮子”有 500 个词，“剑”有 1 000 个词，“蛇”有 200 个词，“骆驼”有 255 个词，“酒”有 100 个词，“灾难”有 400 多个词。这一方面是因为阿拉伯语在形成标准语的过程中吸收了阿拉伯半岛诸多部落的方言，另一方面也是阿拉伯人细腻而丰富情感的集中体现。如：!اذهب اذهب（你走吧，走吧）和.هيهات هيهات الأمر（这件事情是不可能的，不可能的）通过重复动词或动名词来强调动作本身或动名词表达的感情色彩。又如 .يشعر بألم و حزن و لوعة و حسر و حرقة（他感到极度悲伤），句中ألم、حزن、لوعة、حسر和حرقة 五个词都表示痛苦、悲伤的意思，通过同义词的重复使用和叠加表达强烈的、真挚的内心情感。无论是描人绘物，还是叙事说理，诸如此类的语言现象在阿语中频繁出现，描绘出阿拉伯民族发自内心、自然流露、毫不掩饰的丰富情感。

参考文献：

[1] 周烈，蒋传瑛. 阿拉伯语与阿拉伯文化[M]. 北京：外语教学与研究出版社，1998.
[2] 国少华. 阿拉伯语词汇学[M]. 北京：外语教学与研究出版社，1998.
[3] 陈中耀. 阿拉伯语语言与修辞[M]. 上海：上海外语教育出版社，2001.
[4] 刘开古. 阿拉伯语发展史[M]. 上海：上海外语教育出版社，1995.
[5] 王有勇. 阿拉伯语言风格学[M]. 上海：上海外语教育出版社，2000.
[6] 周文巨. 阿拉伯语语言研究[M]. 上海：上海外语教育出版社，2002.
[7] 刘开古. 阿拉伯语汉语翻译教程[M]. 上海：上海外语教育出版社，1991.
[8] 周烈. 阿拉伯语语言学[M]. 北京：外语教学与研究出版社，1995.

[9] 余章荣. 阿拉伯语修辞[M]. 北京：外语教学与研究出版社，1993.
[10] 杨言洪. 阿拉伯语汉语成语谚语词典[Z]. 北京：对外经济贸易大学出版社，1995.
[11] 陈万里. 阿拉伯概况[M]. 上海：上海外语教育出版社，1988.

「うち」与「そと」之词义浅析

饶琼珍

笔者通过多年的教学实践发现，尽管「うち」与「そと」这一组词的词义丰富，但学生很少能完全理解、掌握这一组词的内外层含义。于是，笔者结合自身的教学实践，查阅相关资料，对「うち」与「そと」这两个词的微观词义、构词功能及宏观词义作如下对比分析。

一、「うち」与「そと」的基础词义（微观词义）

（一）「うち」的基础词义

据日语『新明解国語辞典』的注解，「うち」的词义主要有七个方面：

（1）何かで区切られた中（側）、即ち：範囲内（用什么东西将其隔开，即指某个范围之内），汉语相对应的词义为"内"、"中"、"里面"。例如：

①寒いから内へ入りましょう。/冷，到里面去吧。

②この内から一つ選んでください。/请你从这当中，挑一个。

③これもわたしの仕事のうちです。/这也是我工作的分内。

（2）時間、数量の一定の限定内（时间、数量的一定限度）。汉语相对应的词义为：a. "之内"、"以内"；b. "时候"、"趁着"。例如：

①三日のうちにやりとげる。/三天之内完成。

②一時間のうちに帰ってきます。/一小时之内回来。

③増水期 入らないうちにダム工事を完成する。/趁没有进入汛期，把水

库工程完成。

④暗くならにうちに帰る。/趁天还没黑，回去。

⑤若いうちに勉強せよ。/趁年轻学习吧。

⑥さめないうちにお上がりください。/请趁热吃。

(3) 家族の集まりとしてのその人の家（の人）（作为家人团聚的某人的家、家里人）。汉语相对应的词义为“家”、“家里人”。这时相对应的日语汉字为「内」「家」。例如：

①うちへ遊びにいらっしゃい。/到家里来玩。

②うちを持つ。/结婚、成家。

③うちで野球の番組を見る。/在家里看棒球节目。

(4) 自分の住む家。/自己住的房子。

①退職金で初めて家をたてる。/第一次用退休金盖房子。

②明日はうちにいる。/明天在家。

③三階建てのうち。/三层楼的房子。

(5) 自分の夫（妻）。指自己的丈夫或妻子。例如：

①うちの人。/我丈夫。

②うちの者。/我妻子（家属）。

(6) 自分の仲間（属する団体、組織など）。指自己的朋友、所属团体、组织等。例如：その計画はうちでたてよう。

①うちの学校/ 我们学校。

②うちの会社/ 我们公司。

(7) 関西の女性語で（わたし）。日本关西地方妇女用语（我）。

（二）「そと」的基本词义

据日语『新明解国語辞典』的注解，「そと」的词义主要有：

（1）中、内 囲みや仕切りに限定されない、広い部分（外面、外边）。

①そとから帰る。/从外面回来。
②そとで食事する。/在外面吃饭。
③汽車の窓からそとの景色を見る。/从火车的车窗看外面的风景。

（2）表に現れて見える部分（表面、外部）。

①不満をそとへ表わす。/表露出不满。
②喜びをそとへ表わす。/流露出喜悦。

（3）その建物から出たところ（通り）。

①そとは寒い。/ 屋外冷。
②冬にもそとで体を鍛える。/即使冬天也在屋外锻炼身体。

（4）自分の家でない、別の場所（别处、别的地方）。

よそで食事する。/在外就餐。

（5）「そとづら」の略（外面、外表）。

外面だけはりっぱだ。/仅外表漂亮。

从上述所列「うち」与「そと」的基本词义看，「うち」的基础词义中，（1）、（2）项的日语汉字多数可写为「中」，其反义词为「そと」。在（3）、（5）项基本词义中，「うち」的日语汉字通常也可写为「家」。而第（3）、（5）项的反义词为「よそ」。从词义范围分析，「うち」基础的词义比「そと」之基础词义宽。

二、「うち」与「そと」构词功能

（一）由「うち」、「そと」构成的复合词

「うち」与「そと」不仅比一般普通名词词义宽泛，而且还具有复合词的功能，即能和其他名词构成复合词。下面笔者列举部分由「うち」与「そと」构成的复合词，并对所列举的复合词进行分析。

①うちがわ（内側）——そとがわ（外側）
②うちわく（内枠）——そとわく（外枠）
③うちまた（内股）——そとまた（外股）
④うちうみ（内海）——そとうみ（外海）
⑤うちまわり（内回り）——そとまわり（外回り）
⑥うちぶろ（内風呂）——そとぶろ（外風呂）
⑦うちぼり（内堀）——そとぼり（外堀）

上述所列 7 组词是由「うち」与「そと」所构成的复合词，这些都分别为词义相反的复合词。从这些复合词词义上分析，其基本词义没有超出本文“一”中所列「うち」与「そと」基本词义（1）的词义范围。即「うち」词义（1）何かで区切られた中（側）、即ち：範囲内（用什么东西将其隔开，即指某个范围之内）。「そと」词义（1）中、内 囲みや仕切りに限定されない、広い部分（外面、外边）。在上述「うち」与「そと」基本词义部分笔者已将所列词的词义逐一进行了对比。二者在第（1）项词义中是一组词义对等的反义词。所列复合词与原词相比，基本词义没有改变，但所指范围与基本词义相比所指内容更为具体。

（二）由「うち」构成的复合词

在上述文段中，笔者已逐一将「うち」与「そと」的基本词义进行了对比。通过对比，可以看到「うち」词义较「そと」词义宽泛，「うち」中的一部分词义可以与「そと」互为对等的反义词，而其余的部分则不能互为反义词。下面笔者列举部分由「うち」构成的复合词。在下述所列复合词中没有由「そと」所构成的相对应的反义词。如：

①うちべんけい（内弁慶）——窝里横的人
②うちいわい（内祝い）——家庭或内部的庆贺
③うちわ（内輪）——家里、内部
④うちまく（内幕）——内幕、内情
⑤うちわれ（内輪割れ）——内部决裂
⑥うちわもめ（内輪揉め）——内部争吵、内讧
⑦うちうち（内内）——私下、暗地
⑧うちげいこ（内稽古）——在自己家里教授技艺的艺人
⑨うちポケット（内ポケット）——内包、里兜
⑩まつのうち（松の内）——新年门前装饰松枝的期间
⑪まくのうち（幕の内）——盒饭的一种
⑫てのうち（手の内）——手腕、势力范围

三、「うち」与「そと」在语言文化层面的折射（宏观词义）

「うち」与「そと」除具有上述所列举的基础词义及构词功能外，在日常生活中还具有支配日本人的日常语言行为的作用。在文中，笔者把这一作用称为「うち」与「そと」的文化折射，即宏观词义。以下笔者将对这一宏观层面的词义进行分析。

（一）「うち」、「そと」日本人集团意识及语言行为的体现

日本人可以说是世界上集团意识极其强的民族之一。由上下级关系所形成的“序列社会”，即纵向式的社会构成日本社会的一大特点。据说在日本，年轻人在大学或高中毕业就职时，与将来想从事某一工作这种「就職」（就职）观念相比，将来自己进入哪家公司工作这种「就社」（在某一公司就职）的意识更为强烈。年轻人在就职时，大多数人都选择进大公司或一流公司，因此，在日本大公司或一流公司的就职竞争是最为激烈的。之所以如此，据说那是因为在日本规模大的公司或一流公司，除工资、福利等待遇好之外，更主要的是公司内上下级关系秩序严谨，这对即将就职的年轻人来说对将来的不安因素相对要少（在日本，员工的待遇及职务是随着工作年限的增加而不断增加的），因此年轻人会因为自己能在大公司就职而感到安心。公司在录用新员工时，往往不决定其具体的工作种类。最为常见的例子是录用之后具体的工作安排由公

司决定，所以在录用时完全没有听取本人关于工作种类的意愿。这就是年轻人在就职时所注重的不是将来自己“想从事什么工作（どんな仕事をしたいか）”，而是考虑自己将来“想成为哪一家公司的员工（どういう会社の人間になるか）”的原因之一。年轻人一旦就职于某一公司，其归属感及集团意识亦随着自己所就职的公司带来的安心感而日益增强。对于和自己一块儿在同一公司工作的所有人员（包括上司、长辈、同事等）都称为「うちの者」（家里人、自己一方的人）。与此相对应的则是「そとの者（よそ者）」（局外人、集团之外的人）。作为雇用方的公司或集团通常把员工、职员看做家里人，上司通常会在部下的结婚典礼上当媒人，公司举办各种运动会，组织赏花、旅游等活动。无论是上司还是部下，自己生活的一切都与公司或集团有着密切的联系，由此员工、职员之间通常会萌生一种同一组织、同一整体的意识。即通过共有的「場」（公司、集团）而产生一种相互间的同族意识。笔者认为，这大概就是日本人把在同一公司或集团工作的同事称为「うちの者」（家里人）的缘故吧。

日本人在对人的态度方面也往往受「うち」、「そと」所左右，若是「うちの者」，通常会按照「うちの者」的礼仪进行交往。新员工对老员工、上司态度通常比较恭敬、谦虚。在日本经常会看到这样的场景：在拥挤的电车上，某一年轻职员，看见自己的先辈（比自己先进的公司的员工）或公司的上司也乘上了同一辆电车时，通常显得十分慌张，并会立即站起来主动让座。相反，如果有一位素不相识的老者站在自己的座位旁，那个年轻人会装作没有看见的样子，是不可能把座位让给站在自己身边的那位老者的。这就是日本人在对待「うちの者」与对「そとの者（よそ者）」时，在态度上所表现出的如此令人吃惊的明显的差异。在对待「うちの者」时，按照严格的上下级关系及次序进行，下级对上级恭敬、谦虚，热情、礼貌，而对待「そとの者（よそ者）」时，却往往表现得极为冷漠。

（二）「うち」、「そと」日本人日常语言行为的准绳

众所周知，敬语是日语的一大特点之一。由于日本人的日常语言行为受到诸多因素的影响，因此日语措辞往往会因为说话双方的上下、亲疏等各种关系的不同而变化较大。这里所说的上下、亲疏等关系可以用「うち」、「そと」这一概念来替代。因为，现代日语敬语主要是对「そと」这一群体所使用，而且在「そと」这一群体中的「上、下」关系明显存在。与此相对应，「うち」中的「上、下」关系要弱得多。因此笔者认为，在分析日常生活中支配

日本人待人语言行动的原理之时，首先要分析的是「うち、そと」的关系，以及交织于「うち、そと」各层面的「上、下」关系。

在日本，作为「うち」（自己人）可以交往的人际关系，日本语言学家井出祥子列举出如下三种场合：

①くつろいだ時の家族間（身心放松时的家人之间）。
②仲のよい友人間のつき合い（好朋友之间的交往）。
③酒の席での男のつき合い（酒桌上男子间的交往）。

在上述三种场合，③属于临时场合，虽然是一种精神上的临时性放松，但由于存在程度问题，在③的交往中很容易形成一般日常关系，所以③的交往不如①②之间的关系那么固定、持久。据井出先生分析，日本人在「うち」之中，喜欢使用非正式的、强烈建议性的、亲密的语言表达。日本人普遍认为「うち」是一个可以说真心话、允许发牢骚、可以撒娇的地方。此外，日本人在对待「うち」之外（即「そと」）的朋友、同行、熟人等时，无论在社会方面或是心理方面，因为存在一定的利益关系，在与「そと」的交往中，通常仅限于注重情面上的交往，所说的话不是真心话而是场面话，并且有意识地努力保持与对方之间的“和”及“秩序”，极力控制自我，仅作表面上敷衍。换句话说，与「そと」的交往是一个远比理论更须提防自己的言行不刺激、不伤害对方的世界。所以，在与「そと」的交往中，深入交往，说真心话都具有使“和”崩溃的危险。因此，在「そと」（内部之外的世界）这个层面的交往中，日本人通常喜欢使用正式的、委婉的、十分谨慎的语言表达。

如上所述，日本人在「うち」（内部世界）及「そと」（内部之外的世界）的语言行为不仅其差异十分明显，而且其界限也非常分明。如果把在「うち」（内部世界）使用的语言用于「そと」（内部之外的世界）的人，会被认为是「横柄」（傲慢）、「無作法」（没礼貌）、「無教養」（无教养）。相反，如果把「そと」（内部之外的世界）语言措辞带入「うち」（内部世界）的话则会被指责为「水臭い」（见外）、「他人行儀」（外道、多礼）、「お上品ぶっている」（装文雅）等。由此可见，「うち」、「そと」在日本人日常语言行为中不但起着举足轻重的作用，而且通过上述「うち」、「そと」的表层及深层含义的对比分析，可以揭示出日语语言及日本文化的部分重要特点。

参考文献：

[1] 国立国語研究所．敬語教育の基本問題（上）[M]．[出版地不详]：大蔵所印刷局，平成4年．
[2] 国立国語研究所．敬語教育の基本問題（下）[M]．[出版地不详]：大蔵所印刷局，平成4年．
[3] 文化庁．日本語の特色 [M]．[出版地不详]：大蔵所印刷局，昭和63年．
[4] 大森和夫．日本（下）[M]．北京：外语教学与研究出版社，2005.
[5] 山田忠雄．新明解国語辞典 [M]．第3版．[出版地不详]：三省堂，昭和55年．
[6] 大连外国语学院．新日汉辞典 [M]．沈阳：辽宁人民出版社，1983.
[7] 靳卫卫．走进日本 [M]．北京：北京语言大学出版社，2005.

日本語動詞アスペクト「……ている」の意味

——中国語との対照において

劉　一

はじめに

日本語にしても、中国語にしても、発話時を中心にして、その時点との事態を言うのか、それより以前、つまり過去の事態を言うのか、あるいは今より先の未来の事態を言うのかによって、動詞が規則的に形をかえるかと、そうでないとがある。ここでは、ある現象を、現在時を基準にして過去か未来かで描き分けるの出なく、それを一つの幅のある事象の中のプロセスのどの点かによって描き分ける、つまり、始動か、途中継続進行中、未完結のものと見るか、完了したもの、完結したものと見るかに動詞の形を対応させるというシステムつまりアスペクトについて及びたい。日本語動詞アスペクトはそのもっとも基本的な形が「……ている」であるが、中国語の場合は、それに対応する表現は何であろうか、つまり中国語のアスペクトは何であるか及びそれぞれの意味特徴について見てみたい。

一、動きの最中

動きの最中とは、問題となっている基準時において、動きが始まって終わるまでの動きの最中の状態に主体があること表わす。例えば、

① 父は新聞を読んでいる。
爸爸正在（在）看报。爸爸看着报。
② 子供たちが遊んでいる。
孩子们正在（在）玩。孩子们玩着。
③ 和子は走っている。
和子正在（在）跑。和子跑着。
④ 列車が大橋を通っている。
列车正在（在）经过大桥。
⑤ 庭で犬が吠えている。
院子里狗正在（在）叫。院子里狗叫着。

のように「読んでいる」、「遊んでいる」、「走っている」、「通っている」、「吠えている」のは、いずれも動作のある時間内継続すること、または現在継続中であることを表わすものである。中国語の場合は、動作の進行中は、文の通り、「正在（在）」、「着」で表わしているのである。語形の変化はまったくなかった。これは孤立語という中国語の性質に規定されたのである。アスペクトなどの意味を表わすには、必ず動詞とそれ以外の語と組み合わせなければならない。前の例のように、動きの最中即ち動作の進行中の表現は、動詞の「読」、「玩」、「跑」、「経過」、「叫」などの前に「正在（在）」を、後或は真中に「着」を使わなければならない。

二、持続

これは、前の「動きの最中」によく似ているが、例えば、

① 彼は立っている。
他在站着。
② 電燈が点いている。
电灯在点着。
③ 窓が開けている。
窗子在开着。
④ 母は息子の合格をとても喜んでいる。
母亲为儿子的考取在（而）高兴。

⑤ 太郎は恋人のことを悩んでいる。
太郎为恋人的事情在烦恼。

以上の例を見れば、全部同一状態の継続であるが、動きの「最中」ではない。だから持続態を名づける。④、⑤の例の場合、動作、動きの継続ではなく、心的な状態の持続を表わしている。その動きが顕在的、外在的でないことは、さらに動きが希薄になって来た。これは、動きを伴った事態の持続であるものの、典型的な「動きの最中」から「単純状態」へと移り動き傾向がある。中国語の場合は、「在……着」で動作、動きの持続を表わすとわかった。しかし、④、⑤の場合は、動きの表現はすごく薄く、「在……着」を使わなくてもよい。

三、結果の残存

結果の残存とは、動きが終わり、その動きの結果を生じた新しい状態が存在、持続していることを表わす。例えば、

① 彼は結婚している。
他结婚了。
② 花瓶が倒れている。
花瓶倒了。
③ 壁が崩れている。
墙塌了。
④ 今日の気温が三十度を越えている。
今天的气温超过了三十度。
⑤ 梅雨が開けている。
梅雨期过去了。

以上の「……ている」形が、過去の動作、作用の結果から生じた新しい状態がまだ存在、持続していることであるが、例①の「結婚している」は、基準時以前に「結婚する」という事がまたしていなかった主体「彼」に起こり、その結果を生じた新しい状態が即ち基準時の現在は彼は妻帯者になった。つまり「結婚する」という結果を成り立つのである。中国語の文「…

結婚了」、「…倒了」、「…塌了」、「…超過了…」、「…過去了」いずれも動詞+完了助詞「了」で表わしたのである。即ち、結果の残存を表わすのは中国語のアスペクトは「……了」を使わなければならない。

四、経験・完了

経験・完了とは、動きが終わったことを基準時から眺めて捉えたもので、動きが終わり、その結果が間接的に主体に残っていることを表わす。次の例を見ると、

① ここに来る前にすでに知り合っている。
在来此之前就已经相识了。
② 田中先生は息子を失っている。
田中先生失去了儿子。
③ 福岡家は赤字で店をしまっている。
福岗家因赤字关了店。
④ 鈴木先生は自叙伝を出版している。
铃木先生出版了自传。
⑤ 父親が郊外に土地を求めている。
父亲在郊外买了土地。

これらは、いずれも基準時において、主体が動きの最中にあるのでもなければ、基準時以前に起こった動きによって引き起こされた新しい状態の中に主体があるのでもない。基準時以前に起こった動きを基準時との関連において、基準時から眺めることによって、基準時における主体への間接的な影響といった意味合いが出てくるのである。即ち、主体の状態を動きの結果を直接的には規定してこない、動きの結果は、主体の経歴に影響を残すといったものである。この直接的には規定してこないといったところが「結果の残存」との基本の違いである。例えば、

① 太郎は大学に合格している。

② 太郎は二〇〇〇年に大学に合格している。もちろん、①は結果の残存であり、②は経験・完了である。結果の残存の①では、基準時の現在、太郎

は大学生であるということが意味されているが、経験・完了の②では、現在太郎が大学生であるということは必ずしも意味されてはいない。基準時の現在以前に途中退学をしていて、現在大学生ではない可能性もあると考えてもよい。中国語の場合は、前の「結果の残存」同じように「動詞＋了」という形式で表わすのである。

五、単純状態

単純状態とは、動きの契機を持たず、単に持続状態を表わすものである。単純状態は二つの種類がある。次の例を見てみると、

① 赤のネクタイが洋服によく合っている。
红色领带很适合于西装。
② 台風で被害総額が一億円に上がっている。
由于台风被害总额达一億円。
③ 品物が見本と違っている。
实物和样品不尽相同。
④ 弘の成績が妹より劣っている。
弘的成绩不如妹妹。
⑤ 道はその角で左に折れている。
道路在那面向左转了。

以上のように「ている形」と「る形」の双方を有し、それらが共に「単純状態」を表わす場合である。次の例は、

⑥ この料理は辛味が勝っている。
这料理以辛辣而闻名。
⑦ 彼女は母親の面影を残している。
她和母亲很相像。
⑧ この写真はきれいに写っている。
这张照片照得很漂亮。
⑨ 彼は知識の発達が遅れている。
他大脑发育较晚。

⑩ 恵子の話はいつも決まっている。
　恵子的话题总也不变。

以上、動詞そのものは文中の表現が「る」形を持たずに「単純状態」を表わす「ている」形のみの動詞である。もちろん、動詞としては他の用法をも持っているが、「単純状態」を表わす用法ではやはり「る」形を持たず、その「ている」形が「単純状態」を表す動詞である。いわゆる「形容詞的な意味」を表わしている。だから、起こり終わりということは考えられない。つまり、ある状態にあることを表わすのである。中国語は「単純状態」に相当する表現が例のとおりなかったのである。

むすび

以上、日本語動詞アスペクト「……ている」の意味と中国語のアスペクトの表現・意味を見てみたが、

① 日本語の場合、「……ている」はその前の動詞と組み合わせたら、前に見たように、動きの最中、持続、結果の残存、経験・完了、単純状態などいろんな意味を表わされる。

中国語のアスペクトの表現は、「正在…」、「在…」、「…着」、「…了」などがある。動詞と組み合わせたら、「正在…」、「在…」は動きの最中を、「…着」は持続を、「…了」は結果の残存、経験・完了を表わすのである。

② 日本語動詞＋ているの形式は、前の動詞の性格によって、アスペクトの意味を変わるのである。

中国語の場合は逆にアスペクトの表現によってアスペクトの意味を決まるのである。

③ 日本語はある状態にあることを表わす「単純状態」というアスペクトがあるが、中国語の場合はそれに相当するアスペクトの形式はなかった。

最後に本文は中日アスペクトの基本を対照的に触れたが、詳しい展開がしなかった。間違ったところもあろうと思うころである。今後、よく勉強したうえで、より良い論文を書き上げたいと思う。

参考文献：

[1] 金田春一彦．日本語動詞のアスペクト［M］．［出版地不详］：むぎ書房，1976.

[2] 森山卓郎．日本語動詞述語文の研究［M］．［出版地不详］：明治書院，1988.
[3] 国立国語研究所．現代日本語動詞のアスペクトとテンス［M］．［出版地不详］：誠之堂書店，1985.
[4] 井上和子．日本語文法小詞典［M］．［出版地不详］：大修館書店，1989.
[5] 小泉保など．日本語基本動詞用法詞典［M］．［出版地不详］：大修館書店，1989.

编后记

对于高校教师而言，教学与科研是其必须具备的基本职业要求，犹如鸟之双翼，缺一不可。这已经是人所共知的常识，毋庸置疑。然而，在具体的实践中，要处理好二者的关系，却并非所设想的那么简单。重此轻彼或重彼轻此的现象，在不少学校、不少人身上并不鲜见。前者表现为对教学与科研二者关系的认识偏颇上，后者则表现为对二者的处理方式不妥及后果不良上。

作为一所综合性大学的外语学院，由于其学科特点以及其他一些原因，与其他学院比起来，在相当长一段时间内，在学术著作、学术论文的发表数目上存在着一定的差距。这不能不说是一个缺憾。当然，学术著作和论文的发表数量并不能完全代表一个单位、一个人科研水平的高低。然而，在我们所处的这样一个知识大爆炸、信息大传播的数字化时代，这已经成为一项重要的衡量标准，也关系到学校和教师的学术声望。这是不争的事实。

所幸的是，近年来学校和学院领导对外语教师的科研工作给予了高度的重视，采取了切实的措施；结合学科发展和高等院校外语专业教学评估，在政策和经费上都提供了有力的支持。全体教师也进一步提高了从事科研的自觉性，在繁忙的教学工作之余，主动挤时间进行学术研究，撰写学术论文。本书所收编的就是我院教师近期所撰写的部分论文，也算是外国语学院的一次科研成果展示。但愿这样一种上下一心、积极进取的可喜局面能够长期保持下去，成为一种常态。

本书的出版得到了各方面的支持与鼓励。首先，要感谢学校领导的关心与支持，设立专项经费解决了学院的拮据状况。其次，要感谢云南大学出版社施惟达社长和邓立木、唐志成编辑，没有他们的精心编辑，本书是不可能及时付梓的。最后，还要对本书编委会的全体专家表示敬意。正是他们不辞辛苦、不计报酬的工作才使这样一部涉及多领域、使用多语种的论文集得以顺利结集。

编　者

2008 年 6 月

图书在版编目（CIP）数据

外国语言文学与文化研究/徐枫主编．—昆明：云南大学出版社，2008

ISBN 978-7-81112-621-1

Ⅰ．外…　Ⅱ．徐…　Ⅲ．①语言学—外国—文集②文学评论—外国—文集③文化学—外国—文集　Ⅳ．C53

中国版本图书馆CIP数据核字（2008）第092846号

外国语言文学与文化研究

徐　枫　主编

策划编辑：邓立木
责任编辑：纳文汇　唐志成
责任校对：蒋丽杰
封面设计：力印天翌/书籍设计
出版发行：云南大学出版社
印　　装：云南科技印刷厂
开　　本：787mm×1092mm　1/16
印　　张：17
字　　数：315千
版　　次：2008年7月第1版
印　　次：2008年7月第1次印刷
书　　号：ISBN 978-7-81112-621-1
定　　价：38.00元

地　　址：云南省昆明市翠湖北路2号
云南大学英华园（邮编：650091）
发行电话：（0871）5033244　5031071
网　　址：www.ynup.com
E-mail：market@ynup.com